INDIA'S TURN

INDIA'S TURN
UNDERSTANDING THE ECONOMIC TRANSFORMATION

ARVIND SUBRAMANIAN

OXFORD
UNIVERSITY PRESS

OXFORD

UNIVERSITY PRESS

YMCA Library Building, Jai Singh Road, New Delhi 110 001

Oxford University Press is a department of the University of Oxford. It furthers the
University's objective of excellence in research, scholarship, and education
by publishing worldwide in

Oxford   New York

Auckland   Cape Town   Dar es Salaam   Hong Kong   Karachi   Kuala Lumpur
Madrid   Melbourne   Mexico City   Nairobi   New Delhi   Shanghai   Taipei   Toronto

With offices in

Argentina   Austria   Brazil   Chile   Czech Republic   France   Greece   Guatemala
Hungary   Italy   Japan   Poland   Portugal   Singapore   South Korea   Switzerland
Thailand   Turkey   Ukraine   Vietnam

Oxford is a registered trademark of Oxford University Press
in the UK and in certain other countries

Published in India
by Oxford University Press, New Delhi

© Oxford University Press 2008

ISBN-13: 978-0-19-569354-6
ISBN-10: 0-19-569354-X

Typeset in Adobe Garamond 11/14 by Jojy Philip
Printed in India by DeUnique, New Delhi 110 018
Published by Oxford University Press
YMCA Library Building, Jai Singh Road, New Delhi 110 001

To

Rohan, Karti, and Toto
Mukund, and
Parul

for

life and love lessons

CONTENTS

TABLES AND FIGURES

TABLES

FIGURES

ABBREVIATIONS

AMS	Aggregate Measure of Support
BOP	balance-of-payment
CAC	Capital Account Convertibility
CERC	Central Electricity Regulatory Commission
DUP	directly unproductive
ECB	external commercial borrowing
EPW	Economic and Political Weekly
FDI	Foreign Direct Investment
FERA	Foreign Exchange Regulation Act
FTA	Free Trade Area
FTAA	Free Trade Area of the Americas
GATT	General Agreement on Tariffs and Trader
GDP	Gross Domestic Product
GER	Gross Enrollment Ratio
IRDA	Insurance Regulatory and Development Authority
ISI	Import Substituting Industrialization
MFN	most-favoured-nation
MRTP	Monopoly and Restrictive Trade Practices
OBC	Other Backward Classes
OECD	Organization for Economic Co-operation and Development
PMP	Phased Manufacturing Programme
PPP	Purchasing Power Parity
OR	Quantitative Restrictions
RBI	Reserve Bank of India

RTI   Right to Information

SEBI   Securities and Exchange Board of India

T&D   Transmission and Distribution

TRAI   Telecommunications Regulatory Authority of India

TRIPS   Trade-related Aspects of Intellectual Property Rights

USINTA   India-US Free Trade Area

USTR   United States Trade Representative

WTO   World Trade Organization

ACKNOWLEDGEMENTS

When Keynes famously noted that practical men believe themselves to be exempt from any intellectual influences, he probably had in mind some iron law of vanity which says that the debts we really owe (even if to defunct economists) considerably exceed those we recognize and acknowledge. The obligatory filling of an acknowledgements page is a discipline, however weak, to guard against this law. So here goes.

Some of the papers and articles in this book are the product of collective effort, and I would like to thank four of my co-authors Dani Rodrik, Aaditya Mattoo, Raghuram Rajan, and Harsha V. Singh for allowing me to publish these papers and articles. Aaditya Mattoo has been a constant source of ideas and stimulation, and a fount of patience, for nearly thirty years. To Dani Rodrik, I owe particular debts. First, the privilege of observing at close range the workings of a really fine and subtle mind. Second, gratitude for the gift of collaboration. Collaborating with him was the essential stroke of luck that led directly, and in important ways indirectly, to a lot of the research that I have since undertaken—either on my own or with other collaborators—and that features in this book.

Jagdish Bhagwati, Simon Johnson, and Vijay Kelkar have provided consistent encouragement and support on the professional front over a number of years. And similar encouragement has been forthcoming from my parents, grandmother, mother-in-law, and brother, Anand. Deena Khatkhate's episodic visits and touching concern have often acted to revive the sagging spirit.

Kalpana Kochhar, Utsav Kumar, Ioannis Tokatlidis, and Manzoor Gill provided substantial contributions to some of the chapters in this book as did my OUP editors in editing and compiling this volume.

Although the outputs in this book pre-date my joining the Peterson Institute for International Economics and the Center for Global

Development, I am thankful to Fred Bergsten and Nancy Birdsall, heads of these two institutions, for providing a great environment, including the necessary freedom, to pursue my research and writing interests.

I would like to acknowledge the various academic journals and newspapers where these articles first appeared for permission to reproduce them. These journals and newspapers are listed on page 226.

Above all, this book would not have been possible without the five to whom it is dedicated.

INTRODUCTION

INDIA AS CRUCIBLE

At its independence, India was the cynosure of the world. Not just because of the epic, violent beginnings, nor Pandit Nehru's memorable oratory that ushered it in. India was the crucible for three fundamental economic experiments in the then poor parts of the world.

The first related to democracy and development, what might be called the bread versus freedom question. When the Indian founding fathers chose to adopt a political system with universal adult franchise (well before even a number of European countries), they were making not just a political but an economic gamble. It was far from clear that democracy was the way to keep together a highly heterogeneous society with fissures running along several lines—religion, caste, ethnicity, language, and culture. It was even less clear that democracy was the best way to achieve rapid growth and lift millions out of poverty. At least one model that was then considered a success—the Soviet Union—pointed in the other direction. Circa 1950, economic development was dominated by 'capital fundamentalism,' the notion that accumulating capital—that is, investing—was the key to economic growth. And autocracies were generally regarded as more effective than democracy in facilitating accumulation.[1]

The second experiment related to the relative roles of the state and markets in delivering economic development. Drawing lessons from the relevant experiences of the time—the Great Depression and the success of Keynesianism in the United States, the embrace of a larger role for the

[1] If, as Bob Solow said, the only real job of economists is to consign bad ideas to the dustbin, they seem to have failed quite badly: capital fundamentalism reared its head again in the early 2000s, providing the intellectual basis for the call to ramp up foreign aid to the poorest countries so that they could meet the United Nations' Millenium Development Goals.

public sector in the United Kingdom and Europe, and above all the success of the Soviet model—India consciously chose an economic model that privileged the state over the market. Not just were large swathes of the economy to be run by the government and protected from foreign competition but the allocation of all economic resources would be guided by planning and planners. India chose to trade Adam Smith's invisible hand of the market for the intrusive tentacles of the state. A related choice was to privilege the manufacturing sector—through a rapid and planned process of industrialization—at the expense of agriculture.

The third related to the roles of opportunity and guarantee as means of social and economic advancement within the country. The choice made by India was schizophrenic. For those that had been the victims of historical discrimination, India emphatically chose the guarantee route. Affirmative action—in public sector employment and educational institutions—was India's answer to redress historical inequities and bring their victims into the mainstream of social and economic development. These victims of India's history were called the Scheduled Castes and Tribes, the name deriving from the fact that a schedule in the constitution was devoted to identifying the particular social groups that would be the beneficiaries of various affirmative action programmes. The opportunity-creating route was given short shrift for the disadvantaged but was favoured for the elites. This was reflected in the inattention to, and inadequate resources provided for, basic education compared with institutions of higher education and research, which included medical schools, the Indian Institutes of Technology, the Indian Institutes of Management, and other research institutes and laboratories. Thus, opportunities for the elites and guarantees for the disadvantaged was thought to be the way forward.

THE EXPERIMENTS REVISITED

What light does the Indian experience shed on these questions? If this question had been posed circa 1980, the answer would have been straight-forward: Never do as India does. With the exception of a stubbornly persistent democracy, Indian economic performance had been unremarkable, and India remained the poster child for development policy choices gone wrong.[2]

---

[2] It is telling that in a famous paper authored by the Nobel Prize winner, Robert Lucas, as

Nearly thirty years on, though, these questions have acquired a new relevance because the answers are no longer as unambiguously negative. India is the new kid on the economic bloc. After nearly three decades of disappointing but not disastrous growth, famously dubbed the 'Hindu growth', it has in the following three decades posted solid growth of 6 per cent per year (and rising): for the average person this translates roughly into a four-fold increase in the standard of living. As a result, poverty has declined from close to 50 per cent in the 1970s to about 25 per cent today, and nearly all indicators of social outcomes have improved substantially. And although it is struggling to get out of China's shadow, and despite Lord Meghnad Desai's dashing of Indian hopes and perhaps pretensions when he pronounced that 'China will be a Great Power but India will just be a Great Democracy', the buzz that is India is now becoming impossible to ignore.

Bread versus Freedom

Of the four or five big postcolonial experiments in fashioning a functioning whole out of multi-ethnic, multi-religious, or multi-linguistic parts, the Soviet Union and Yugoslavia have disintegrated; Sudan is on the verge of a divorce between its Muslim and Christian parts; and Nigeria teeters perennially on the cusp of implosion. India has survived despite its ethnic, religious and linguistic diversity, and while many problems loom and fissiparous tendencies do erupt periodically, disintegration does not appear to be a serious possibility.

India has not only survived but done so democratically. That achievement, widely noted and not easily explained, seems all the more remarkable in retrospect given how inhospitable the terrain was for democracy to strike secure roots: low levels of income and literacy, high levels of inequality, a small middle class, and a society that was predominantly agrarian and fractured along religious and linguistic lines.

The important development question was whether this political model would be compatible with generating economic wealth for the average person. For about three decades, it seemed that the answer was in the negative. The weight of evidence seemed to be in favour of the East Asian

---

recently as 1988, India was chosen as the archetypal 'poor' country, the exemplar of underdevelopment.

model in which the chronology seemed to be bread first and freedom later as in the case of Korea, Taiwan, Malaysia, and Indonesia (and also Chile); or bread first and freedom not yet or not at all as in the case of China, Singapore, and Hong Kong, which despite their rapid growth have yet to fully or meaningfully democratize.

But the growth in India over the last twenty-five years have come as somewhat of a relief for those who still refuse to see the two—economic growth and political liberties—as incompatible. At the Hindu rate of growth, the question of whether freedom was an unaffordable luxury may have been meaningful. At 6 per cent rate of growth, the question has become increasingly moot: one can have one's cake, expect its size to increase, and also expect as a fundamental right to be able to walk to the polling booth to cast one's vote. Looking back though at the Indian experience, one can say a little more than just that democracy can deliver economic growth even if it takes time. One can say that the lack of growth in the past may have had origins in policies taken in the economic domain that were largely orthogonal to democracy: certainly, no democratic compulsion underlay the system of industrial licensing and other controls that taxed domestic manufacturing activity..

But the bread versus freedom question should be evaluated on many more economic dimensions than just growth. There are the important dimensions of economic instability, including macroeconomic price fluctuations, proneness to crises, and of course, vulnerability to extreme deprivation brought on, for example, by famines. On each of these scores, not only had India fared reasonably, but this performance has had a lot to do with India's democratic practice.

On famines, the Nobel laureate Amartya Sen has famously contrasted the Chinese and Indian experience with famines, in which India came out a lot better because of the openness of its political regime. Such openness, according to Sen, led to swift responses in India, averting famine and starvation; in contrast, China's system was less willing to acknowledge the extreme catastrophe and hence less able to avert massive starvation which led to about thirty million deaths.

While the experience with famines is widely known, less recognized has been India's ability to maintain macroeconomic stability and avoid financial crises. Amongst developing countries, long-run inflation has been amongst the lowest in India and India's record of macroeconomic prudence has, until recently, been exemplary. One surprising manifestation of this has been the reaction of markets to the sharp increase in India's fiscal deficit and accumulation of debt. India's government debt-to-GDP (Gross Domestic Product) ratio, at about 90 per cent, exceeds that of many of the other emerging market countries, including Brazil and Argentina. Yet, the sense of risk or imminent crisis has not been as acute for India. Of course, markets, given their notoriously procyclical proclivities, might be understating the risks, with this being the boom phase of the bust that might follow. However, it is worth noting that part of this apparent market sanguineness could stem from a confidence in Indian creditworthiness, which is in turn based on an unblemished record of no-default and low inflation (which is, after all, expropriation by other means). Research shows that markets set different debt thresholds for different countries, with lower levels set for countries with past records of high inflation or default. The relatively large slack that markets appear to have cut for India may therefore be grounded in the institutional checks in India against instability and expropriation. The joke about the Indian political and economic system possessing the wheels of a bullock-cart and brakes of a Rolls-Royce captures well the over-proliferation of checks and balances. But this arrangement has not been without benefits for macroeconomic stability and crisis avoidance.

State versus Markets

A lot has been written on this dichotomy and especially on the choices that India has made. Three brief remarks are worth making here. First, the characterization of the Indian development model as one of 'import substitution,' is misleading in one important respect. Yes, India created a huge public sector and yes, India throttled foreign trade. But if the point of erecting barriers to foreign competition was to favour domestic activity, especially in the private sector, the raison d'etre of import substitution, India certainly failed. It failed because India did something quite unique. It also simultaneously through licensing and other measures taxed domestic (private sector) activity in manufacturing, which was at loggerheads with the import substitution motive. Why this came to be so, or what possible political economy led to industrial licensing and the other panoply of regulations, defies easy explanation? But with some exaggeration, one could even claim that the only time that India truly adopted import substitution was the 1980s, when foreign trade was controlled and restrictions on domestic activity were eased.

Turning to today, the state versus markets debate in India is largely settled. True, India has a long way to go in terms of shedding all the traces of its dirigiste past, but the principle of the primacy of markets over the state is now not seriously questioned.

However, the state versus markets debate in India is settled largely in terms of the scope or the reach of the state's activities. But there is insufficient recognition of and emphasis accorded to addressing the weaknesses of the state in its performance of certain core functions that cannot be performed by markets. While it is undoubtedly true that the state has retreated progressively both in terms of production and regulatory roles, there has been no significant improvement in the effectiveness and quality of the state's core role.

This question merits further examination because of the increasing recognition of the role of the state or public institutions in fostering development. Institutions—in the definition of Nobel Prize winner Douglass North—are the rules of the game in a society that affect economic behaviour, including the protection of property rights, the rule of law and order, and sanctity of contracts. Recent research suggests that these institutions are one of the key deep determinants of long run economic development.

Opportunity versus Guarantee

The democracy versus development question has been settled, in favour of democracy because they no longer seem opposed. So too has the state versus markets question, in this case by reversing the original choice. Yes, India still has a long way to go in terms of policy reforms, but the principle of the primacy of markets is no longer seriously questioned. The same, however, cannot be said of the choice between opportunities and guarantees. As noted earlier, India has indeed provided opportunities for the elite and guarantees for the downtrodden. For a poor country India spent, and still spends, relatively far more resources on higher education than on primary education. For example, India spent 86 per cent of per capita GDP on each student in tertiary education in 2000 while it spent 14 per cent of per capita GDP per student in primary education. By contrast, China spent 10.7 per cent and 12.1 per cent, respectively, of per capita GDP per student in tertiary and primary education. Put another way, India spent substantially more in PPP adjusted dollars per student in tertiary education than China, and even South Korea or Indonesia in 2000.

The historically disadvantaged groups could have been pulled up through a massive programme of basic education such as South Korea or China. But as the figures above reveal, India forswore this option. The elitism of Indian policy is also reflected in the pattern of specialization above, namely the greater use of skilled-intensive activities at the expense of low-skilled activities which would have more clearly benefited the poor.

To offset this bias in opportunity, guarantees were provided in the form of massive affirmative action programmes in education and public sector employment. Over time, the scope of such programmes widened as these groups acquired political power through the ballot and legislated greater guarantees. In the late 1980s (Mandal Commission), for example, the scope of affirmative action which broadly reserved 23 per cent of jobs and educational opportunities to the Scheduled Castes was considerably expanded to 50 per cent when newer categories of disadvantaged groups were identified and brought within the scope of affirmative action programmes. In the state of Tamil Nadu, for example, about 90 per cent of college admissions in higher educational institutions are reserved for the so-called backward castes. Resistance to privatization in recent years has stemmed in large part from politicians from backward castes: having acquired political power, they would feel cheated if the key sources of patronage for their communities—handing out public sector employment to their constituencies—were now taken away from them.

More recently, the focus has been on expanding the scope of Other Backward Classes (OBC) reservations to higher educational institutions. Talk is slowly gaining ground of expanding reservation even to private sector employment. Interestingly, whereas reservation has always been a politically polarizing issue with the Bharatiya Janata Party being opposed to it, reservation today seems to be becoming more bipartisan.

Thus, in the popular discourse and in practical politics, the provision of opportunity through education received surprising little attention compared to the fight over guarantees and targeted benefits. While it might be argued that affirmative action in education was a recognition of opportunity as salvation, the problem was that educational outcomes were poor and the there was seldom any real pressure to hold the culprit—public education—accountable. Thus, in not actively promoting education or redressing the massive failures that had emerged in this sector, the revealed preference of politicians seemed to be that education and opportunity were not very important.

If in the arenas of public policy and politics, guarantees are the preferred options to pursue, individuals and the private sector are behaving quite differently, indeed moving in the opposite direction. Individuals are voting with their feet and choosing the opportunity over the guarantee route and the rapid growth over the last three decades has been the decisive, endogenous, transforming factor. How so?

Until the early 1990s, India's education indicators were abysmal when compared with a number of countries, including those in Africa. In the last ten years, the sector has undergone a radical transformation. Between 1991 and 2001, the gross enrolment ratio (GER) in primary education (grades 1) rose from 82 per cent to 95 per cent, and in upper primary education (grades 6) from 54 per cent to 61 per cent (see table). Available government data suggest that in that age group, the number of children not in school fell sharply from about 60 million in the early 1990s to 25 million in 2002, and this decline is continuing. What India has accomplished is no small feat—especially given that its population grew from about 840 million to nearly one billion between 1991 and 2001, with the number of children age six to fourteen rising by 35 million to 205 million. While specific numbers in such a large federal system may be viewed with caution, and questions remain about the quality of education received, the magnitude of the progress appears to be in little doubt. Why and how have this happened?

Amartya Sen had drawn attention to the disappointing post-Independence performance of the Indian state in delivering education, reflected in very slow improvements in literacy rates, especially amongst women. While the supply of educational services by the state was inadequate, Sen raised the puzzle as to why there was not greater demand for education and hence greater pressure on the state to meet this demand. One answer to this puzzle was that the private returns to literacy and basic education were low. When Indian growth rate was poor, parents often made the choice of keeping the child on the farm over sending him, and certainly her, to school.

But with growth unleashed, there is a significantly increased demand for educational services and hence in educational outcomes. The dynamic of education has seen a tectonic shift as a result of growth. But the interesting twist documented by Harvard researchers, Michael Kremer and Karthik Muralidharan, is that much of the increased demand is being met by the private sector—the public sector is being by-passed. It turns out that the growth of private primary education is directly and strongly correlated with the dysfunctionality of the public education system. In states, where teacher absenteeism is greatest, private schools are growing most rapidly. Moreover, this substitution of private for public seems to be a win-win situation: private sector schools charge lower fees, lead to greater contact between teacher and student, and hence in superior performance on test scores, and involves greater teacher accountability.

India is witnessing a similar phenomenon in higher technical education, where private engineering colleges have mushroomed in the last ten years. To be sure, these are all not MITs or Caltechs but their rise is related again to the combination of a rapid increase in demand for such skills combined with the inability or reluctance of the public system to meet this demand.

As the demand for education increases and as educational attainment rises, spurred by growth, so too will the opportunities for advancement. To be sure, there will always be fight for guarantees, but slowly over time, there might even be a self-initiated effort by those who partake of the benefits of growth through better education to wean themselves off the state.

THIS BOOK

India, at last, being a 'happening' country, is thus one provocation for this book, which is a collection of articles that I have written or co-written, over the last decade, on the two major economic developments in India: its growth and the globalization of its economy and policies. The articles have all appeared either in academic and policy journals or in edited volumes.

But India as a noteworthy subject can only be a necessary condition for this or any other book. It is not a sufficient one, especially for a compilation of already written articles. In other words, compiling a collection of previous writings provokes the obvious question: why? If the constituent elements are noteworthy on their own, a compilation is unnecessary. On the other hand, if they are not, and have eluded the eyes of a curious audience, a compilation seems an unwanted infliction, like an unwelcome visitor.

One rationale for a compilation is a late-in-life look back at a significant body of work, where the significance and quality of the work justifies the indulgence of a retrospective, with hindsight making clearer the themes and their coherence. In short, it affords the author a chance to luxuriate in happy fulfillment, and move on to inactivity and silence.

But that is not my excuse. Inactivity is hopefully not in prospect. And, clearly, 'significance' and 'quality' cannot be asserted by the provider but are assessments that will have to be made by the user.

On the assumption that the constituent elements are reasonably interesting, one objective of putting together a collection of writings is to reach an audience that is broader than the somewhat narrower audience at which many of the academic articles were originally targeted. There is also the hope (much like the corporate raider who goes for an acquisition) that the whole will be somehow and somewhat greater than the sum of the parts.

But instead of dwelling on the why, I want to describe the broad themes underlying the articles in this compilation and also, where possible, to provide a history and context that might be of interest to readers. The articles fall into two broad categories. The first set of four articles all relate to India's current and future growth. These articles are largely analytical in nature and mostly free of prescriptive content. The broad theme that runs through these articles is that the Indian growth experience say in the past three decades has been special or atypical or, to sound more dramatic, unique. The articles then address different aspects of this unique experience.

The second set of articles relates to the integration of India into the world economy in trade in goods, in ideas, and capital flows. Unlike the first part of this book, where the articles are almost exclusively positive or analytical in nature, contributions in this section are highly prescriptive, offering advice to Indian policy-makers on policy options to consider and even policy choices to make. If there is a theme, it is one of how contingent or time-sensitive the choices are, especially at a time of rapid change. Some of these articles may not have retained relevance beyond their own time and context. But even in their datedness, they might have their uses, serving as useful history, shedding light on the global trading context and the opportunities and constraints that India faced at a certain point in time, and importantly, how quickly these change.

SECTION 1: INDIA'S GROWTH: UNIQUE?

India's growth has been unlike many other or most other growth experiences. The uniqueness relates to three aspects:

1. When it happened?
2. Why it happened?
3. And what happened/is happening?

While a lot of current discussion centres on the last question, it is at least of equal interest to understand the first two questions. The first paper in the book (written with Dani Rodrik), which generated a lot of controversy, sheds light on the first two questions.

It is by now a universally acknowledged 'truth' that the Indian growth miracle began in 1991 in the wake of the macroeconomic crisis which led to the implementation of sweeping policy reforms. The currency of this truth does not just circulate outside the borders amongst those who are only superficially knowledgeable about India. It circulates very much within India amongst the cognoscenti. Take this quote of Tarun Das in Thomas Friedman's bestseller *The World is Flat*:

Our Berlin Wall fell,' said Das, 'and it was like unleashing a caged tiger. Trade controls were abolished. *We were always at 3 per cent growth, the so-called Hindu rate of growth—slow, cautious, and conservative.* To make [better returns], you had to go to America. Well, three years later [after the 1991 reforms] we were at 7 per cent rate of growth. (Friedman 2005, p. 50, emphasis mine)).

Or take this multiple choice question which I often ask audiences. Did India's growth turnaround happen:

1. At the same time as China's?
2. Ten years after China's?
3. Fifteen years after China's?

Audiences overwhelmingly chose the second or last option. At which point, I present the following numbers: Indian growth averaged 3.8, 3.0, 5.9, and 5.6, per cent, respectively in the 1960s, 1970s, 1980s, and 1990s. The sharp turnaround in India's fortunes occurred sometime in the late 1970s/early 1980s.

If the numbers are just numbers, that is facts, why is it still universally acknowledged that growth turned around after 1991? Keynes famously asked, 'When the facts change, I change my opinions, what do you do, sir?' But about Indian growth, there seems to be a stubborn immunity to facts. Why might this be so?

One plausible answer is the tyranny of ideology. Since the early 1980s, the reigning, pervasive ideology around the world is that economic growth follows structural and policy 'reforms'. We are all, to varying degrees, predisposed to believing it. In the Indian case, the irresistible force of ideology, however, ran into the immovable object of inconvenient fact. The fact being that growth took off nearly ten–twelve years before the market-based reforms were seriously undertaken. To accommodate this inconvenient fact would require some revisions of one's ideological priors. But it is a sign—of something what I am not quite sure—that these revisions have become nearly impossible. And, as we argue in the first chapter, the revisions need not be so serious as to fatally undermine the prior. They can in fact be easily accommodated but at the cost of more nuanced understanding.

The way inconvenient fact has been accommodated to rule out any shift in ideological priors is to change the interpretation of the facts. This has taken the form of arguing that the growth of the 1980s was 'bad' or unsustainable growth. In the first chapter, we address both these interpretations and rule them out.

The unsustainable growth argument is that growth during the 1980s was driven by fiscal expansion and hence unsustainable. We did discuss this possibility and found it wanting. Briefly, we argued that the demand-pull argument is inadequate to explain the large increase in trend productivity, even under the most favourable circumstances for that argument. The rise in capacity utilization, such as it was, cannot explain more than part of the increase in labour or total-factor productivity. We can adduce additional evidence to support our point of view. Consider the Latin American experience prior to the 1982 debt crisis. Fiscal-expansion-led growth there hardly produced an increase in productivity growth.

Moreover, we do not consider India's balance-of-payments crisis of 1991 to constitute compelling evidence that the growth of the 1980s was unsustainable. Countries can make macro policy mistakes both when they are stagnating and when they are growing rapidly. Once more, comparative evidence is useful: How many analysts seriously believe that the Asian financial crisis of 1997–8, arguably much bigger in magnitude than India's in 1991, proves that the rapid growth of South Korea, Thailand, Malaysia, and Indonesia in the decades prior was unsustainable? How many argued that the Mexican peso crisis of 1994 was unsustainable because of the preceding and comprehensive market-based reforms?

In any case, the case that growth in the 1980s was fiscally driven and unsustainable needs to be made; it is not enough to assert it. We suspect that there is a tendency to dismiss the growth of the 1980s because it makes the subsequent reforms look less good (since the system was not reformed, any growth that came out should have been unsustainable— that is, bad growth). But that would be just ideology, not analysis.

This naturally leads to the second unique aspect of India's growth— why? Again, the universally acknowledged view that reforms were the key driver runs up against the obvious question: why did growth take-off in the 1980s? We discuss this in some detail in the first paper, arguing that something significant happened in the 1980s, which is still not entirely clear. For lack of positive evidence in the form of a paper trail of actual and significant policy changes, we offered an attitudinal shift on the part of the government as a plausible reason. We characterized this shift as pro-business rather than pro-market because the policies, implicit and explicit, served to improve the opportunities for domestic business without exposing them to greater competition. The real pro-competitive reforms were only introduced after 1991.

We also need to correct a misunderstanding—indeed there has been an attempt to create a straw-man. We did not argue that the attitudinal shift of the early 1980s led to a 'once-and-for-all' increase in growth. We argued that the attitudinal shift was a plausible reason for the increase in growth during the 1980s. We explicitly mentioned the possibility that, without the reforms of the 1990s, growth may have petered out.

The essential point is that the growth turnaround has been a longer and more continuous process than votaries of the 'reform matters school' would like to have it, who view the change in fortune as a discrete and dramatic event located in 1991.[3] The more nuanced understanding is also consistent with the broader view that growth is not a simple matter of policy changes but a more complex one arising from an interaction of triggers (in this case, the policy reforms) and certain fundamentals, which in this case were India's institutions as well as its supply of high-skilled labour; the latter playing a

---

[3] Ed Luce's excellent book articulates this view well: 'The second and even more dramatic moment came in 1991 (the first being the 1966 devaluation), when India's economy went into a tailspin after its foreign-exchange reserves dropped almost to zero…. Nehru's socialist dream of creating an economy that would be immune to the influence of former colonial powers had culminated in bankruptcy…' (p. 32)

key role in the IT-revolution that India has profited from over the last two decades.

The first article also touches upon a few aspects of 'what' is unique about India's growth. First, unlike many countries in Latin America and East Asia, India's growth has been stable, less susceptible to the vagaries of foreign capital, and hence escaped some of the turbulence experienced by nearly all emerging markets.

And most surprising of all, India's growth performance is not a reflection of adding more men and machines but extracting more from the existing stock of them. In 1994, Paul Krugman in his article in *Foreign Affairs*, 'The Myth of Asia's Miracle' was famously sceptical about the East Asian economic performance and dire about its future prospects. Both diagnosis and prognosis were based on the observation that East Asian growth had been based on deferred gratification (greater investments) than on productivity growth. India's growth over the last twenty-five years has turned out to be of the right kind, fueled predominantly by productivity. For an economy that had been the byword for inefficiency and waste, this was indeed sweet revenge.

Lee Kuan Yew, delivering the 37th Jawaharlal Nehru Memorial Lecture, asserted that, 'Since the Industrial Revolution, no country has become a major economy without becoming an industrial power'. India has not yet become a major economy so it is too early to say whether India will defy this trend. But if India continues to grow at current rates, and if the current pattern of development is also maintained—for which there is some evidence—it is possible that India will become a major economy without becoming an industrial or manufacturing powerhouse. India might yet prove the sage of Singapore wrong.

This pattern of development is the subject of the second article ('India's Pattern of Development: What happened, What Follows?', co-authored with Kalpana Kochhar, Utsav Kumar, Raghuram Rajan, and Ioannis Tokatlidis). Here, the focus is on Indian uniqueness in terms of what is happening.

India's pattern of development has been unique in many ways much of it relating to the idiosyncratic policy choices made in the 1950s and 1960s. India has followed a highly unusual pattern of development which very different from that of the very successful pattern followed by the East Asian countries. The typical successful country specialized first in unskilled labour-intensive activities (e.g., textiles and clothing) and then moved up the value-added chain, shifting toward the higher skilled and technology-intensive as it started getting richer. A corollary of this is that most of these countries moved from agriculture toward manufacturing and then over time toward services.

India, by contrast, has been specializing in skill-intensive activities both within manufacturing and now of course in services. Reflecting this, the share of GDP in manufacturing has not grown, despite the rapid growth of income over the last twenty-five years. What has happened instead is that the decline of agriculture has been mirrored in a commensurate increase in the service sector.

The reasons for this can be located in the idiosyncratic set of policies that India followed in its early years. First, higher education was emphasized over basic education which led to the creation of a pool of highly skilled engineers and managers that have been the backbone of the booming IT-sector in India. Second, in addition to the extensive controls on the private sector, there was a generalized phobia against size (it is a difficult question whether the Indian planners had a greater phobia against markets or size). This manifested itself in labour laws that protected workers, with the protection increasing as the size of the firm expanded, policies that earmarked certain sectors of the economy for small-scale firms, and anti-monopoly laws that acted as a deterrent for large firms. The consequences were a smaller role for manufacturing, especially formal manufacturing, and within manufacturing a much lower size of firms than in comparator countries. In sum, a whole panoply of policies prevented the manufacturing sector from using the vast pools of unskilled and from achieving some normal scale of operation.

But this constellation of choices also led to a highly diversified skill and production base—India produces more skill-intensive products than countries at similar levels of development and produces a wider range of products than comparators—which again unexpectedly contributed to the rapid growth since the 1980s by making India ready to exploit the new technological opportunities afforded by globalization. Those who blamed Nehru for neglecting basic education, while retaining the high ground and being essentially correct nevertheless had to concede that Nehruvian choices were not unambiguously flawed, and may even have had many (at least partially) offsetting benefits.

The interesting thing, however, is that this pattern of specialization has not been altered over the last twenty-five years despite the progressive reform of policies. While India has opened up the economy and chipped away at the opaque regulatory framework, it continues to specialize in skill-intensive activities with no real move to do more manufacturing. In other words, there may be some hysteresis or persistence in the Indian economy which might lead it to continue to behave unlike other developing economies.

One implication of India's skill-intensive pattern of development that this chapter serves to highlight is what we have called the 'Bangalore Bug', which is India's version of the Dutch disease problem. Dutch disease refers to the contractionary effect exerted on traditional manufacturing as a result of a sudden discovery of a natural resource like oil. The mechanism through which this happens is the appreciation of the exchange rate that renders traditional manufacturing uncompetitive. In the Indian variant, the surge in the IT sectors has similarly led to a sharp increase in wages that either directly or via the rupee appreciating adversely affects the profits of unskilled-based manufacturing.

Another spectacularly unique aspect of India's pattern of development has only recently become evident. This relates to capital flows. Capital is normally expected to flow from rich countries (where the risk-adjusted returns to capital have declined) to poor countries (where many unexploited investment opportunities remain). In the post-war period, this has not always happened and poorer countries have occasionally exported capital. But a stronger version of the capital flow hypothesis, that a certain kind of capital—foreign direct investment (FDI)—always flows from rich to poor countries, has not been violated empirically. The remarkable thing is that India seems to be defying this strong version of the capital flow hypothesis. In 2006–07, India, although not quite a *net* exporter of capital was a sizable gross exporter of capital. Even more strikingly, Indian exports of FDI have been not to poorer countries and have not been confined to oil; rather a substantial share of FDI is to rich countries and has been very diversified in terms of the sectors covered. Although a full-blown economic analysis needs ot be written, I wrote a short op-ed piece, highlighting this unusual phenomenon, which is included in this volume at the end of Capter 2 (called 'Precocious India').

As I have just suggested, some of the uniqueness relating to the pattern of development stemmed from idiosyncratic economic policy choices favoured by the founding fathers. But what is perhaps idiosyncratic about

India is the initial political choice: opting for democracy.[4] This unusual starting point—relatively strong economic and political institutions—has bred its own set of opportunities and problems. The irony is that, on the one hand, these strong institutions played a key role in turning growth around since the 1980s. On the other, these institutions themselves have not demonstrably improved over time, and the question is whether this could have been the consequence of not opting for the more traditional East Asian route where institutions evolve as a result of growth.

This is the issue discussed in Chapter 3 on institutions. This chapter documents what might be interpreted as a decline in India's key institutions—judiciary, bureaucracy, and police—that play such an important role in allowing a market-based economy to flourish.

Even allowing for the distorted prism of nostalgia, few would disagree that the quality of politicians, bureaucrats, and judges, and hence the public roles they served and the institutions they inhabited were considerably stronger in the first two–three decades after independence. The decline set in thereafter, a process that was aggravated by the rent-seeking that the Kafkaesque system of controls gave rise to. While difficult to quantify, the anecdotal evidence points to a decline in the quality of all the meta-institutions—the rising levels of pending cases in the state courts, the increase in the number of 'political' scandals, the politicization of the judiciary and the bureaucracy, and rising teacher absenteeism in public schools.

To be sure, one needs to be careful about over-generalizing because of Joan Robinson's point that everything and its opposite are true in India, and this is true also of institutions. Islands of excellence, or at least competence, do exist. The election commission has been studiously unbiased and efficient in conducting elections; the civil service at the all-India level is still recruited through merit-based procedures; and important successes have been scored by public interest litigation initiatives (such as the move to make New Delhi environmentally cleaner).

But accountability—a key aspect of all public institutions—has been systematically undermined. One important and ominous statistic reflective of institutional decline is the incidence of armed insurgency by revolutionary

---

[4] India is one of four countries in the post-war era that began with strong political institutions and have done reasonably well in terms of growth performance. The other three are Botswana, Mauritius, and Sri Lanka.

leftist groups against state institutions in over a quarter of India. Thus, basic law and order, stemming from state monopoly over violence and a precondition for a functioning political system, cannot be taken for granted in vast swathes of the country.

Two paradoxes arise from the two-way relationship between growth and institutions. The first paradox is really to explain why India's growth fortunes have improved so dramatically despite the relatively modest pace of reforms. Especially, when compared to many countries around the world (especially in Latin America), which reformed faster, deeper, and earlier than India, India's growth has been greater, better founded, and more stable. The second paradox is about why India's institutions have proved so immune to improving economic prospects. Normally, institutions are to use economic jargon a superior good; that is the demand for them rises faster than the rise in underlying incomes. Put differently, as countries grow rich, their citizens demand more of the government—better law and order, safety, security, public goods such as parks, education, health etc. In India, it is hard to see that these services provided by public institutions have improved. The question is why and Chapter 3 seeks to provide some preliminary answers.

Having reviewed the past, the temptation to look into and pronounce on the future is irresistible, despite George Eliot's stricture against it: 'Among all forms of mistake, prophesy is the most gratuitous', she warned. In Chapter 4 (written with Dani Rodrik), India's economic future is predicted. Back in 2004, well before India's growth trajectory moved up and prior to the euphoria that that gave rise to, we predicted that India's medium run growth rate would be at least 7 per cent a year. The essay also spelt out the upside potential and the downside risks. Even though only three years have elapsed, while the projection seems to be reasonably accurate and holding up to events, the discussion of the potential and especially the risks have evolved. If that essay had been written today, there are things that should have been emphasized more—such as the shortage of skilled labour and the constraints from weak institutions—and these changes would have been informed by the other chapters (especially Chapters 3 and 4) that were written after the rash prediction was made. The salutary lesson from this is of course that Eliot's admonition should be heeded more carefully, but more that nothing is more certain than the uncertainty of things especially at times of rapid change—of the sort that India is witnessing these days.

SECTION II: GLOBALIZATION

Trade in Goods: Multilateralism and Preferentialism

The first chapter in this section was co-authored with Harsha V. Singh (currently the Deputy Director General at the WTO). As relatively junior staff at the GATT, facing constraints on our public utterances, we wrote this under a pseudonym for the *Economic and Political Weekly (EPW)*. In the piece, we wanted to instill some calm and rationality into the heated and charged debate in India at that time on whether to accept the results of the Uruguay Round. This was a historic moment and choice for India because accepting the Uruguay Round would mean a decisive break with its dirigiste past but also with its role as recalcitrant, defensive player in the multilateral trading system. Hitherto, India was a self-styled leader of the so-called 'Group of 77', a motley collection of developing countries. India's main role in the GATT was to curry special favours for developing countries. These included being free of the GATT's obligations not to protect one's economy and also asking industrial countries to provide preferential access to the exports of developing countries. Both of these ensured a second-class status for India in the GATT, a fact that somehow got obscured by the grandstanding that India's skilled bureaucrats always managed to pull off in Geneva.

In some ways, history has not been unkind to the pitch we made for India to start becoming a serious and credible player in the international trading system. A few aspects of this short piece are worth repeating. We openly stated that India should re-assess its role as spokesman for the 'South'. We asserted that southern solidarity was a bit of a myth. We said: 'the prospect of preferential access to the North American market has lulled or lured Latin America into acquiescence' with regard to US demands; as to East Asia, we said that 'not for it the posturing and striding the world's political stage if it meant forsaken exports'. Above all, 'And the sweeping winds of liberal economic policy have blown apart the ideology of protectionism on which tenuous Southern solidarity in the GATT was in part founded'.

Another theme of this piece was for India to get serious and dispassionate about assessing its own benefits and costs of staying in, and as importantly, of comparing these with opting out (at that stage a serious possibility given the reactions the Uruguay Round provoked) of the multilateral trading system. To self-important Indian policymakers, we wanted to send the message that India's influence in international trade was not unlimited as policymakers had led themselves to believe. It was time to stop posturing, a stance that found free rein in the GATT previously because the rest of the world did not need India as a profitable market opportunity and could hence, condescendingly, indulge Indian sloganeering. Instead, it was time to become a serious player in the multilateral trading system.

Another paper that I co-authored with Aaditya Mattoo (which is not a part of this volume but can be found at *http://www.petersoninstitute.org/ publications/papers/subramanian0300.pdf*), pushes this same line of argument a bit further. It was written after the debacle of the Seattle Summit in 1998, when the multilateral trading system seemed in trouble because of the strong backlash against globalization in general. The thrust of the piece was that India should be more proactive in the multilateral trading system because it had a number of market access (i.e., export) interests—in textiles, agriculture, and services—which could be pursued in the WTO. And if these could be obtained, they could facilitate domestic reform in a number of areas within India. As we put it: '... active multilateral engagement can be incrementally helpful in facilitating domestic reform and gaining access for India's export of goods and labor services'. It identified India's interests in each of the sectors and suggested what it should seek in multilateral negotiations on each of these topics.

At first blush, the second piece, also co-authored with Aaditya Mattoo, seems to intellectually inconsistent with the second. In this, which is actually a review of a book by the brilliant trade economist, Jagdish Bhagwati, we set out the case for a free trade agreement (FTA) between India and the United States, a proposal we first made in 2000, on the eve of President Clinton's visit to India. How could we justify advocating Indian proactivity on the multilateral trade front while actively campaigning for an FTA with one of India's largest trading partners? Was this a case of having one's cake and eating it too, hypocrisy masquerading as expediency? Actually, in retrospect, it turns out there was coherence between the two. Our advocacy of the multilateral approach was than qualified by what we called 'negotiating pessimism'. We concluded our paper on India and the WTO with the following: 'The value of such engagement might be limited if prospects for securing increased market access seem dim. Such negotiating pessimism is not without basis, but the launch of a new round of negotiations at Doha marks an improvement over the fiasco at Seattle'.

And this is how we motivated our case for a US–India FTA:

There are two problems with using the multilateral approach to impart impetus to India's trade reform. First, the prospects for the current multilateral round of trade negotiations appear uncertain, if not bleak. The more important point is that the WTO is unlikely to be a forum where significant progress can be made to further India's market access interests in labour-intensive manufacturing (textiles and clothing) and in skills-based services. These are the areas in which India has a comparative advantage and in which, at this juncture, India needs access to help revive the flagging growth momentum. Even if the Doha Round 'succeeds', it is quite probable that India's export interests will remain largely unaddressed.

The second problem with an exclusive reliance on multilateralism, is that the space of pure multilateral trade is fast shrinking. The US, EU, and even Japan are striking regional deals galore. The EU has negotiated deep integration agreements with countries in Eastern Europe and North Africa. Mexico has FTAs with the US and the EU. The US is negotiating the Free Trade Area of the Americas (FTAA), which will include Brazil and Argentina. The US and Japan are similarly striking deals with Singapore and other Asian countries. As a result of these, India's major developing country competitors are gaining a competitive advantage over India in the major industrial country markets. And China, by joining the WTO, has caught up with India in terms of its treatment by trading partners. To use a cricketing metaphor, when the world around us has chosen to have the freedom of playing on the front-foot or the back-foot, should India continue to grope forward on principle, oblivious to the flight and pitch of the ball?

Thus, our advocacy of regionalism was predicated on the failure of multilateralism to address India's needs, and to that extent was not a case of undermining multilateralism. That said, it is interesting to see how the changing economic landscape within India in the last few years since this piece was written, may have modified the case we made for a US–India FTA. The most telling example relates to labor mobility. In the 1990s and early years of this millennium, India had a keen interest in increasing the size of the H-1B visas to allow more Indian professionals to enter the US. But with the intensive use of skilled labour by India and emerging skilled labour shortages in India, it is less clear that exporting this labour is in India's best interest—the Indian growth engine is too reliant on skills for exporting them to be a reasonable option.

The general point here, again, is that at a time of rapid change, policies and interests are highly time-contingent. It must be an article of faith that as times change, these too will have to change.

Intellectual Property or Trade in Ideas

The first chapter in this section is the first paper that I wrote after my Ph.D. It was written when I was a low-level bureaucrat at the GATT when the TRIPs negotiations were under way. I can reasonably claim that I was amongst the first to assert that the provisions of any future TRIPs agreement relating to the protection of pharmaceutical product patents would be harmful for India and the first to calculate, albeit crudely, the magnitude of the costs to India (about US$1 billion on my calculation) and a group of other developing countries.

When this paper was written, my immediate bosses refused to grant permission for publication on the grounds that GATT officials involved in the negotiations could not be allowed to publicly take positions on what was turning out to be a highly contentious subject, pitting developed countries that were predominantly producers of ideas and hence likely beneficiaries of extending patent protection against developing countries that would likely lose from TRIPs. I took the matter up to Arthur Dunkel, who was then the Director General of the GATT. Despite his Swiss origins (Switzerland's pharmaceutical industry stood to gain substantially from TRIPs), and to his eternal credit, Dunkel over-ruled my bosses and granted permission for the paper's publication.

For me, the paper was really gratifying also because it seemed to have some impact, however small, on the debate on the merits of the TRIPs agreement within and outside India. Carla Hills (known as the 'crowbar' for her strident vow to pry open foreign markets for US exports), who was then the United States Trade Representative (USTR) came to India in 1991 to try and persuade India out of its overly obstructionist stance, an obstructionism she argued was based on a misguided economic understanding of the issues. She presented Chidambaram, India's then Commerce Minister, with a set of studies purporting to show that India would benefit from TRIPs. Chidambaram reciprocated by giving Carla Hills my paper that came to the opposite conclusion. Clearly, it was not enough to deflect Hills from her conviction but at least it helped to make the intellectual debate less one-sided. Wider dissemination of my paper and its results was helped considerably by three top economists—Jagdish Bhagwati, Dani Rodrik, and Andre Sapir—who supported the work and used it in their own writings and pronouncements on TRIPs and the Uruguay Round.

The TRIPs debate, for me, was also an eye-opener. It exposed the less savoury and less well-known side of the way knowledge and policy research are generated and disseminated, and more depressingly, the way they are suppressed. It was pretty clear that had my research come to the opposite conclusions, namely that TRIPs was good for developing countries, there would have been no opposition to its publication by GATT officials. But research that ran counter to the interests of large corporate interests and powerful governments in the trading system had to battle to find utterance.

As interesting was the intellectual role played by the World Bank during the nearly fifteen years—from about 1988 to 2003—that the TRIPs debate raged. In its intellectual capacity, the World Bank's research is meant to, among other objectives, identify policies that increase the welfare of developing countries. During this whole period, it would be difficult to find a single research or policy document that explicitly stated the costs to developing countries from the TRIPs provisions on pharmaceutical protection.

To be sure, there were a number of hedged outpourings on TRIPs: on the one hand and on the other. But, pronouncements and assessments on the benefits of trade liberalization, which actually needed to be more hedged, were in fact stated more categorically. The intellectual case on the costs of TRIPs was clear cut, a point that has been subsequently acknowledged by most analysts.[5] But the World Bank was simply unwilling to state the obvious. Why? That remains a mystery, especially given the enlightened intellectual leadership it had during those years.[6] This omission is especially striking given that during this period, sub-Saharan Africa— the World Bank's key client and moral responsibility—was being ravaged

---

[5] Nobel Prize winner James Tobin once remarked: 'A heapful of Harberger triangles cannot fill an Okun gap.' What he meant was that efficiency benefits of policies (usually depicted as Harberger triangles in the basic supply and demand diagram of economics) can seldom be justified if they are associated with underutilization of resources; Okun gaps refer to the macroeconomic costs of these unemployed resources. In TRIPs, there was a similar geometric comparison. The losses to developing countries were rents or profits (depicted as rectangles) that had to be given up to foreign pharmaceutical companies while the efficiency gains were the same Harberger triangles. It was therefore easy to assert that in the case of TRIPs, a heapful of Harberger triangles could not fill a Schumpeterian rectangle.

[6] A top official at the Bank even called upon a young, rising star of the economics profession and asked him to write a paper, arguing that developing countries stood to gain from TRIPs. So, instead of supporting the obvious developing country position, there was an intellectual effort to undermine it.

by one of the worst epidemics of all time—AIDS—and TRIPs' impact on the access of these countries to AIDS drugs was clear and unambiguously negative.[7] Was this was an dereliction of intellectual duty on the part of the Bank?

While this piece tried to fight TRIPs, another piece (again not part of this volume but available at *http://www.petersoninstitute.org/publications/papers/subramanian0300.pdf*), recognized that the battle had been lost. Once it became clear that India would have to accept TRIPs, the question was how to use the flexibility provided by the agreement to maximize the good and minimize the harm from the agreement.

One of the more interesting suggestions in this chapter, which unfortunately was not taken up by the Indian authorities when they revised the Indian patent bill to bring it into conformity with the TRIPs provisions, was to use IP as an enforcement device by India against its trading partners in the event that they did not live up to their WTO obligations vis-à-vis India. So, for example, if the US did not open up its textiles markets to Indian exports or implemented an illegal safeguard, India could threaten to revoke the patent of an American company. I argued that the credibility of this threat would then ensure that the US would think very hard before imposing trade restrictions against India's exports in the first place: the trade equivalent of gaining greater ex ante peace by ensuring mutually assured destruction ex post. To me, this proposal would have been part of the process of India becoming a fully engaged member of the WTO, reducing asymmetries between India and its richer trading partners—in this case by adding to the armoury of trade weapons that India could deploy—and making the trading system symmetric more generally.

Even in relation to IP, though, it is striking how much economic developments in the last few years have changed India's outlook. Consider the following thought experiment: Suppose the TRIPs negotiations were being conducted today rather than in 1992, what would India's stance be?

---

[7] On this too, there is an interesting asymmetry. At least in the international press, a lot of the credit for the reduction in drugs prices in AIDS-ravaged countries in Africa is attributed to the efforts of leaders like Bill Clinton, who managed to successfully appeal to the goodwill of pharmaceutical companies. That competition rather than compassion had at least as important a role is less well-recognized. Indian companies like Cipla were producing generic versions of AIDS drugs at the fraction of the price charged by large pharmaceutical companies, forcing the latter to charge more reasonable prices.

In three important areas, the Indian negotiating position would probably be quite different than it was in the Uruguay Round. On copyright and the protection of software, the rise of India's IT sector would surely make India less inclined to be on the side of weak protection. On films, given Bollywood's global reach and popularity today, India would have had a really strong stake in the strong protection and enforcement of copyright protection and the prevention of piracy. And even on pharmaceuticals, India's position would be a little less strident because the domestic industry is no longer comprised just of generic producers: the nascent R&D-based drugs industry with tie-ups with foreign multinationals would have had some influence in steering India's position away from strident resistance to a degree of ambivalence on patent protection.

Trade in Capital

The final chapter in this section relates to an issue of great contemporary relevance. Should India open up to foreign capital, and if so, how rapidly? The first draft of this chapter was prepared nearly two years ago, and in some ways anticipated the recent tensions between monetary policy, exchange rates, and foreign capital—what is known in the profession as the international trilemma. The Indian economy has been overheating and foreign capital has been pouring in. The RBI has tried to tighten monetary policy but this has only served to increase the flow of capital that has put further pressure on the exchange rate. The RBI faces the classic dilemma of having to meet two objectives—containing inflation and maintaining currency competitiveness—but with only one instrument, namely monetary policy.

The chapter anticipated these developments and discusses the policy options for India in relation to the contentious question of how and when to open up the capital account. In some ways, the main point of the chapter was to show that discussions in India of capital account policies were being conducted somewhat unmindful of the exchange rate implications of such opening. Both the Tarapore Committee reports in 1996 and 2006 devote only a few paragraphs to exchange rate issues, making the unobjectionable but unhelpful observation that India's exchange rate should remain competitive.

To some extent, Indian policymakers have been lulled into complacency about exchange rate management because of having done it so well in the past: indeed, Indian exchange rate policy must rank as one of those few areas where policy has been consistently sensible and successful. But the problem is that exchange rate management has become a very different beast given the growth of the Indian economy and the rapid increase in capital inflows. The past, in this instance is not the best guide to future action. The philosopher, Santayana cautioned against repeating the mistakes of the past. But wisdom also consists in knowing when not to repeat the successes of the past, or when not to fight the last battle, even if the outcome was victory.

The chapter outlines why exchange rates are important for development and makes the case for a more cautious attitude toward opening up to foreign inflows because of the exchange rate consequences which can be damaging for exports and overall growth. It also suggests some markers that can guide policymakers in moving more rapidly toward capital account convertibility. As with all the other chapters in this section on globalization, it is almost certain that some of the analysis in this chapter will be rendered moot by future events.

A final note for the reader. Although this is a book mainly for policy wonks—broadly defined to include economists, bureaucrats, journalists, political scientists, sociologists, development practitioners, etc.—it also tries to reach out to a wider audience. This is done by including at the end of each of the more technical chapters—a summary (or summaries) that is written non-technically and hopefully without too much jargon. In fact, all these summaries are reproductions of newspaper articles or op-eds which should serve to reassure the general reader that they will in fact be comprehensible.

Section 1

INDIA'S GROWTH

CHAPTER 1

FROM 'HINDU GROWTH' TO PRODUCTIVITY SURGE
THE MYSTERY OF THE INDIAN GROWTH TRANSITION

The only duty we owe to history is to rewrite it.
—Oscar Wilde

India's economic performance during the first three decades since independence was christened the 'Hindu' rate of growth, a term connoting a disappointing but not disastrous outcome, and playing to the cliché of the acquiescence in the present that the religion supposedly imbues, because of a greater emphasis on the hereafter.

That cliché, of course, is gradually lapsing into disuse, thanks to the remarkable transformation in India during the last two decades. Since 1980, its economic growth rate has more than doubled, rising from 1.7 per cent (in per capita terms) in 1950–80 to 3.8 per cent in 1980–2000. Shackled by the socialist policies and the 'license-permit-quota raj' (to use Rajaji's memorable phrase) of the past, India used to serve as the exemplar of development strategies gone wrong. It has now become the latest poster child for how economic growth can be unleashed with a turn towards free markets and open trade. India has yet to catch up with China's growth rates (or even to China's level of income)[1], but thanks to its solid democratic institutions and impressive performance in information technology, the country is increasingly vying with, if not displacing, China as the country of the future in the eyes of many knowledgeable observers.[2]

---

[1] According to Penn World Tables (PWT) 6.1, India's purchasing-power adjusted per capita Gross Domestic Product (GDP) stood at $2479 in 2000, compared to $3747 for China. However, there are reasons to believe India's Purchasing Power Parity (PPP) level of income is understated (see Deaton et. al., 2004).

[2] See Huang and Khanna (2003).

The improvement in India's economic performance is obviously good news for its one billion people. But equally important, this transformation also holds hope for other poor countries around the world, insofar as it sends the message that rapid economic growth is attainable under appropriate policies.

But what exactly are those 'appropriate' policies that made the Indian miracle possible? The conventional story about India, which can be glimpsed in any number of policy-oriented papers and newspaper articles, goes like this. Until 1991, India's policymakers followed misguided policies that closed the economy to international trade, erected inefficient industries under state guidance, riddled the private sector with extraordinarily cumbersome and detailed regulations, and suffocated private economic activity with controls and bureaucratic impediments. Then, in 1991 the big breakthrough happened. Spurred by a balance of payments crisis, Indian policymakers turned to technocrats such as Manmohan Singh, who promptly began the process of liberalizing the economy. Trade barriers were slashed, foreign investment was welcomed, the license raj was dismantled, and privatization began. The economy started to boom, with software exports and call centres leading the way.

Like all caricatures, this story has elements of truth in it. It is indeed the case that until recently India had one of the most over-regulated and closed economies of the world. It is also true that the economic liberalization of 1991 constitutes a watershed event for the Indian economy. But the main difficulty with the standard account, as summarized in the preceding paragraph, is that the pick-up in India's economic growth precedes the liberalization of 1991 by a full decade. Even a cursory glance at the growth record reveals that the more-than-doubling of India's growth rate takes place sometime around 1980, with very little discernible change in trend after 1991. In fact, some indicators, such as economy-wide total factor productivity, even go in the 'wrong' direction, showing a deceleration after 1991. Therefore, the striking post-1980 improvement in performance cannot be attributed to the liberalization of 1991. The latter may well have played a role in sustaining and deepening an ongoing process of growth, but we need to look elsewhere than the reforms of 1991 to understand how India made the transition to high growth. A related implication is that more recent phenomena such as the boom in IT and related services cannot have been the original source of India's economic growth.

We present in this chapter a somewhat different interpretation of India's experience. We argue that the trigger for India's economic growth was an attitudinal shift on the part of the national government in 1980 in favour of private business. The rhetoric of the reigning Congress Party until that time had been all about socialism and pro-poor policies. When Indira Gandhi returned to power in 1980, she realigned herself politically with the organized private sector and dropped her previous rhetoric. The national government's attitude towards business went from being outright hostile to supportive. Indira's switch was further reinforced, in a more explicit manner, by Rajiv Gandhi following his rise to power in 1984. This, in our view, was the key change that unleashed the animal spirits of the Indian private sector in the early 1980s.

It is important to characterize appropriately this attitudinal change that took place in the early 1980s. We make a distinction here between a *pro-market* and a *pro-business* orientation. The former focuses on removing impediments to markets and aims at achieving this through economic liberalization. It favours entrants and consumers. A pro-business orientation, on the other hand, is one that focuses on raising the profitability of the established industrial and commercial establishments. It tends to favour incumbents and producers. Easing restrictions on capacity expansion for incumbents, removing price controls, and reducing corporate taxes (all of which took place during the 1980s) are examples of pro-business policies, while trade liberalization (which did not take place in any significant form until the 1990s) is the archetypal market-oriented policy. This distinction can be observed, for example, in the contrasting approaches towards reform in East Asia and Latin America. South Korea's reforms in the 1960s and 1970s were primarily pro-business rather than pro-market. Latin America's reforms in the 1990s were primarily pro-market.

The change in India in the early 1980s are accordingly best described as pro-business rather than pro-market. True liberalization was by and large anathema to organized business at the time. Indira Gandhi was far less interested in opening up the economy and removing impediments to competition than in garnering political support from existing business groups. Rajiv Gandhi, who was somewhat more prone to liberalize, had to step back when he reached too far out of line and when the Bofors scandal undermined his effectiveness. The primary beneficiaries of growth were therefore incumbents and preexisting activities rather than entrants and new activities. Nevertheless, we view this shift towards a pro-business orientation as the essential trigger that set off the boom of the 1980s. That this was a powerful trigger can be deduced from the fact that the genuine liberalization after 1991 added very little to aggregate economic performance. Apparently, this attitudinal shift was in itself a very powerful stimulant for economic growth, even in the presence of price and other market distortions.

The fact that an attitudinal change on the part of the national leadership could have such a strong impact on growth is in turn grounded in India's initial conditions. India has very strong political and economic institutions for a country at its income level. It is a democracy where the rule of law generally prevails and property rights are protected adequately. Judged by cross-country norms, it ought to have a level of income that is several times higher. The implication is that relatively minor changes in the policy environment can produce a large growth impact. We interpret the suspension of the national government's hostility to the private sector as one of these changes, something that left little paper trail in actual policies but had an important impact on investors' psychology.

We begin this chapter by documenting India's growth transition in the 1980s and placing this experience in comparative context. We show that this transition is grounded in an impressive increase in productivity (rather than in factor accumulation). We also show that India has moved from being a global underperformer before 1980 to a strong overperformer since then.

We next present a series of possible explanations for this shift and show that none of them can satisfactorily account for the boom of the early 1980s. There was not much liberalization in the 1980s, and the little that took place happened during the second half of the 1980s. The Indian economy remained closed to world trade, and in some ways more protected than ever. The Green Revolution is unlikely to have been the source of the boom in non-agricultural activity, because we do not observe the requisite changes in the internal terms of trade. Demand-side explanations are inadequate to explain the rise in productivity. Public sector investment is unlikely to have been the story either, unless we make demanding assumptions on time lags.

We then lay out our own explanation and provide some empirical evidence in support of it. We show in particular that post-1980 growth was strongest in activities and states that were most advantaged by the national government's attitudinal shift—namely in the formal manufacturing sector built up under the earlier policy regime. Hence to some extent, the learning generated under the earlier policy regime and the modern manufacturing base created thereby provided a permissive environment for eventual takeoff once the policy stance softened vis-à-vis the private sector. So, unlike what one may have otherwise expected (from accounts of how costly Import Substituting Industrialization (ISI) was), growth occurred where the earlier investments had been made.

Our analysis focuses on the transition to high growth in the 1980s, and we have little to say about the 1991 reforms and the experience of the 1990s. We take the view that igniting growth and sustaining it are distinct challenges, requiring different sets of policies and approaches (Rodrik 2003, Hausmann et al., 2004). This chapter is concerned exclusively with the challenge of igniting growth and the story of how India seems to have overcome it.

THE FACTS

A key fact that we establish at the outset of this chapter is that the turnaround in this performance—the decisive break with the Hindu past—occurred around 1980 and not in the 1990s as most accounts have it. We are not the first to make this point: De Long (2003) and Williamson and Zagha (2002) have both emphasized that the approximate doubling of India's growth rate took place a full decade before the 1991 reforms. Nonetheless, it is impossible to read the standard policy-oriented accounts and not leave with the impression that it is were reforms of the 1990s that have brought superlative economic performance to India (Ahluwalia, 2002; Srinivasan and Tendulkar, 2003).

Figure 1.1 illustrates that three measures related to aggregate growth performance—real GDP per capita, real GDP per worker, and total factor productivity—displayed a sharp upward trend beginning 1980 after remaining virtually flat for the preceding two decades. Table 1.1 confirms that the pick-up in labour and total factor productivity between the 1970s and 1980s amounted to about 3 percentage points. While the 1990s continued to see strong growth, the productivity measures show a *deceleration* of between 0.3 and 0.6 percentage points between the 1980s and 1990s.[3]

---

[3] Micro-level evidence is also consistent with the absence of any significant break associated with the reforms of 1991. Deaton and Dreze (2002) show that measures of poverty reduction, real wage growth, health and education exhibit trends in the 1990s similar to those prior to the 1990s.

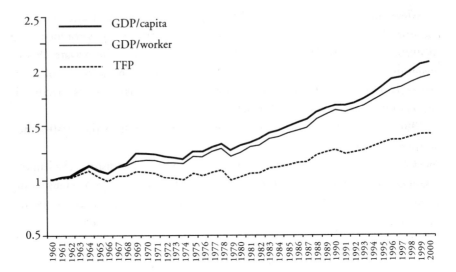

Figure 1.1: Economic performance in India 1960–2000 (log scale, 1960–1)

Source: Penn World Tabler, Bosworth and Collins (2003)

Regardless of whether the 1990s were slightly worse (or slightly better) than the 1980s, it is abundantly clear that India's economic performance improved sharply sometime around 1980.[4]

More formal evidence that the break occurred around 1980 comes from a variety of sources. First, using the procedure described in Bai and Perron (1998, 2003), we computed the optimal one, two, and three break points for the growth rate of four series: per capita GDP computed at constant dollars (World Bank) and at PPP prices (PWT), GDP per worker (PWT), and total factor productivity (Bosworth and Collins, 2003).[5] In all four cases, we find that the single break occurs in 1979.[6] Second, Hausmann et

[4] We note that this improvement is also evident when Indian GDP is expressed in PPP terms (that is, using Penn World Tables data). So it cannot be argued that the pickup in growth is artificial due to the interaction of price distortions with differential sectoral expansion.

[5] We thank Andy Berg and Marcos Souto for suggesting and estimating this procedure. For the case of a single break, the Bai and Perron procedure minimizes the sum of squared deviations of the growth rate around the means of the two resulting subsamples. For multiple breaks, we use the method described in Bai and Perron (2003), which employs a dynamic programming algorithm to compare all possible combinations, so that a minimum global sum of squared residuals is achieved. Details are available from the authors upon request.

[6] The two breaks occurred in 1970 and 1979, and the three breaks occurred in 1970, 1979, and 1994 (with the procedure suggesting that there was a trend decline after 1994).

al. (forthcoming) have analysed transitions to high growth in a large cross-national sample and date the Indian growth transition in 1982.[7] Finally, Wallack (2003) has analysed GDP and its disaggregated components for structural breaks. She finds evidence for a break in the GDP growth rate in the early to mid-1980s. The highest value of the F-statistic associated with the existence of a break is reached in 1980 (Wallack 2003, p. 4314).[8]

Was this improved aggregate productivity performance since the 1980s simply a consequence of re-allocation of resources from low productivity (agriculture) to high productivity (manufacturing and services) or was there a trend improvement in the performance of individual sectors? There has been a substantial structural change in the composition of the labour force employed in the three major sectors, with the most pronounced one being the decline in agriculture's share of about 10 percentage points between 1975 and 1995, offset by an increase in the share of services (about 7.5 percentage points) and industry (2.5 percentage points). But this shift explains a very small fraction (less than 10 per cent) of the improvement in economy-wide productivity. For example, when the aggregate labour productivity growth is computed with fixed (base-period) employment shares, the pick-up in the 1980s is between 2.6 and 2.9 percentage points, and the deceleration in the 1990s about 0.4–0.6 percentage points (Table 1.1).

A number of studies have argued that manufacturing experienced a surge in productivity in the 1980s (Ahluwalia, 1995; Unel, 2003) although some of these estimates have been contested (Hulten and Srinivasan, 1999; Balakrishnan and Pushpagandan, 1994).[9] For example, Ahluwalia's (1995)

---

[7] The Hausmann et al. (forthcoming) filter looks for a year such that the growth rate in the seven years following it is at least 2 percentage points or more higher than the growth rate in the prior seven years.

[8] She finds less evidence for a break in growth rates in specific sectors (such as manufacturing and agriculture), attributing the post-1980 growth to the changing composition of GDP. Note that Wallack's study focuses on value added and not productivity.

[9] Hulten and Srinivasan (1999) make the point that conventional TFP measures understate the true contribution of productivity performance by ignoring the additional capital formation induced by an increase in productivity. Balakrishnan and Pushpagandan's (1994) critique is based on the failure of conventional measures to use separate deflators for gross output and intermediates in arriving at TFP measures. Another study (RBI, 2004), using the double deflation methodology, however, shows that manufacturing TFP grew at 3.9 per cent in the 1980s and declined to 2.1 per cent in the 1990s.

Table 1.1: India: Aggregated and Sectoral Growth Accounting
(annual average growth rates, unless otherwise specified)

	1960–70	1970–80	1980–90	1990–99
Bosworth-Collins (B-C)				
Output	3.84	2.98	5.85	5.59
Output per worker (Q/L)	1.87	0.69	3.90	3.27
Capital per worker	0.83	0.61	1.06	1.32
Education	0.29	0.58	0.32	0.34
Total factor productivity (TFP)	0.74	-0.50	2.49	1.57
IMF				
Output	3.75	3.16	5.64	5.61
Output per worker	1.77	0.86	3.69	3.30
Total factor productivity[a]	1.17	0.47	2.89	2.44
Total factor productivity[b]	-0.94	-2.07	1.28	0.94
Disaggregated growth of Q/L based on current employment shares				
Agriculture[c]	1.20	0.13	2.57	1.29
Manufacturing[d]		2.00	6.30	6.00
Services (B-C)[e]		2.12	6.32	6.57
Services (IMF)[f]		3.14	5.30	6.69
Growth rate of Aggregate Q/L with base-period employment shares as weights				
Aggregate (Bosworth-Collins)		0.69	3.66	3.08
Aggregate (IMF)		0.86	3.49	3.11
Contribution of labour-shifts to aggregate Q/L growth				
Aggregate (Bosworth-Collins) n.a.			0.24	0.19
Aggregate (IMF) n.a.			0.20	0.19
Employment Share[g]		1975	1985	1995
Agriculture		70.8	64.4	60.8
Industry		12.4	15.2	15.8
Services		16.8	20.4	23.4

Sources: Bosworth and Collins (2003); Ghose (1999); and authors' estimates

Notes: [a] Based on labour force; [b] Based on average years of schooling in population above 15 years of age; [c] From World Bank's World Development Indicators; [d] For 1980s and 1990s, data from IMF Working paper; for 1970s, estimate based on Ahulwahlia (1995); [e] Calculated as a residual by deducting weighted average sectoral productivity growth rates from B-C agg. Q/L growth rate; [f] Calculated as a residual by deducting weighted average sectoral productivity growth rates from IMF agg. Q/L growth rate; [g] Obtained from Ghose (1999). His number for 1977–78 is extrapolated backward to 1975 by applying trend between 1977–8 and 1983 and his number for 1993–4 is extrapolated forward to 1995 by applying the trend from 1987–8–1993–4.

figures suggest that the increase in TFP growth during 1981–9 over the previous two decades was 3.2 percentage points.

A break in growth performance is also suggested by the evidence on economic growth at the level of the Indian states. Figure 1.2 plots per capita GDP for all states for every ten years beginning in 1960. Beginning in 1980, there is both an upward trend in the average as well as a wider spread in the distribution of incomes. A more formal test of (unconditional) convergence between states for the four decades confirms this break (Table 1.2). For the 1960s and 1970s, the convergence coefficient is positive and insignificant. For the 1980s and 1990s, this coefficient increases and becomes statistically significant. The magnitude of the coefficient suggests that in the latter two decades, states are diverging at an annual rate of about 1.2 per cent a year, very much a case of 'Divergence, Big Time' (Pritchett, 1997).

The surge in India's performance since the 1980s is also confirmed by cross-national evidence. Table 1.3 provides basic data on the average growth

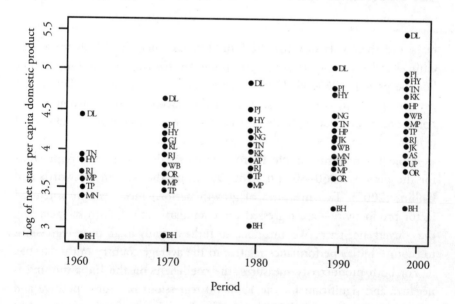

Figure 1.2: Real per capita net state domestic product,
1960–2000 (at 1993–4 prices)

Source: EPW Research Foundation.

Table 1.2: India: Unconditional State-Level Convergence

Period	1960s and 1970s	1970s and 1980s	1980s and 1990s	1960s– 1990s
Initial Income	0.006	0.008	0.011	
	1.15	1.34	2.04	
1960s convergence dummy				0.008
				1.75
1970s convergence dummy				0.007
				1.65
1980s convergence dummy				0.011
				2.71
1990s convergence dummy				0.011
				2.88
R-square	0.04	0.04	0.09	0.38
No. of observationss	38	41	42	80

rates and their volatility for the four decades since the 1960s for India, China, and the other regional groupings (Bosworth and Collins, 2003). For the period, 1960–80, India's growth rate of output per worker, at 1.3 per cent per year, is the lowest in the world except for sub-Saharan Africa. For the next two decades, however, its average growth exceeds, by a substantial margin, that of all other regions, except East Asia.

Table 1.4 presents simple Barro-type cross-country growth regressions for the periods 1960–80 and 1980–99, using the data in Bosworth and Collins (2003). Two measures of growth performance—labour and total factor productivity—are regressed on a standard set of controls, including the convergence term. We introduce an India dummy in all these regressions to capture India's performance relative to the average country in the sample.

For both productivity measures, the coefficient on the India dummy is negative and significant for the 1960–80 regressions but turns positive and significant for the period 1980–99. The Total Factor Productivity (TFP) regressions suggest that, after controlling policies, endowments, and initial income, India grew 0.7 per cent per year slower than the average country in 1960–80 period, but grew 2.1 per cent per year faster than the average

Table 1.3: India in the Cross-Section: Mean and Volatility of Growth Rate of Output per Worker, 1960–2000[a]

	1960–1970	1970–1980	1980–1990	1990–2000	1960–1980	1980–2000	1960–2000
Industrial Countries							
Mean	4.12	2.12	1.54	1.47	3.12	1.51	2.34
Standard deviation	2.26	2.61	1.98	2.06	2.71	2.08	2.63
Coefficient of variation	0.55	1.23	1.29	1.41	0.87	1.38	1.13
East Asia (incl. China)							
Mean	4.19	4.11	4.15	3.98	4.15	4.07	4.11
Standard deviation	3.99	2.80	3.24	3.91	3.69	3.74	3.98
Coefficient of variation	0.95	0.68	0.78	0.98	0.89	0.92	0.97
China							
Mean	1.66	2.82	6.86	8.85	2.24	7.85	5.05
Standard deviation	12.45	3.40	3.59	2.37	8.90	3.13	7.17
Coefficient of variation	7.50	1.20	0.52	0.27	3.97	0.40	1.42
Latin America							
Mean	2.38	1.69	(1.65)	0.83	2.03	(0.48)	0.81
Standard deviation	3.47	4.00	4.40	3.03	4.07	4.17	4.43
Coefficient of variation	1.46	2.36	(2.66)	3.66	2.00	(8.70)	5.47
India							
Mean	1.91	0.77	3.91	3.22	1.34	3.57	2.45
Standard deviation	3.24	4.16	1.87	2.05	3.68	1.94	3.11
Coefficient of variation	1.69	5.40	0.48	0.64	2.74	0.54	1.27
Africa							
Mean	1.87	0.69	(0.47)	(0.03)	1.28	(0.26)	0.53
Standard deviation	5.41	5.25	4.48	4.48	5.54	4.89	5.55
Coefficient of variation	2.90	7.56	(9.53)	(170.29)	4.33	(18.85)	10.47
Middle East[b]							
Mean	4.61	3.47	1.81	1.19	4.04	1.51	2.81
Standard deviation	5.83	6.64	3.42	2.77	6.55	3.21	5.44
Coefficient of variation	1.26	1.91	1.89	2.33	1.62	2.12	1.94

Source: Bosworth and Collins (2003) and authors' calculations.
Note: The box highlights the argument about the volatility of growth rate of output per worker for India. Parenthesis indicate negative values.
a All regional aggregates are unweighted averages.
b Excludes Jordan.

Table 1.4: India's Growth in Comparative Perspective

Dependent variable period	Labour productivity		Total factor productivity	
	1960–80	1980–99	1960–80	1980–99
Initial income	–7.24	–5.92	–3.28	–3.60
	–7.25	–5.28	–4.76	–4.59
Life expectancy	0.06	0.04	0.05	0.03
	2.84	1.27	2.56	1.22
Terms of trade	0.13	–0.01	0.11	–0.13
	2.13	–0.12	2.13	–1.67
Instability in terms of trade	–0.12	0.00	–0.08	–0.01
	–3.23	0.04	–2.38	–0.48
Budget balance	0.05	0.03	0.02	0.01
	0.79	0.56	0.36	0.38
Inflation	–0.01	–0.01	0.01	–0.01
	–0.44	–2.53	0.60	–2.29
Openness	0.53	2.03	0.12	0.82
	1.83	2.72	0.33	1.59
Geography	0.34	0.33	0.03	0.20
	2.08	1.11	0.15	0.98
Institutions	2.94	5.19	0.93	4.41
	2.07	2.94	0.70	3.33
India dummy	–1.72	2.99	–0.71	2.11
	–5.35	4.74	–2.08	4.63
R-square	0.65	0.61	0.36	0.57
No. of observations	73	3	73	73

Note: For description of variables, see Bosworth and Collins (2003).

country in the 1980–99 period. These results indicate that India's turnaround is not a consequence of merely catching-up. In the cross-section, the magnitude of over-performance in the latter period has been substantial and exceeds the magnitude of under-performance in the 1960–80 period.

Table 1.3 also sheds light on the variability of India's growth in the various decades in absolute and relative terms. India's growth has not been more variable than other developing regions in the period 1960–80. Indeed,

Table 1.5: Contributions to Growth: India in the Cross-Section, 1960–99

Region/ Period	Output	Output per worker	Contribution of in percentage points Physical capital	Education	Factor productivity	in % of total Factor productivity	Physical capital
Industrial Countries							
1960–80	4.42	3.05	1.22	1.61	1.30	43%	40%
1980–99	2.68	1.60	0.78	0.98	0.64	40%	49%
1960–99	3.57	2.34	1.01	1.30	0.98	42%	43%
East Asia (incl. China)							
1960–80	5.64	2.98	1.45	1.93	0.96	32%	49%
1980–99	8.03	6.02	2.44	2.85	3.25	54%	41%
1960–99	6.80	4.45	1.93	2.38	2.07	46%	43%
China							
1960–80	4.04	1.83	0.76	0.43	0.64	35%	41%
1980–99	9.75	7.85	2.63	0.36	4.71	60%	33%
1960–99	6.78	4.72	1.66	0.39	2.60	55%	35%
Latin America							
1960–80	6.10	2.90	1.08	1.42	1.45	50%	37%
1980–99	2.20	−0.54	0.09	0.48	−1.02	189%	−17%
1960–99	4.18	1.21	0.60	0.96	0.24	20%	49%
India							
1960–80	3.4	11.2	80.7	20.4	30.1	29%	56%
1980–99	5.73	3.60	1.18	0.33	2.05	57%	33%
1960–99	4.53	2.40	0.95	0.38	1.06	44%	39%
Africa							
1960–80	4.36	1.78	1.06	1.21	0.66	37%	59%
1980–99	2.02	−0.70	−0.12	0.25	−0.93	134%	18%
1960–99	3.21	0.57	0.48	0.74	−0.12	−21%	85%
Middle East							
1960–80	5.71	3.14	2.74	3.25	0.28	9%	87%
1980–99	3.68	0.85	0.20	0.81	−0.08	−9%	23%
1960–99	4.71	2.02	1.50	2.06	0.11	5%	74%

Source: Bosworth and Collins (2003).

it has the lowest standard deviation amongst all regions although the coefficient of variation is higher than for the Middle East, Latin America, and Asia. Between 1980 and 1999, however, India's growth exhibits the lowest variation in terms of both the standard deviation and the coefficient of variation. Thus, India outperformed all regions, except East Asia, in terms of average growth, and outperformed all regions, including East Asia, in terms of the stability of growth.[10] Interestingly, and contrary to some claims, Indian growth was more stable in the 1980s than in the 1990s.

A really striking feature about the Indian performance that emerges from the cross-national comparison is the respective contributions of capital accumulation and total factor productivity growth to overall labour productivity growth (Table 1.5). Prior to 1980, the contribution of TFP growth to overall labour productivity growth, at 10 per cent, was lower in India than in any other region, except the Middle East: even sub-Saharan Africa fared better. Since 1980, however, India almost tops the list for TFP contribution to overall growth. Nearly 60 per cent of overall growth was accounted for by TFP, a feature matched only by China. Amazingly, the Indian TFP performance in 1980–99 surpasses that of East Asia even in the first twenty years of the East Asian miracle. Evidently, India has relied less on deferred gratification and more on productivity to motor its growth even compared to the fast-growing countries of East Asia. If productivity-based growth is more sustainable than accumulation-based growth, it would appear that India's future prospects appear quite promising.

THE EXPLANATIONS THAT DO NOT WORK

What explains the dramatic rise in India's growth, and in particular its productivity, performance since 1980? In this section, we discuss a number of explanations that could explain this turnaround, including those that have been put forward by recent studies. For the most part, we argue that these explanations are inadequate or unsatisfactory in some way. In the next section, we propose some alternative hypotheses for which we provide some direct and indirect evidence.

India's performance in the 1980s has elicited a number of distinct explanations. We consider each in turn.

[10] India's superior performance on the variability of growth in the 1980–99 period is confirmed in simple cross-section regressions (available from the authors upon request).

Was it a Favourable External Environment?

The first explanation that we need to consider whether the improved productivity performance was simply a consequence of a more favourable external environment. There is very little to suggest that such a factor was at play. On the whole, the 1980s did not present a hospitable environment for developing countries, something that can be readily gauged by the slowdown in growth pretty much everywhere (with the notable exception of China).[11] The long decline in industrial country productivity began with the oil shocks of the 1970s. Figure 1.3 plots the temporal evolution of India's terms of trade, which is a gauge of external environmental conditions. It turns out that since 1960, the terms of trade were most unfavourable for India in the 1980s, during which period they declined by about 20 per cent relative to the previous period. This, of course, only serves to deepen

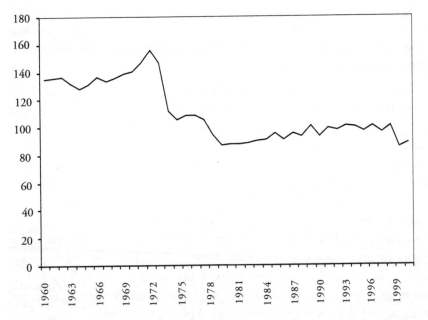

Figure 1.3: India's external terms of trade, 1960–2000

Source: IMF's World Economic Outlook

[11] For example, the real price of oil was 15 per cent higher in the 1980s than in the 1970s (and nearly 75 per cent higher than in the 1990s); and industrial country growth averaged 3.5 per cent in the 1970s versus 3.2 per cent in the 1980s.

the mystery of the 1980s productivity performance because it appeared to have occurred at a time when exogenous external conditions were most adverse.[12]

Aggregate Demand and the Unsustainability of 1980s Growth

A common argument used in downplaying the growth of the 1980s is that it was led by fiscal expansion and hence unsustainable. This view is expressed clearly, for example, in Ahluwalia (2002) and Srinivasan and Tendulkar (2003).[13]

This (the 1990s) growth record is only slightly better than the annual average of 5.7 per cent in the 1980s, but it can be argued that the 1980s growth was unsustainable, fuelled by a buildup of external debt that culminated in the crisis of 1991. In sharp contrast, growth in the 1990s was accompanied by remarkable external stability despite the east Asian crisis. (Ahluwalia, 2002, p. 67)

The fiscal expansionism of the 1980s, accompanied by some liberalization of controls on economic activity, generated real GDP growth of more than 5.8 per cent a year. This expansionism, however, was not sustainable and led to the macroeconomic crisis of 1991. (Srinivasan and Tendulkar, 2003, p. 9)

This Keynesian-run-amok explanation is, at first blush, supported by the data. During the 1970s, the average consolidated government deficit averaged 5 per cent of GDP. During the 1980s, this had soared to 9 per cent, an annual increase of 4 percentage points. But the fiscal expansion has two distinct consequences, relating respectively to its unsustainability and its impact on productivity, which the quotes above fail to distinguish. Indeed, the two consequences work at cross-purposes with each other.

Fiscal expansion can lead to rising current account deficits, and hence to a build-up of external debt which in the Indian case proved to be unsustainable, triggering the crisis of 1991. But the more this happens, that is, the more the fiscal expansion 'leaks abroad' and leads to a debt build-up, the less the demand that is generated for domestic goods and services, and the less likely that measured productivity increases could have resulted. It is because the current account deficit did not deteriorate one-for-one relative to the fiscal impulse (the current account deficit was about 1.7 percentage points higher during the 1980s than the 1970s),

---

[12] By the same token, the 1990s productivity performance looks less impressive.
[13] See also Chopra et al. (1995).

that the demand explanation has potential traction for explaining productivity growth.

The component of fiscal expansion that leads to increased demand for domestic goods and services can explain output growth over short periods, strictly speaking relative to trend, but it is not clear how it can explain a large and sustained rise in *trend productivity*. The only possible explanation would rely on sustained differences in capacity utilization across time. A demand expansion can then increase output, which in the presence of idle capacity would also show up in the measured productivity aggregates. One way to control such a demand-induced increase in productivity is to compute the productivity aggregates incorporating changes in capacity utilization. In the Indian case, this argument would suggest that the TFP measures for the 1970s and 1980s should be corrected for capacity utilization.

Data on capacity utilization in Indian manufacturing for the period under consideration are produced by different sources and are difficult to reconcile. For example, for the 1970s, the World Bank (1995) reports an estimate of 72.7 per cent while Ahluwalia's (1991) numbers yield an estimate of 77.6 per cent. Estimates for the 1980s are similarly dispersed. One consistent estimate for the 1970s and 1980s (World Bank, 1995) implies an increase in capacity utilization of about 2.7 per cent, which would have the effect of reducing measured TFP growth in the 1980s by about 1 per cent per year.[14] Even on the strong assumption that all this change in capacity is demand-induced, the turnaround in TFP growth between the 1970s and 1980s would remain substantial (about 2–2.2 per cent per year). Of course, the turnaround in labour productivity growth would remain unaffected by changes in capacity utilization.

More broadly, however, the explanation of increased demand is likely to be unsatisfactory or incomplete because the break in the 1980s that we have presented: (i) related to a number of productivity aggregates and not just at aggregate but also at the level of the states; (ii) appeared to hold not just in a time series context for India but also in the cross-section; (iii) even on the most favourable interpretation cannot account for a large share of the trunaround. A lot remains unexplained.

---

[14] Effectively, the contribution of capital accumulation to labour productivity growth is increased by an amount equal to the percentage increase in capacity utilization multiplied by the share of capital in output (assumed to be 0.35).

External Liberalization

Was the pickup in India's trend productivity growth in the 1980s caused by external liberalization? We present below evidence—relating to trade policies and trade outcomes—which paints a remarkably consistent picture of little, if any, liberalization taking place during the 1980s, significant liberalization taking place in the 1990s, with its full effects being felt in the late 1990s.

Table 1.6, based on Das (2003), presents data on the actual trade policy reform that was carried out since the early 1980s. We can see that during the early 1990s, trade protection declined unambiguously and markedly. However, during the 1980s, protection through tariffs (measured in terms

Table 1.6: India: Measures of Trade Protection, 1980–2000

	1980–85	*1986–90*	*1991–95*	*1996–2000*
All Industries				
Average effective rate of protection	115.1	125.9	80.2	40.4
Import coverage ratio	97.6	91.6	38.0	24.8
Import penetration rate	10.0	11.0	12.0	16.0
Intermediate Goods				
Average effective rate of protection	147.0	149.2	87.6	40.1
Import coverage ratio	98.3	98.3	41.8	27.6
Import penetration rate	11.0	13.0	15.0	18.0
Capital Goods				
Average effective rate of protection	62.8	78.5	54.2	33.3
Import coverage ratio	95.1	77.2	20.5	8.2
Import penetration rate	12.0	12.0	12.0	19.0
Consumer goods				
Average effective rate of protection	101.5	111.6	80.6	48.3
Import coverage ratio	98.7	87.9	45.7	33.4
Import penetration rate	4.0	4.0	4.0	10.0

Source: Das (2003).

of effective protection) increased, and protection through quantitative restrictions (measured in terms of the coverage of these restrictions) declined only marginally. This is true for manufacturing as a whole and for the different use-based sectors. It is important to note here that these numbers likely understate the increase in effective protection for final/consumer goods for much of the 1980s and 1990s stemming from the liberalization, albeit limited, of the capital goods sector.

This broad pattern of trade policy reform is confirmed by the data on tariff collections and by data related to trade outcomes. Figure 1.4 illustrates that duties collected as a share of imports and GDP rose substantially during the 1980s, peaking in the early 1990s. Duty collection as a share of imports rose from over 30 per cent in the early 1980s to nearly 45 per cent in the late 1980s. As a share of GDP, duty collections declined steadily only after the mid-1990s. The figure also computes a broader measure of trade protection—the anti-export bias—which incorporates the export subsidies granted to manufacturing under various schemes. Incorporating export subsidies reduces the level of protection but confirms the pattern of sharply rising protection during the 1980s. In 1991, the important export subsidies were eliminated, which imparted a one-off increase to the level of overall protection.

The pattern of trade outcomes is also consistent with the pattern of trade protection (see Figure 1.5 and Table 1.7).

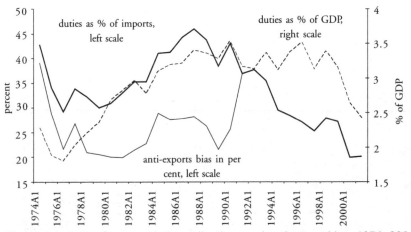

Figure 1.4: India: Customs duties collections and anti-export bias, 1974–2001

Source: Duties (WB, *World Development Indicators*), Imports (IMF, *World Economic Outlook*), Export subsidies (Joshi and Little).

Table 1.7: Trade Outcome for India

(in per cent)

	1970s	1980s	1990s
Annual growth of non-oil import volume	1.1	2.8	12.9
Annual growth of export volume	4.6	4.0	10.7
Openness ratio	9.8	12.7	19.3

Source: IMF's *World Economic Outlook*.

Crude outcome indicators such as the openness ratio tell a story of modest increases in openness during the 1970s and 1980s of 1.5 and 2.2 percentage points, respectively, over the preceding decades followed by a more dramatic increase of 6.6 percentage points in the 1990s. The same is true for import and export volumes: export volumes grew at a slower pace in the 1980s than in the 1970s.

These indicators have the usual problem of leaving open the question of the causes of increase in openness. A more sophisticated way of assessing trade outcomes is to use a gravity model, which controls many of the possible determinants of trade. Table 1.8 presents the estimated coefficients for India

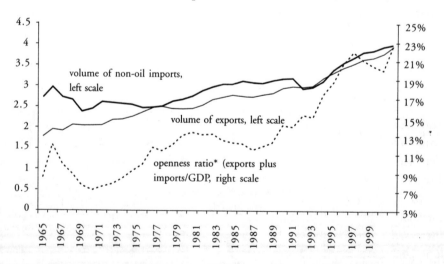

Figure 1.5: India: Evolution in merchandise trade, 1960–2000

Source: IMF's *World Economic Outlook*.

Table 1.8: Gravity Model Results of Trade Outcome for India
and China

	1980	1985	1990	1995	2003
India	−0.39	−0.49	−0.82	−0.68	0.04
	0.13	0.13	0.15	0.12	0.10
China	0.52	0.39	0.39	−0.30	0.71
	0.15	0.12	0.14	0.13	0.12

Source: Based on data in Subramanian and Wei (2003).
Note: Standard errors below coefficients. Coefficient estimates for the standard covariates not reported.

and China dummies in gravity estimations for the period 1980 to 2000 based on the dataset and methodology used in Subramanian and Wei (2003). The India dummy is negative and significant for all periods except in 2000, with the value of the dummy increasing in absolute value through the 1980s, and starting to decline only in the mid-1990s, consistent with the timing of the trade policy reform. If the results are to be taken at face value, they suggest that India only become a normal trader in 2000. In contrast, the China dummy is positive and significant for most of the 1980–2000 period.

External liberalization could also encompass exchange rate changes that could have an impact on trade and productivity. Figure 1.6 depicts the movement in India's real exchange rate since 1970. After remaining broadly unchanged during the first half of the 1980s, the rupee experienced a large real depreciation of over 40 per cent in the second half of the 1980s. Could this have caused the productivity spurt? In terms of timing, the real depreciation followed the pick-up in productivity growth in the early 1980s. But could it have contributed to sustaining this spurt in the late 1980s?

We would argue that exchange rate changes are an unlikely candidate. First, a real depreciation boosts aggregate demand and while it could have increased output growth in the short term, its consequences for raising long-run productivity growth are less clear. Of course, a real depreciation could have an effect on overall productivity through an import substitution-induced reallocation effect: if tradables are generally more productive than the rest of the economy, raising the share of tradable goods in overall GDP

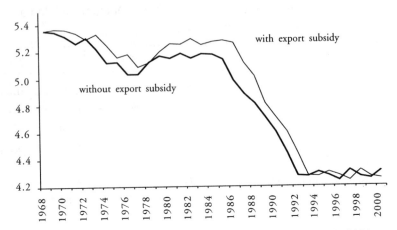

Figure 1.6: India: Real effective exchange rate, 1968–2000

Source: IMF's Information Notice System.

can result in an economy-wide productivity increase. In India, the share of manufacturing in GDP is small, and more importantly, the increase in this share in the aftermath of the real depreciation was too small to help explain overall productivity growth.[15]

Was it the Green Revolution?

Another possible explanation for the growth pickup in the 1980s is agriculture, which witnessed an increase in labour productivity growth from 0.1 per cent in the 1970s to 2.6 per cent in the 1980s. The difficulty with agriculture as the source of the improvement in overall performance is fourfold. First, in quantitative terms, the turnaround in agriculture's performance was actually less impressive than that in manufacturing and services, where the acceleration in productivity growth was actually larger. Second, if rising agricultural productivity were the underlying cause for improved productivity performance elsewhere in the economy, a necessary condition that would have to be met is a deterioration in the agricultural terms of trade. This classic 'Preobrazhensky effect' relies on improved productivity driving down agricultural prices and releasing resources for use in manufacturing. But as Figure 1.7 illustrates, quite the converse

---

[15] Between 1986 and 1992, the share of manufacturing in GDP remained unchanged at about 16 per cent.

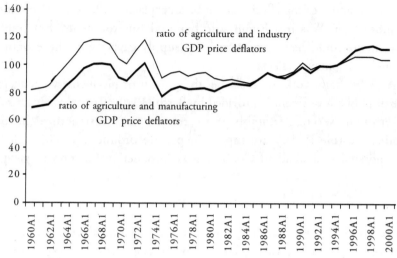

Figure 1.7: India: Agriculture's terms of trade, 1960–2001

Source: World Bank's World Development Indicators.

happened. During the 1980s, the terms of trade of agriculture with respect to industry and manufacturing actually improved. Moreover, as we showed above, the sectoral reallocation brought about by improved agricultural productivity performance would be too small to explain improvements in overall productivity. Third, recent work by Burgess and Venables (2003) and Foster and Rozenzweig (2003) shows that agricultural productivity plays a comparatively small role in explaining the interstate variation in total, urban, and surprisingly, even rural poverty.[16] It is non-farm productivity that appears to be the driver of aggregate outcomes. Finally, in our econometric analysis described in the following pages, we too found no evidence of a role for agriculture in explaining the overall productivity improvement.

Was it Public Investment?

The period between the late 1970s and the late 1980s witnessed a marked rise in public investment of about 4 percentage points of GDP (Figure 1.8). Could this have played a role in accounting for the 1980s productivity performance? It should be emphasized that the impact of public investment

[16] At the level of the states, agricultural growth and overall growth are negatively correlated.

via its demand-creating effects cannot be an explanation for reasons outlined
in subsection 'Was it a Favourable External Environment?' But public
investment could have augmented the supply capacity of the economy
through its spillover effects.

A useful framework for analysing the growth or productivity-enhancing
role of public investment is provided by Barro (1990). Conceptually, certain
government services (notably those related to infrastructure) have a
productive role if they are inputs in private production. This can be
incorporated in a standard Cobb-Douglas production function to yield:

$$Y/K = A \ (G/K)^{\alpha} \tag{1.1}$$

where Y and K are expressed in per worker terms, G is the flow of government
services in infrastructure (that is, excluding output of government
enterprises). The parameter a is the productivity of public services relative
to private services (which should theoretically be close to the average tax
rate, about 15 per cent in the case of India). In turn, this yields the growth
accounting decomposition:

$$y - k - a = a/(1- a) \ (g/y) \tag{1.2}$$

where the lower case variables are the proportional rate of growth analogues
of the underlying variables. This equation makes clear that the standard
growth accounting decomposition could overestimate total factor
productivity growth if the spillover effects of government investment are
ignored. Given data on government investment, we can compute the
possible contribution of government services to overall growth for given
values of a. The results of this exercise are illustrated in Tables 1.9 and
1.10. Under the assumption that the effects of public investment are
contemporaneous or that only the infrastructure component of public
investment is productivity enhancing, we estimate that the contribution
of public investment to overall growth is quite small (0.2–0.3 per cent).
If, on the other hand, the effects are lagged (by say five years), public
infrastructure investment, and especially total public spending could
explain a substantial part of overall growth (1.5–2.9 per cent). The bottom
line is that the surge in public investment could in principle explain
India's growth in the 1980s, but only if we make an appropriate

Table 1.9: India: Growth of Public Investment Ratio

| | | Rate of growth of G/Y | | | |
| | | Contemporaneous | | Lagged 5-years | |
	TFP growth (%)	Infrastructure (%)	Total public (%)	Infrastructure (%)	Total public (%)
1961–70	0.7	3.2	−1.5		
1971–80	−0.5	3.9	5.1	−0.5	−5.7
1981–90	2.5	−1.0	0.9	1.3	8.6
1991–2000	1.6		−3.7		−2.2

Source: Authors' calculations. Infrastructure spending data are from Joshi and Little (1994, Table 13.7). Data on total public investment are from Joshi and Little (1994) for 1961–70 and WEO for 1971–2000.

Table 1.10: Estimates of Contribution of Public Capital to TFP growth, 1960–2000

| | | Contribution of public capital to TFP growth | | | | | | | |
| | | Contemporaneous | | | | Lagged 5-years | | | |
	TFP growth (%)	Infr.[a] (%)	Total Pub.[b] (%)	Infr.[a] (%)	Total Pub.[b] (%)	Infr.[a] (%)	Total Pub.[b] (%)	Infr.[a] (%)	Total Pub.[b] (%)
	Bosworth-Collins	alpha= .25		alpha= .15		alpha= .25		alpha= .15	
1960–70	0.7	1.1	−0.5	0.6	−0.3				
1971–80	−0.5	1.3	1.7	0.7	0.9	−0.2	−1.9	−0.1	−1.0
1981–90	2.5	−0.3	0.3	−0.2	0.4	2.9	0.2	0.2	1.5
1991–2000	1.6		−1.2		−0.7		−0.7		−0.4

Source: Authors' calculations. Infrastructure spending data are from Joshi and Little (1994, Table 13.7). Data on total public investment are from Joshi and Little (1994) for 1961–70 and WEO for 1971–2000.
[a] Government spending on infrastructure.
[b] Total public spending.

assumption about the nature of the lags between public investment and its productivity-enhancing effects.

Was it 'Internal' Liberalization?

A promising candidate for explaining the 1980s turnaround is what in India is called 'internal liberalization'. This relates to the dismantling of the vast controls on domestic investment and competition implemented through a Kafka-esque array of licences, regulations, and other forms of control.

We discuss these in greater detail in the following paragraphs, but for the purposes of our narrative it is enough to note at this stage that the timing and magnitude of internal liberalization are not quite compatible with a productivity take-off in the early 1980s. Indeed, contemporaneous accounts of these internal reforms make clear the limited range of liberalization that was attempted. In what is probably the best account of this period, Joshi and Little (1994, pp. 71–72) express this sentiment as follows:

In summary, liberalization in our period (1964/65–1990/91) consisted of little more than the piecemeal deregulation of industrial licensing and the introduction of a measure of exchange rate flexibility. These changes were not trivial and did improve economic performance. But ideology and vested interests prevented any significant action in the more difficult areas such as trade liberalization, financial liberalization, and reform of the labor market and public sector enterprises.

Srinivasan and Tendulkar (2003, p. 2) imply the same when they talk of the '*shift in 1991* from an inward-oriented, state-led development strategy to a policy of active reintegration with the world economy' (our italics).

Others have, however, drawn attention to the important steps taken between 1985 and 1988, under Rajiv Gandhi, to dismantle the industrial licensing system in India. We shall describe these in greater detail below but a rough magnitude of the importance of these steps can be gauged by the assessment that in 1991, prior to the sweeping deregulatory effort, between 60 per cent and 80 per cent of industry was still subject to licensing and controls.[17] Thus, the magnitude of the reform effort not only seems modest, but it also lags behind the turnaround in the productivity surge.

---

[17] The 60 per cent estimate is due to Chopra et al. (1995, Table 7.6, p. 60), while the 80 per cent estimate is due to Hasan (1997, p. 27). Also, data compiled by Balakrishnan and Babu (2003) suggest that gross margins in industry did not decline in the 1980s relative to the 1970s.

POSSIBLE EXPLANATION

So what explains the Indian growth take-off in the early 1980s? In this section, we propose an alternative explanation and offer some econometric evidence in support. First, a few points on our data set and approach, which rely largely on exploiting variations in performance between the twenty-one states for which we have data. Accordingly, we use state-level data for the period 1960–2000 which is disaggregated by seventeen sectors in the national income accounts. For one of these sectors—manufacturing—data are also available for the output of the registered and unregistered sectors. These data have been compiled and recently released by the EPW Research Foundation.

We created a panel data set with variables defined for four decades—1960s, 1970s, 1980s, and 1990s. Since we are interested in changes in impact across these decades, particularly in the 1980s, we interacted the explanatory variables with the appropriate decadal dummies. Data on the political variables were gathered from the website of the Election Commission of India (http://www.eci.gov.in/infoeci/key_stat/keystat_fs.htm) and supplemented by state-level sources.

Our explanation comprises four elements. First, that there was an attitudinal change on the part of the government in the 1980s, signaling a shift in favour of the private sector, with this shift validated in a very haphazard and gradual manner through actual policy changes. Second, this shift and the limited policy changes were pro-business rather than pro-competition, aimed primarily at benefiting incumbents in the formal industrial and commercial sectors. Third, these small shifts elicited a large productivity response because India was far away from its income possibility frontier. Finally, manufacturing, which was built up through previous efforts, played a key role in determining the responses to the shifts.

We posit that sometime in the early 1980s there was a significant attitudinal change towards the private sector on the part of the national government, led by Indira Gandhi's Congress Party. Congress went from being hostile to private business[18] to mildly supportive, and eventually quite supportive. This change was inaugurated with the return of a much-

---

[18] Basu (2003) describes the general attitude of mistrust towards business in postcolonial India, tracing it back to India's experience with the East India Company and the trader mentality of the colonial rulers.

chastened Indira Gandhi to political power in the 1980s after a three-year rule by the Janata Party. It gathered momentum (after her assassination) under Rajiv Gandhi. The transformation has some antecedents in the 1970s, as reflected for example in the appointment of a high-level committees to propose changes to the trade regime and to industrial licensing. One important manifestation of this change, noted by Joshi and Little (1994), was the fact that import controls were not tightened in the wake of the balance of payments crisis in 1979–80.

But the attitudinal change was grounded primarily in political calculation, and not in a desire to enhance the efficiency of the economic regime. As Kohli (1989) notes, Indira's main objective was to counter the perceived threat posed by the Janata Party, which had trounced Congress in the Hindi heartland in the 1977 elections. Her political rhetoric consequently became less secular and populist and more communal and private-sector oriented. In Kohli's words, 'in India's political culture ... the two packages of secularism and socialism and Hindu chauvinism and probusiness have tended to offer two alternative legitimacy formulae for mobilizing political support' (1989, p. 308). After 1980, Indira dropped the first package in favour of the second. From our perspective, what is particularly important is that Indira Gandhi now actively sought to woo the business and industrial establishment.

As we have already noted, there were few significant policy changes in the early 1980s, and the changes later on (beginning in 1985) were restricted largely to some internal liberalization relating to the relaxation of industrial licensing. The limited nature of these changes, as well as the form that they took, is best understood by appreciating the political logic of Indira's (and later Rajiv's) efforts. These were aimed to gather support from the business establishment rather than to alienate them. Hence there was more action where business support existed—for example, in reducing taxes, easing access to imported capital inputs, or liberalizing capacity restrictions—than where it did not—for example, in external liberalization.

As we have noted, most observers agree that the actual policy framework did not change significantly until 1991. That is why we describe the shift as an 'attitudinal' one, having to do with the government's attitude towards business and the private sector, rather than as policy reform per se. This shift had more to do with currying favor with existing business interests (essentially large, politically influential firms in the formal manufacturing sector) than with liberalizing the system as a whole.

We explore the implications of the first two elements of our explanation: if the causal mechanism is a shift in the attitudes of the national government, we should see differences in growth rates depending on the nature of the political alliance between state governments and the national government. In particular, growth post-1980 should be more pronounced in states where the ruling government was in alliance with the national government (mostly Congress in this period) than where it was not. To test for this, we coded state governments according to the party in power and constructed variables for each of the decades depending on the number of years the party ruling in a state was either the same as, or had an alliance with, the party in power at the centre. Table 1.11 displays the results.

As column 1 shows, states that were allied with the national government had growth rates in the 1960s and 1970s that were indistinguishable from others. This changes dramatically in the 1980s and 1990s—when states allied with the national government had dramatically higher growth rates.[19] We would expect the change in policy attitudes to have a particularly marked effect on the formal sectors of the economy because as explained above both the attitudinal and policy shifts were in their favour. So in column 3 we look more narrowly at the growth of registered manufacturing. As expected, states that were allied with the national government had significantly higher growth rates in registered manufacturing in the 1980s.[20] Column 4 analyses the difference between growth rates in registered and unregistered manufacturing, on the theory that an attitudinal shift towards business should have a larger impact on registered than unregistered businesses.[21] Once again, we find this intuition confirmed: states that were allied with the national government experienced differentially higher growth rates in registered manufacturing.[22]

[19] This result holds whether the political variable is defined as parties being allied to that in the centre or as being the same as that in the centre.

[20] Column 2 reports results when this political variable is interacted with the share of registered manufacturing. Again the coefficients for the 1980s and 1990s are positive and significant.

[21] The differential between the growth of the registered and unregistered sectors in aggregate was 4.3 per cent in the 1980s compared with 1.7 per cent in the 1970s.

[22] Interestingly, in the equation for registered manufacturing and for the difference in growth between registered and unregistered manufacturing, the political variable for the 1990s ceases to be significant. This suggests that the impact of the 1990s liberalization was broader than that in the 1980s.

Table 1.11: India: Attitudinal Shift[*]

Dependent variable	Growth rate of per capita domestic product		Growth rate of reg. manuf.	Difference in growth between reg. and unreg. manuf.
Initial income	0.011	0.009		
	2.53	1.93		
State party allied with Centre 60	0.000		0.029	0.027
	0.01		1.51	1.40
State party allied with Centre 70	−0.006		0.015	−0.002
	−0.85		0.57	−0.08
State party allied with Centre 80	0.021		0.097	0.058
	2.68		3.07	2.09
State party allied with Centre 90	0.027		0.004	−0.035
	2.48		0.10	−1.17
Initial level of registered manufacturing			−0.005	−0.008
			−1.28	−1.98
Party[*] share of registered manufacturing 60		−0.077		
		−0.94		
Party[*] share of registered manufacturing 70		−0.151		
		−1.73		
Party[*] share of registered manufacturing 80		0.266		
		2.48		
Party[*] share of registered manufacturing 90		0.241		
		3.04		
R square	0.41	0.40	0.23	0.29
No. of observations	58	58	59	59

Source: Unless otherwise specified, data are from the EPW Research Foundation. Data on political parties compiled from @http://www.eci.gov.in/infoeci/key_stat/keystat_fs.htm. T-statistics reported below coefficient estimate.

[*] Suffixes indicate that the underlying variable has been interacted with the appropriate decadal dummy.

In addition to the differential impact on formal manufacturing, another suggestive piece of evidence in support of the proposition that the shift was pro-business comes from investment behaviour. While aggregate private investment does not increase greatly in the 1980s, there is a striking shift in the early 1980s in private investment towards corporate sector investment (and away from the household sector, comprising largely unincorporated enterprises).

Figure 1.8 shows the corporate-sector investment rate rising by about 2–3 percentage points in the 1980s. It looks like the corporate form of investment became considerably safer sometime in the early 1980s.

We turn next to the third element. Why did this apparently small trigger elicit such large productivity responses? It is worth noting at the outset that India was very far from its long-run or steady-state level of income given the level of its domestic institutions. If the recent literature's emphasis on the importance of institutions on development is correct, India appears to be far inside the possibility frontier. Table 1.12 illustrates this under-achievement. It reports regressions of income on the deep determinants of income (based on Acemoglu et al., 2001; Rodrik et al., 2002) with an India dummy.

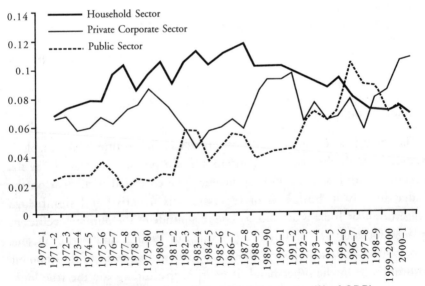

Figure 1.8: India: Investment rates, by sector (% of GDP)

Source: Reserve Bank of India.

Table 1.12: How Far Below is India from its Steady-state Level of Income?

Period	1980	1999	1980	1999	1980	1999	1980	1999
Geography	0.04	−0.07	0.03	−0.01	0.02	0.00	0.01	0.03
	5.19	−1.51	2.74	−0.93	1.72	0.21	1.23	4.55
Openness	0.27	−0.89	0.43	−0.54	−0.10	−0.54	−0.04	0.01
	1.07	−1.18	0.66	−2.03	−0.28	−0.71	−0.17	0.03
Economic institutions	0.51	2.60	1.53	1.47				
	4.32	3.05	1.36	6.80				
Political institutions					0.38	0.65	0.46	0.45
					3.24	2.90	5.39	5.92
India dummy	−1.36	−1.40	−1.06	−1.33	−2.61	−2.34	−2.61	−1.69
	−4.61	−2.36	−1.28	−4.92	−4.59	−3.27	−6.82	−5.95
Instrument for institutions	Settler morality		EURFRAC, ENGFRAC		Settler morality		EURFRAC, ENGFRAC	
No. of observations	48	66	76	114	58	58	91	91

Source: Rodrik et al. (2004)
Notes: For description of geography and openness variables and the instruments for institutions, see Rodrik et al. (2002)
For 1980, economic institutions measured as the protection against expropriation in 1982 from ICRGE.
For 1999, economic institutions measured as in Rodrik et al. (2002).
Political institutions are measures as the constraint on the executive.
T–statistics reported below coefficient estimates.

The first four columns report results where the institutional variable is economic while the last four columns contain political institutions as the relevant determinant of long-run income. The estimated coefficient on the India dummy in both sets of regressions is negative and significant, suggesting that India is an outlier. The magnitude of the dummy coefficient is large: for example, column 1 suggests that in 1980, India's level of income was about a quarter of what it should be given the strength of its economic institutions. On the other hand, if political institutions are the true long-run determinant of income, India's income is about 15 per cent of what it should be. India has thus been a significant under-achiever in the sense that it has not exploited the potential created by having done the really hard work of building institutions.

Next we turn to the role of manufacturing, and in particular registered (or formal) manufacturing, in mediating the changes. We begin by noting a very strong regularity in the data: starting in the 1980s, it is states with the largest formal manufacturing base ('registered manufacturing') that take off. Figure 1.9 shows how the simple correlation between growth and the share of registered manufacturing in total output, which is weakly negative in the 1970s (rho=−0.08), turns significantly positive in the 1980s (rho = 0.42). Table 1.13 tests this more formally. When we introduce state-level registered manufacturing shares in the growth regression and allow the coefficients to vary by decade, not only are the shares for 1980s and 1990s highly positive and significant, but also these variables can 'knock out' the pure period dummies (see columns 1 and 2).[23] In other words, whatever it is that happened in the early 1980s, it stimulated growth primarily in states with high level of formal manufacturing activities.

We note also that this is not simply an artifact of the fact that it is the richer states that take off after 1980 (the richer ones also having in general larger manufactures shares). Column 4 shows that manufacturing shares are still significant for the 1980s, when period-specific convergence terms are added to the regression (while the latter are insignificant).

The importance of the registered manufacturing sector in the productivity surge is confirmed in the robustness checks that we report in Table 1.14. In columns 1–4, we check whether agriculture or infrastructure, which account for a larger share of output than registered manufacturing, play a similarly important role. Not only are these variables insignificant on their own, they are also unable to 'knock down' the significance of the decadal dummies. In columns 5–7, we undertake a different kind of check on the role of manufacturing. If the mechanism by which manufacturing was affecting overall GDP growth was spillovers, for example, in the form of human and managerial capital built up in industry and being applied elsewhere in the economy, it seems plausible that these spillovers should occur more in relation to services than agriculture. To test this, we change the dependent variable in columns 5–7 to per capita non-agricultural GDP growth. In all these specifications,

---

[23] To minimize endogeneity-related problems, the beginning-period value of the share of registered manufacturing is used as the regressor.

Table 1.13: Role of Manufacturing in Productivity Surge*

(Dependent Variable is Annual per Capita Growth of State Net Domestic Product)

Initial income	0.010	0.008	0.009	0.007	0.019	0.007
	2.64	*1.84*	*2.27*	*1.54*	*3.86*	*1.27*
70s dummy	−0.003	−0.002				
	−0.78	*−0.30*				
80s dummy	0.014	0.007				
	3.85	*1.14*				
90s dummy	0.013	0.005				
	2.61	*0.51*				
Initial income 70				−0.001		
				−0.37		
Initial income 80				0.002		
				0.94		
Initial income 90				0.001		
				0.51		
Share of registered manufacturing 60		−0.046	−0.079	−0.050		−0.030
		−0.73	*−1.70*	*−0.73*		*−0.45*
Share of registered manufacturing 70		−0.050	−0.104	−0.044		−0.046
		−0.94	*−2.43*	*−0.81*		*−1.01*
Share of registered manufacturing 80		0.076	0.119	0.080		0.170
		1.79	*3.37*	*1.78*		*3.76*
Share of registered manufacturing 90		0.100	0.113	0.096		0.157
		1.44	*2.64*	*1.31*		*2.81*
Labour regulation 60					0.004	−0.001
					0.73	*−0.23*
Labour regulation 70					0.012	0.008
					2.14	*1.45*
Labour regulation 80					−0.008	−0.008
					−2.21	*−3.56*
Labour regulation 90					0.000	0.000
					0.05	*0.11*
R square	0.38	0.42	0.40	0.42	0.34	0.55
No. of observations	80	78	78	78	59	59

Sources: Unless otherwise specified, data are from the EPW Research Foundation. Data on labour regulation from Besley and Burgess (2002). T-statistics reported below coefficient estimate.

* Suffixes indicate that the underlying variable has been interacted with the appropriate decadal dummy.

Table 1.14: Role of Manufacturing in Productivity Surge: Robustness Checks[*]

Dependent variable	Per capita growth				Per capita non-agri. growth		
Initial income	0.012	0.009	0.011	0.010	−0.003	−0.003	0.018
	2.39	2.22	2.43	2.13	−0.21	−0.19	1.50
70s dummy		0.005	0.003				
		0.59	0.39				
80s dummy		0.020	0.016				
		2.06	2.22				
90s dummy		0.044	0.014				
		3.26	1.03				
Initial income 70					−0.003		
					−0.78		
Initial income 80					0.002		
					0.55		
Initial income 90					−0.001		
					−0.24		
Share of registered manufacturing 60					−0.096	−0.122	−0.010
					−0.75	−0.70	−0.06
Share of registered manufacturing 70					−0.157	−0.032	−0.124
					−1.31	−0.20	−0.99
Share of registered manufacturing 80					0.301	0.194	0.294
					3.40	2.18	3.01
Share of registered manufacturing 90					0.150	0.180	0.128
					1.28	1.01	0.80
Share of agriculture 60	−0.008	0.020					
	−0.62	1.14					
Share of agriculture 70	−0.016	0.006					
	−1.12	0.54					
Share of agriculture 80	0.019	0.010					
	1.27	0.58					
Share of agriculture 90	0.013	−0.061					
	0.81	−2.06					
Share of infrastructure 60[b]			−0.332	0.083			
			−1.44	0.27			
Share of infrastructure 70[b]			−0.518	−0.244			
			−2.26	−0.97			
Share of infrastructure 80[b]			0.288	0.110			
			1.75	0.73			

Dependent variable	Per capita growth				Per capita non-agri. growth		
Share of infrastructure 90[b]			0.193	0.106			
			1.23	0.35			
Labour regulation 60							−0.006
							−0.29
Labour regulation 70							0.020
							1.70
Labour regulation 80							−0.015
							−2.65
Labour regulation 90							−0.001
							−0.07
R square	0.33	0.43	0.45	0.48	0.19	0.21	0.37
No. of observations	80	80	63	63	77	77	59

Sources: Except as otherwise specified, all data are from the EPW Research Foundation. Data on labour regulation from Besley and Burgess (2002). T-statistics reported below coefficient estimate.
* Suffixes indicate that the underlying variable has been interacted with the appropriate decadal dummy.
[b] Infrastructure includes railways, electricity, gas and water supply, and communication.

the registered manufacturing variable for the 1980s is highly significant. Interestingly, the magnitude of this coefficient is more than twice its value in the specification with overall GDP as the dependent variable (Table 1.14, col. 3), suggesting that any spillover benefits from manufacturing are greater in the non-agricultural than in the agricultural sector.

So these registered manufacturing shares are capturing something about the nature of the change that occurred. The question is what. We interpret these findings in the following way. It is reasonable to suppose that an anti-business attitude on the part of top political leaders entails a disporoprtionate 'tax' on formally registered entities. That is because these firms' operations are intensive in transactions with the government (paying taxes, complying with regulations, seeking licenses, etc.). When political attitudes become more pro-business, it is formal firms that should receive a particularly strong boost. That is exactly how we read the results with respect to the registered manufacturing.

We also show evidence that the labour regulation data recently compiled by Besley and Burgess (2002) has some traction for the turnaround in the

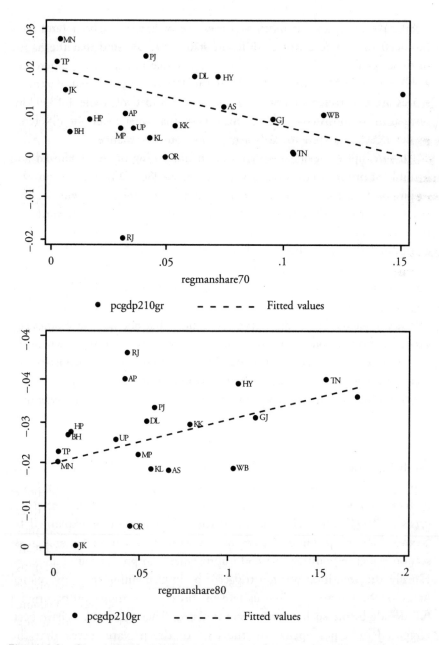

Figure 1.9 : Correlation between growth and share of registered manufacturing, 1970s and 1980s

1980s. We interpret this index as a measure of how pro-labour (and anti-business) the environment in different states was. We find that the nature of these regulations in different states plays a role in explaining differential performance in the crucial decade of the 1980s (whether manufacturing shares are controlled or not—see columns 5 and 6 of Table 1.13). This once again is consistent with our hypothesis that what made the difference in the 1980s is a shift towards a more pro-business stance.

To sum up, the evidence points to an unleashing of the organized and incumbent private sector sometime in the early 1980s. While it is impossible to pinpoint exactly the source for this, there is circumstantial evidence that the trigger was a shift in the national government's attitude towards the private sector. This evidence also indicates that the beneficiary of this attitudinal shift was the formal sector built up under the earlier policy regime. Hence to some extent, the learning generated under the earlier policy regime and the modern manufacturing base created thereby provided a permissive environment for eventual take-off once the policy stance softened vis-à-vis the private sector. So, unlike what one may have otherwise expected (from accounts of how costly ISI was), growth occurred where the earlier investments had been made. This is, of course, in contrast to the experience of the transition countries where post-transition growth was greatest where the drag exerted by the previous state sector was smallest.[24]

CONCLUSION

We believe that our findings raise a number of issues related to growth and, in particular, growth transitions. We would summarize them as follows.

India's growth transition began in the early 1980s rather than after the crisis of 1991. The performance of the 1980s cannot be explained by Keynesian pump priming because there is a variety of time-series and cross-section evidence pointing to trend improvements in productivity indicators. Equally, this transition was not triggered by implementing the conventional litany of Washington Consensus reforms because the transition occurred a full decade before such reforms were initiated. They appeared to have been triggered by a perception on the part of the private sector that the

---

[24] Sachs and Woo (1997) argue that this drag was important in explaining the differential performance of China and the East European countries in the wake of liberalization.

government's attitude toward it had changed, a perception that was subsequently (in the mid-to-late 1980s), mildly validated by piecemeal reforms of the industrial licensing system. The attitudinal shift signaled by the Congress governments in the 1980s elicited a large productivity response, a phenomenon facilitated by the fact that India was far away from its income possibility frontier.

Manufacturing, and in particular registered manufacturing, which had been built up in the previous decades, appears to have played an important role in determining which states took advantage of the changed attitude of the private sector. Thus, while the costs associated with these investments may have been high, they may have generated some spillover benefits in the post-1980s period.

Most observers, focusing on the 1990s, and to some extent the 1980s, have emphasized gradualism as the hallmark of the Indian approach to reforms in contrast with the shock therapy in some of the transition countries and the ambitious liberalization in Latin America since the mid-1980s (Ahluwalia, 2002). Equally important but somewhat neglected has been the approach to reforms adopted by India in the 1980s, where the distinctiveness has had arguably less to do with pace than with the manner and sequencing.

We would stress that our characterization of the 1980s reform is not about whether 'liberalization' took place but about how it happened. Some accounts of the 1980s point to the easing of access to foreign technology, to foreign capital goods, and to foreign direct investment (with the entry of Suzuki into the domestic car market as the most telling example) as examples of 'liberalization.' To us, these reforms in the 1980s, were not pro-liberalization but pro-business in the important sense that they served to boost the profits of existing businesses without threatening them with real competition. Allowing a single foreign firm, Suzuki, to enter the domestic car market under existing conditions of limited external liberalization (and subject to local content requirements) is very different from opening the domestic car market to all foreign producers, which is the normal liberalization strategy and the approach adopted in the 1990s.[25]

---

[25] Guaranteed profits were arguably why Suzuki accepted the onerous conditions—joint-venture with the public sector, requirement to fulfill local content requirements—associated with its entry.

This pro-business rather than pro-market/pro-competition orientation manifested itself in the greater focus on 'internal' rather than 'external' reforms. In addition, even the internal reforms which favoured business were slanted more toward favouring pre-existing activities rather than facilitating new businesses (that is, through entry by domestic firms).[26] This approach had the political economy merit of avoiding the creation of losers. And it appears that the economic impact of favoring existing activities, which must have entailed some inefficiency, was not only not negative but actually positive. This is reflected in the fact that the growth of the 1990s also appears to have taken place in states with a large initial share of registered manufacturing, some of it built up during the 1980s. Thus, India's 'reforms' in the 1980s, which essentially amounted to more import substitution, were attractive from a political economy perspective because they created virtually no losers. This is reminiscent of China's reforms as well, although the latter obviously took on a very different form.

But just as in China, economic dynamism created a fertile environment not just for incumbents, but also for entrants and new activities. It is perhaps not a coincidence that some of the IT powerhouses that would begin to fuel India's growth a decade or so later got established in the early 1980s, just as the economic environment was turning more business-friendly. For example, Wipro first ventured into IT in 1980, and Infosys was founded in 1981. These firms eventually were able to reap handsome benefits from India's prior public investments in higher education (the IITs in particular) once the policy environment turned permissive. Their story is in many ways similar to the one we have laid out for the more traditional activities during the 1980s: pre-existing strengths unleashed by more pro-business policy attitudes.

[26] The four major internal liberalization measures that were implemented in 1985 and 1986 involved: (i) Eliminating the licensing of 25 categories of industries subject to certain fairly onerous conditions; (ii) extending delicensing to large companies in 22 industries which were previously restricted by the Monopolies and Trade Restrictive Practices Act (MRTP) and Foreign Exchange Regulation Act (FERA); (iii) allowing companies in 28 industries to expand the scope of their operations into related activities; and (iv) allowing companies that had reached 80 per cent capacity utilization to expand their capacity upto 133 per cent of that reached in any of the previous years. Apart from the first, all the remaining measures essentially allowed incumbents to operate more freely rather than facilitate the entry of new domestic firms and promote competition. Even the limited reduction in protection of capital goods industries served to increase the effective protection of incumbents in final goods industries.

What about the reforms of the 1990s? It may well be the case that the performance of the 1980s would have run out of steam and that the 'true' reforms of the 1990s were essential to keep the productivity growth alive. The reforms of the 1990s were, of course, triggered by the crisis of 1991. The quick rebound from the crisis has been almost entirely attributed to the decisive break from the dirigiste past. But if the 1980s experience was as successful as we think it might have been in creating a strong base of manufacturing and productivity growth, it is hard not to draw the conclusion that the quick rebound was also rendered possible by the strength of the 1980s performance.[27] In some ways, although India was reforming in response to a macroeconomic crisis, it was reforming from a position of strength in the real sector of the economy. That might explain why the response to the reforms in India in the 1990s was so different from that in Latin America (or in sub-Saharan Africa).

Finally, one consequence of the conventional story that we sketched out at the beginning—that the 1990s marked the watershed for India—has been the unfortunate neglect of research on policies and performance in the 1980s. We hope that this paper will kindle research interest in a number of very interesting issues relating to the 1980s, which could be important in deriving broader lessons for growth transitions across the world.

REFERENCES

Acemoglu, D., S. Johnson, and J. A. Robinson (2001), 'The colonial origins of comparative development: An empirical investigation,' *American Economic Review*, 91(5), pp. 1369–1401.

Ahluwalia, I.J. (1991), *Productivity and Growth in Indian Manufacturing*, Oxford University Press, New Delhi.

——— (1995), *India: Industrial Development Review*, The Economist Intelligence Unit and UNIDO.

Ahluwalia, M. S. (2002), 'Economic reforms in India since 1991: Has gradualism worked,' *Journal of Economic Perspectives*, 16(7), pp. 67–88.

Bai, J., and P. Perron (1998), 'Estimating and testing linear models with multiple structural changes', *Econometrica*, 66 (1), pp. 47–78.

——— (2003), 'Computation and analysis of multiple structural change models', *Journal of Applied Econometrics*, 18, pp. 1–22.

[27] This is supported by cross-industry studies, which show that the positive impact of liberalization on productivity in the 1990s is small in magnitude (Topalova, 2004).

Balakrishnan, P., and K. Pushpagandan (1994), 'Manufacturing industry: A fresh look,' *Economic and Political Weekly*, October, pp. 2028–35.

Balakrishnan, P., and Babu, M.S. (2003), 'Growth and distribution in Indian industry in the nineties,' *Economic and Political Weekly*, (September), pp. 3997–4005.

Barro, R. (1990), 'Government spending in a simple model of endogenous growth,' *Journal of Political Economy*, 98(5), pp. S103–19.

Basu, K. (2004), 'The Indian economy: Up to 1991 and since,' Kaushik Basu (ed.), *India's Emerging Economy: :Problems and Prospects in the 1990's and Beyond*, Cambridge, MA, MIT Press.

Besley, T., and R. Burgess (2002), 'Can labor regulation hinder economic performance? Evidence from India', CEPR Discussion Paper No. 3260, Center for Economic Policy Research, London.

Bosworth, B., and S. Collins (2003), 'The Empirics of Growth: An Update', mimeo, Brookings Institution, Washington.

Burgess, R., and A. J. Venables (2003), 'Towards a microeconomics of growth', mimeo, London School of Economics, London.

Chopra, A., C. Collyns, R. Hemming, K. Parker, W. Chu, and O. Fratzcher (1995), 'India: Economic Reform and Growth,' *Occasional Paper No. 134*, International Monetary Fund, Washington.

Das, D. K. (2003), 'Quantifying trade barriers: has trade protection declined substantially in indian manufacturing', *Indian Council for Research on International Economic Relations, Working Paper No. 105*, New Delhi.

Deaton, Angus, and Jean Dreze (2002), 'Poverty and inequality in India: A re-examination', *Economic and Political Weekly*, (September), pp. 3729–48.

Deaton, A., J. Friedman, and V. Atlas (2004), 'Purchasing power exchange rates from household survey data: India and Indonesia,' mimeo, Princeton University, New Jersey.

De Long, B. (2003), 'India since independence: An analytic growth narrative,' in D. Rodrik (ed.), *In Search of Prosperity: Analytic Narratives on Economic Growth*, Princeton University Press, New Jersey.

Foster, A. D., and M. R. Rozenzweig (2003), 'Agricultural development, industrialization and rural inequality,' mimeo, Harvard University, Cambridge, Massachusetts.

Ghose, A. K. (1999), 'Current issues of employment policy in India', *Economic and Political Weekly*, 4 (September), pp. 2592–2608.

Government of India, *Economic Survey*, Various Issues.

Hasan, R. (1997), 'Productivity growth and technological progress in a reforming economy: Evidence from India,' Ph.D. dissertation, University of Maryland, Maryland.

Hausmann, R., and D. Rodrik (2003), 'Economic development as self-discovery', *Journal of Development Economics*, December.

Hausmann, R., L. Pritchett, and D. Rodrik (2005), 'Growth Accelarations', *Journal of Economic Growth*, 10(4), December, pp. 303–29.

Hulten, C., and S. Srinivasan (1999), 'Indian manufacturing Industry: Elephant or tiger? New evidence on the Asian miracle', *National Bureau of Economic Research Working Paper No. 7441*.

Joshi, V., and I. M. D. Little, 1994, *India: Macroeconomics and Political Economy, 1964–1991*, The World Bank, Washington.

Y. Huang and Khanna, T. (2003), 'Can India overtake China?', *Foreign Policy*, July/August.

Kohli, A. (1989), 'Politics of economic liberalization in India,' *World Development*, 17(3), pp. 305–28.

Pritchett, L. (1997), 'Divergence, big time,' *Journal of Economic Perspectives*, 11(3), pp. 3–17.

Reserve Bank of India (RBI) (2004), *Report on Currency and Finance*, 2002–03, India.

Rodrik, D., A. Subramanian, and F. Trebbi (2002), 'Institutions rule: The primacy of institutions over integration and geography in development', *Journal of Economic Growth*, 9(2), June, pp. 131–65.

Rodrik, D. (2003), 'Growth Strategies,' NBER Working Papers 10050, October, National Bureau of Economic Research, Cambridge, MA.

Sachs, J., and W. T. Woo (1997), 'Understanding China's economic performance,' *National Bureau of Economic Research Working Paper No. 5935*.

Srinivasan, T. N., and S. Tendulkar (2003), *Reintegrating India with the World Economy*, Institute for International Economics, Washington.

Subramanian, A., and S-J Wei (2003), 'The WTO promotes Trade Strongly, But Unevenly', *Journal of International Economics*, 72, p. 1.

Topalova, P. (2004), 'Trade liberalization and firm productivity: The case of India', *IMF Working Paper, 04/28*, International Monetary Fund, Washington, D.C.

Unel, B. (2003), 'Productivity trends in India's manufacturing sectors in the last two decades', *IMF Working Paper, WP/03/22*, International Monetary Fund, Washington.

Wallack, J. S. (2003), 'Structural breaks in Indian macroeconomic data,' *Economic and Political Weekly*, October, pp. 4312–15.

Williamson, J., and R. Zagha (2002), *From Slow Growth to Slow Reform*, Institute for International Economics, Washington, D.C., July.

World Bank (1995), *India: Recent Economic Developments and Prospects*, The World Bank, Washington.

Summary

The Indian Economy: The Last Two Decades

Luckily for India, the 'Hindu Growth' rate was not eternal. Most conventional accounts associate the decisive departure from this unremarkable economic performance with the liberalization of 1991. But the turnaround actually occurred around 1980 and encompassed a number of developments. Growth of per capita GDP between 1980 and 2000 doubled compared with the period 1960–80—an increase that seems to have been the result of a surge in productivity. Growth was also more stable in the post-1980s period. And, the economic performance of the Indian states started diverging significantly.

The post-1980s performance stands out not just in relation to India's past but also relative to other developing countries around the world. India grew faster and with less volatility relative to Asia (with the exception of China), Latin America, and Africa. And significantly, the contribution of productivity growth to overall performance was also amongst the highest in the world.

Why and how did this happen? Two mutually exclusive explanations have been offered by observers. The first view emphasizes the exceptional nature of the fiscal policy stance in the 1980s, which temporarily ignited temporary growth, but received its deserved comeuppance in the crisis of 1991. In this view, Indian policy only broke with the past in the aftermath of the 1991 crisis, with the associated implication that 1990s growth was 'good' and 'sustainable' as opposed to that in the 1980s.

In the second view, India broke from its dirigiste past in the 1980s, started the process of 'liberalization,' and reaped the consequent benefits. Liberalization measures included easing access to foreign technology, foreign capital goods, and foreign exchange, lowering tax rates, easing licensing etc. Allowing the entry of Suzuki into the car market came to symbolize the new, reformed approach to policy-making. The 1990s were then a continuation of this process of reform, albeit with its scope broadened and its pace accelerated, which yielded handsome pay-offs.

In a recent paper (available at http://www.nber.org/papers/w10376), which has elicited considerable debate in the Indian press, we advanced a third explanation that seems to fit the evidence somewhat better. Our explanation for the 1980s' performance is based not on fiscal pump-priming or liberalization, but on a pro-business shift in the attitudes of the central government. We argue that the Congress Party's traditionally hostile attitude to the private sector was the binding constraint on economic growth, the slight lifting of which around 1980 stimulated the animal spirits of the business and industrial class.

It is hard to attribute the pick-up in performance in the 1980s to old-fashioned Keynesianism. The sharp increase in the fiscal deficit in the 1980s could have increased growth in output and for a brief period, but it cannot explain the growth in output per worker (that is, productivity) and for such a long period of time. Even allowing for the existence of spare capacity, we find that the magnitude of the turnaround in productivity exceeded anything that demand expansion alone could deliver.

Second, the view that there was meaningful or significant economic liberalization in the 1980s is on the face of it appealing. But one immediate problem with this explanation is timing: the pick-up in growth began in 1979–80 whereas real policy change, limited as it was, began in the mid-1980s with Rajiv Gandhi coming to power.

We prefer to characterize the trigger for the turnaround as an attitudinal change on the part of the national government. While difficult to document, a variety of evidence points to such a change. There were economic acts of omission: for example, the government chose not to impose controls in response to the foreign exchange crisis in 1979. There were political acts of commission: the government started courting business in order to have access to greater financial resources that became imperative as electoral competition intensified. But to some extent, the inference about the attitudinal change is negative and indirect because there is little paper trail in actual policies that can explain the surge in performance.

A significant distinction we make relates to the nature of policy actions that were taken in the 1980s compared with the 1990s. A variety of policy and outcome-based indicators for the 1980s suggests that there was very little, if any, trade liberalization. This continuing protection against foreign competition formed the backdrop against which other 'liberalization' measures were taken. Because external barriers remained unchanged, reforms in the 1980s, were not pro-competition but pro-business in the important sense that they served to boost the profits of existing businesses without facilitating the entry of new participants. Allowing a single foreign firm, Suzuki, to enter the domestic car market under existing conditions of limited external liberalization is very different from opening the domestic car market to all foreign producers, which is the normal liberalization strategy and the approach adopted in the 1990s. Similarly, reducing tariffs on inputs and capital goods or providing foreign exchange for purchasing foreign inputs favors domestic business (in effect increasing their 'protection') but does not necessarily contribute to more competition.

Did these measures amount to 'liberalization?' Sure, in the sense of providing more freedom and greater incentives to domestic producers, thereby increasing their profitability. But, in another day and age this combination of favoring domestic producers while maintaining external barriers used to go by the much-reviled term 'import substitution.' It is more than ironic to see critics of import substitution take up the cause of 1980s reform under the banner of 'liberalization.'

Another difference in our interpretation has to do with *how* growth took place. Conventional views on India's economic performance seek to relate changes in outcomes directly to changes in policies. Our explanation, on the other hand, relies on the interaction between triggers and pre-existing conditions, certain 'fundamentals.' We find that manufacturing, which had been built up in previous decades, played an important role in determining which states took advantage of the economic opportunities created by the attitudinal and policy changes (the triggers). States that were more industrialized and had a large share of formal manufacturing surged ahead of states that were less industrialized. Thus, while the costs associated with these manufacturing investments may have been high in the 1960s and 1970s, they appear to have generated some economy-wide benefits in the post-1980 period.

Our analysis sheds a different light on the Indian development experiment. For one, it suggests that India's development policies during the 1960s and 1970s departed from classic import substituting industrialization (ISI) policies in an important way. ISI is usually interpreted as erecting barriers to foreign competition in order to favor domestic entrepreneurship and activity. In India, while the barriers were erected, the domestic private sector, far from being favoured, was actually throttled through a combination of reservation for the public and small scale sectors, and industrial licensing. Ironically, the failure of the Indian development strategy in the first three decades, routinely ascribed to trade protection, may have stemmed from the failure to provide sufficient freedom to and incentives for the domestic private sector.

The pro-business tilt in the 1980s, which was a rectification of a previous distortion, may have been the first decade of true import substitution. And, by following-up with the reform of the 1990s, India seemed to have pulled off an interesting experiment in policy sequencing. The limited pro-business reform in the 1980s had the great political economy merit of avoiding the creation of losers, and appeared to have built up the kind of dynamic efficiency that helped India in good stead, when the deeper, but more dislocating, reforms of the 1990s were implemented. The one-two act that was the 1980s and 1990s may have been what the import-substituting doctor prescribed in the early post-war period: a dose of temporary protection to allow domestic industries to learn and become efficient in order to brace themselves for the subsequent and necessary unleashing of the forces of international competition.

It is important to stress what we do not contend. We do not, for example, argue that the superior productivity performance in the 1980s implies that the reform of the 1990s was undesirable or that it had no positive impact. We also do not rule out the possibility that the 1980s' performance may well have run out of steam without further reform of the kind India witnessed in the 1990s. We would argue, though, that the impact of the 1980s on performance in the 1990s has been significantly understated because of an excessive focus on reforms in the 1990s.

But more controversially, the hypothetical question we would pose to the critics is whether the combination or sequencing of reforms that India saw in the 1980s and 1990s would have yielded higher economic pay-offs and remained politically sustainable had

India implemented in the 1980s the kind of reforms it did in the 1990s? Even more to the point, would India have done better to adopt a more ambitious, Latin American-style strategy of rapid liberalization and opening up (as many of the critics implicitly are arguing for)? To us, the answer is not obviously in the affirmative: given the actual performance—annual growth rates of 6 per cent with little social disruption—the onus is on the critics to make that case.

Should India have turned pro-private sector earlier and made the mid-course correction to its development path in the 1970s? Of course. But the main point of our analysis is that India's 1980s–1990s style of reform has a lot to recommend to itself, and was not clearly dominated by a more conventional shock-therapy type of economic liberalization.

CHAPTER 2

INDIA'S PATTERN OF DEVELOPMENT
WHAT HAPPENED, WHAT FOLLOWS?

*Since the industrial revolution, no country has become
a major economy without being an industrial power.*
—Lee Kuan Yew

With an average of thirteen million people expected to enter India's labour force each year for the next four decades, many have expressed concerns about the relatively jobless growth of the last fifteen years (see, for example, Acharya, 2006; Mehta, 2005). While China, the world's manufacturing powerhouse, appears to be absorbing surplus labour from agriculture into manufacturing, there is growing concern that India has failed to match its neighbour in this process. To many, India's emergence as a world-class services hub offers scant comfort because of the relatively limited prospects of such skill-based development for employment growth. In addition, worries are mounting about the uneven distribution of opportunities across states (the fast–growing peninsula versus the slow-moving hinterland), sectors (services versus manufacturing or agriculture), and skill and education levels. Will India foster growth in labour-intensive manufacturing? If yes, how? If not, how can jobs be provided for India's vast, growing, pool of low-skilled labour? These are some of the questions addressed in this chapter.

To preview the answers, we argue that the nature of the policies India followed after independence in 1947 created unique specializations prior to the economic reforms that started in the 1980s. Relative to other comparable poor countries, India's manufacturing was concentrated in skill-intensive industries rather than in labour-intensive manufacture, the usual specialization in a populous developing country. India had a greater presence in industries that required scale (and capital) than other developing countries, though within industries, the average size of enterprise was abnormally small compared to other countries. Perhaps because of the policy distortions, India had a far more diversified presence across manufacturing industries than the typical developing country. Interestingly, it had a lower-than-normal presence in services in the early 1980s, where the skill-intensive segments such as telecommunications were still dominated by the slow-moving public sector.

Recent trends reflect a continuation of some of the patterns that existed prior to economic reforms in the 1980s, especially in the continuing movement away from labour-intensive industries and towards skill-intensive industries. The big change has been in services, which have grown substantially for a variety of reasons—for example, telecommunication perhaps because the private sector has been allowed in, software and business process outsourcing because of the opening of the economy, and construction perhaps because of the growth of retail finance. Nevertheless, even here growth has been in skill-intensive areas.

We then look ahead, using the growth of fast-moving Indian states as a crystal ball. Despite economic reforms that have removed some of the policy impediments that sent India down its idiosyncratic path, it appears unlikely that India will revert to the pattern followed by other poor countries. States are not increasing their presence in labour-intensive industries.

In part, this may be because not all the policies have been reformed—for example, there has been little effective change in labour laws. In part, though, valuable capabilities may have been built up during the period of heavy policy intervention. Instead of reverting to the development norm, the advanced Indian states seem to be taking advantage of the freeing up of the economy to utilize fully their acquired capabilities.

On the one hand, this freedom has increased India's overall growth rate. On the other, it has led to a considerable divergence between states in growth and incomes and in the pattern of specialization. The fast-growing peninsular states are starting to resemble industrial countries in their specialization, moving towards skill-intensive services and manufacturing. But the populous, institution-and infrastructure-poor states of the hinterland have fallen behind. Whether these states can develop appropriate growth strategies and whether these strategies will be impeded or helped by the growth of the more advanced states is a central question for India's economic future. We offer some conjectures and discuss policy implications.

The structure of the chapter is as follows. We first examine India's pattern of development circa 1980 on the grounds that a snapshot at this point reflects the legacy of India's unique and much-commented-upon development strategy: a curious combination of simultaneously favouring and disfavouring domestic entrepreneurship with a rich overlay of arcane rules and procedures. We then examine what happened between 1980 and 2001 to see how the shift in policies from dirigisme to greater reliance on the market affected the pattern of development, especially for fast-moving states. We then use this post-1980s' experience as a basis to speculate about the future.

INDIA CIRCA 1980

How should India's development strategy since Independence in 1947 and until the early 1980s be characterized? Many excellent books and papers have been written about this, and we refer the reader to them for details.[1] A (perhaps overly) simplified view of the main aspects, however, would include:

1.   Indian planners emphasized self-sufficiency to avoid excessive external influence on domestic affairs, an understandable view in a country emerging from colonialism. This translated into an emphasis on rapid industrialization, especially the creation of industries producing capital goods.[2] An additional focus was to reduce dependence on foreign exchange through import substitution. Trade restrictions were the inevitable side effect of these policies.

2.   Given that India was capital poor, and given Indian planners distrusted market forces, they devised a combination of heavy public sector involvement in production (with some industries—the 'commanding heights'—being reserved only for the public sector) and controlled

---

[1] The canonical references are Bhagwati and Desai (1970), Bhagwati and Srinivasan (1993), Joshi and Little (1994), and Krueger (1975).

[2] Recall that Soviet Russia was a successful example of development around the time of India's independence, and many of India's leaders, including Jawaharlal Nehru, were greatly influenced by it. P.C. Mahalanobis, the father of Indian planning viewed the capacity to 'make machines that make machines' as crucial to the economy's long-term rate of growth.

private sector involvement. Licenses were required for investment, production, and imports, while foreign exchange, credit allocation, and even prices were controlled. Also, the government reserved the right to enter even those industries which were not explicitly reserved for the public sector (the threat was realized in 1969 when Indira Gandhi nationalized a number of private banks).

3. A separate reason to control the private sector was to avoid undue concentration of economic power. Additional mechanisms to enforce this objective included the Monopoly and Restrictive Trade Practices (MRTP) act—which imposed severe constraints on expansion by large firms and groups, and the Foreign Exchange Regulation Act (FERA).

4. Geographically balanced development was also an objective; therefore investment was directed towards underdeveloped areas, even if these areas were not near markets or even if scale was inefficiently small. The rents generated by the controls probably helped paper over inefficiencies.

5. In order to encourage labour-intensive manufacture in the private sector, significant benefits were given to small-scale firms (these included tax concessions and holidays, preferential access to credit, subsidized interest rates, and preferential treatment in procurement by the government). In addition, some goods were exclusively reserved for production by the small-scale sector.[3]

6. At the same time, however, significant protections for labour, especially in large firms, were enacted. For example, an amendment to the Industrial Disputes Act (1947) in 1976 made it compulsory for firms with 300 or more workers to seek the permission of the relevant government to dismiss workers. In 1982, the ceiling for seeking permission to dismiss workers was lowered to 100 workers.

7. Also, for a variety of reasons [see Wiener (1991) for one view], for a poor country India spent, and still spends, relatively far more resources on higher education than on primary education. For example, India spent 86 per cent of per capita GDP on each student in tertiary education in 2000 while it spent 14 per cent of per capita GDP per student in primary education. By contrast, China spent 10.7 per cent and 12.1 per cent, respectively, of per capita GDP per student in tertiary and primary education. Put another way, India spent

---

[3] See Mohan (2002) for more details.

substantially more in purchasing-power-parity (PPP) adjusted dollars per student in tertiary education than China, and even Korea or Indonesia in 2000.

In the next section , we examine the legacy of this complex web of policies on the pattern of development. But before we do that, a caveat. Historically, India has been gifted with many clever theorists and statisticians. Unfortunately, the quality of Indian data has not matched the quality of its users [see, for example, Srinivasan (2003)]. As a result, much extant work focuses on deploring the quality of Indian data and attempting to correct problems through careful econometrics. Unfortunately again, this focus has also dampened the quantum of empirical work, especially policy relevant empirical work. While acknowledging problems with the data, we will not dwell on their inadequacies. Instead, we will attempt to tease out broad patterns, and in a variety of ways, both of which might make the work less susceptible to concerns about the data. That said, all findings are subject to the caveat that the data are what they are.

Value-added Shares in 1981[4]

Did thirty years of dirigisme post-independence distort manufacturing? In Table 2.1, we present the share of output in the different sectors in India in 1981 and compare it with that in a number of developing and developed countries. At a little over 16 per cent of GDP, India's share in manufacturing seems low, especially when compared with a number of East Asian countries and China. But from the work of Kuznets and Chenery, we know that the manufacturing share varies with the level of development, rising and then falling off once a country approaches a high level of income. So one way to check whether India's share of manufacturing is too low is to see if it is 'too low' correcting for its level of income and its square (to account for non-linearities).[5]

[4] That the data are what they are does not mean we ignore problems. For example, there are aberrations in the Indian data for 1980 that do not appear in subsequent years. This is why we use data from 1981.

[5] Of course, other factors also affect sectoral shares [see, for example, Chenery and Taylor (1968)], but our intent here is primarily to see whether India is an outlier after controlling for obvious factors, rather than to do an exhaustive study of the sectoral composition of growth per se. Also, we report results for the largest sample of countries, though the results are qualitatively similar, when not specifically noted, for a smaller cross-section restricted to non-OECD countries.

Table 2.1: Sectoral Shares in Value Added and Employment

	Value Added as Per cent of GDP				Employment in sector as per cent of total employment		
	(1) Agriculture	(2) Manufacturing	(3) Industry	(4) Services	(5) Agriculture	(6) Industry	(7) Services
1980							
India	38.9	16.3	24.5	36.6	68.1	13.9	18.6
Brazil	11.0	33.5	43.8	45.2	29.3	24.7	46.1
China	30.1	40.5	48.5	21.4	68.7	18.2	11.7
Indonesia	24.0	13.0	41.7	34.3	55.9	13.2	30.2
Korea	15.1	28.6	40.5	44.4	34.0	29.0	37.0
Malaysia	22.6	21.6	41.0	36.3	37.2	24.1	38.7
Mexico	9.0	22.3	33.6	57.4	23.5	26.5	49.0
Thailand	23.2	21.5	28.7	48.1	70.8	10.3	18.9
Turkey	26.4	14.3	22.2	51.4	43.0	34.9	22.1
Low income	36.4	14.8	24.4	39.2	74.6	8.7	16.5
Lower middle income	21.5	29.1	41.7	36.8	64.0	18.5	16.4
2000							
India	24.6	15.9	26.6	48.8	59.3	18.2	22.4
Brazil	7.3	17.1	28.0	64.7	24.2	19.3	56.5
China	16.4	34.7	50.2	33.4	46.9	23.0	29.9
Indonesia	17.2	24.9	46.1	36.7	45.3	17.3	37.3
Korea	4.3	26.1	36.2	59.5	10.9	28.0	61.0
Malaysia	8.8	32.6	50.7	40.5	18.4	32.2	49.5
Mexico	4.2	20.3	28.0	67.8	17.5	26.9	55.2
Thailand	9.0	33.6	42.0	49.0	48.8	19.0	32.2
Turkey	15.4	15.7	25.3	59.4	34.5	24.5	40.9
Low income	27.3	14.1	26.6	46.1	64.5	12.3	23.2
Lower middle income	12.5	24.2	38.3	49.1	43.2	18.5	38.3

Sources: World Bank, World Development Indicators 2005, except Korea, OECD-Structural Analysis Database, and India, National Accounts Statistics, Indiastat.com.
Notes: For the low income, and lower middle income groups as classified by the World Bank, we report the respective averages. Employment shares are reported for the years indicated, except India (1983), Brazil (1981 and 1999), and Turkey (1982). Employment shares for the low-income group for 2000 are estimates.

Table 2.2: India in the Cross-section: Share of Manufacturing and Services, Early 1980s

	Share of output (1981)				Share of employment (1983)			
	Manufacturing		Services		Industry		Services	
	(1)	(2)	(3)	(4)	(5)	(6)	(7)	(8)
Log GDP per capita	15.37	21.58	36.27**	27.81	26.76	22.09	66.5**	67.20**
	(14.58)	(13.75)	(17.01)	(17.79)	(20.8)	(20.8)	(29.07)	(30.07)
Log GDP per capita	−0.73	−1.09	−1.95*	−1.46	−1.17	−0.92	−3.15*	−3.19*
	(0.88)	(0.83)	(1.03)	(1.08)	(1.2)	(1.2)	(1.71)	(1.76)
India indicator	4.58***	2.33	−6.50***	−3.55**	−0.260	0.560	−7.41**	−7.53**
	(1.25)	(1.76)	(1.3)	(1.61)	(2.52)	(2.82)	(3.27)	(3.63)
Control for country size	No	Yes	No	Yes	No	Yes	No	Yes
Observations	101	101	122	122	44	44	43	43

Notes: Robust standard errors are reported in parentheses.
***represents significance at 1 per cent, **represents significance at 5 per cent, *represents significance at 10 per cent levels.
Country size is measured by area in sq. km.

In Table 2.2, we report the results of cross-section regressions of a country's sectoral share in total output on these variables and an indicator for India. We also present a specification which includes, in addition, country size (proxied for by land area). Correcting only for the income terms, India is a positive outlier among countries in its share of value added in manufacturing in 1981. Its share significantly exceeds the norm by 4.6 percentage points (see Table 2.2, column 1). However, after correcting for country size, the coefficient on the India indicator declines to 2.3 percentage points in 1981 which is not statistically significant (column 2).[6] We focus in what follows on estimates from specifications including country size.

[6] The picture is slightly different when one looks at the share of value added in the industrial sector—which includes manufacturing, mining, construction and core infrastructure industries like electricity, water, and gas. We find that the coefficient on the India indicator is *negative* 3 percentage points, although it is not statistically significant.

Given that India is not an outlier in manufacturing share in 1981, the conventional wisdom that India is underweight in manufacturing could either be because it underperfomed over the next twenty years or because it is typically compared with China. The coefficient for the China indicator suggests that China's share of manufacturing in 1981 was an astonishing 29 percentage points of GDP greater than that for the average country.[7]

Finally, India is an outlier in services in 1981 (columns 3 and 4) and a *negative* one at that. India's share of services in value added is significantly below that for other countries in 1981 (about 3.6 percentage points lower in column 4).

Employment Shares in 1981 and Productivity

When we compare the shares of industrial sector employment in total employment across countries, India is again not an outlier (Table 2.2, columns 5 and 6).[8] In the case of services (columns 7 and 8), however, India has a significant 7.5 percentage point lower employment share than other countries, after controlling for income and size.

In estimates that are not reported, we find that India was a significant positive outlier with respect to relative labour productivity in industry and services in the cross-section in 1981, suggesting productivity in agriculture was low.

Use of factors: Labour intensity, skill intensity

What did the policies do in terms of industry specialization? We look at the manufacturing sector where we have comparable cross-country data from the UNIDO. The first industry characteristic we examine is labour intensity, for which we use as a proxy the share of wages in value added for the industry in a country, averaged across a broad group of developing countries. Examples of industries that score highest on labour intensity are clothing, printing and publishing, and non-electrical machinery, while those that score lowest are beverages, tobacco, and petroleum refineries (Table 2.3).

---

[7] By contrast, China was a large negative outlier in services in 1981, with a share in GDP about 15 percentage points less than that for the typical country, controlling for income and size.

[8] Comparable cross-country data on employment shares are not available separately for the manufacturing sector, only for industry (manufacturing, mining, and core infrastructure sectors), and services. Thus the analysis of employment shares is conducted for industry and services.

Table2.3: Classification of Industries by Labor Intensity, Size, and Skill Intensity

	Isic code	By Labour intensity Industry description	Isic code	By Relative size Industry description	Isic code	By Skill intensity Industry description
	322	Wearing apparel	353	Petroleum Refineries	353	Petroleum Refineries
A	342	Printing & Publishing	314	Tobacco	342	Printing & Publishing
B	382	Machinery except electric	371	Iron & steel	352	Other chemicals
O	332	Furniture, except metal	351	Industrial chemicals	385	Professional and scientific equipment
V	324	Footwear, except rubber or plastic	313	Beverages	383	Machinery, electric
E	321	Textiles	372	Non-ferrous metals	384	Transport Equipment
	331	Wood products, except furniture	352	Other chemicals	382	Machinery except electric
M	384	Transport Equipment	354	Misc Petroleum and coal pdts	351	Industrial chemicals
E	361	Pottery, China, earthenware	341	Paper and products	332	Furniture, except metal
D	323	Leather products	383	Machinery, electric	381	Fabricated Metal products
I	381	Fabricated Metal products	384	Transport Equipment	371	Iron & steel
A	362	Glass and products	362	Glass and products	390	Other manufacturing products
N	385	Professional and scientific equipment	361	Pottery, China, earthenware	356	Plastic products
	390	Other manufacturing products	385	Professional and scientific equipment	355	Rubber products
	355	Rubber products	355	Rubber products	314	Tobacco
B	341	Paper and products	324	Footwear, except rubber or plastic	354	Misc. Petroleum and coal products
E	371	Iron & steel			313	Beverages
L	383	Machinery, electric			311	Food products
O	369	Other non-metallic mineral products	321	Textiles	369	Other non-metallic mineral

	Isic code	By Labour intensity Industry description	Isic code	By Relative size Industry description	Isic code	By Skill intensity Industry description
	352	Other chemicals	382	Machinery except electric	372	Non-ferrous metals
M	356	Plastic products	342	Printing & Publishing	321	Textiles
E	351	Industrial chemicals	323	Leather products	341	Paper and products
D	372	Non-ferrous metals	322	Wearing apparel	324	Footwear, except rubber or plastic
I	354	Misc. Petroleum and coal products	381	Fabricated Metal products	362	Glass and products
A	313	Beverages	390	Other manufacturing products	323	Leather products
N	314	Tobacco	331	Wood products, except furniture	331	Wood products, except furniture
	353	Petroleum Refineries	332	Furniture, except metal	361	Pottery, China, earthenware

	Correlation		Rank Correlation	
	Labour intensity	Skill intensity	Labour intensity	Skill intensity
Skill Intensity	0.10		0.01	
p-value	(0.63)		(0.97)	
observations	26		26	
Relative size	-0.59***	-0.01	-0.74***	0.13
p-value	(0.00)	(0.94)	(0.00)	(0.53)
observations	28	26	28	26

Sources: Labour intensity, Rajan and Subramanian, (2005), Relative Size (as defined in text), UNIDO, 2003, Skill intensity, South Africa's National Accounts.

Notes: In each subgroup, the industries are ranked by descending order of the corresponding measure of intensity or size. Labour intensity is measured by the share of wages in value added for the industry in a country, averaged across a broad group of developing countries, as in Rajan and Subramanian (2005). Relative size is the ratio of value added per establishment within the industry over the value added per establishment within the country, averaged across countries for each industry. Skill is measured by the ratio of the remuneration of highly skilled and skilled labour over the total value added of the industry.

For each country, we calculate the ratio of value added in above-median-labour-intensity industries to the value added in below-median-labour-intensity industries. If Indian manufacturing generated relatively more value added in labour intensive industries in 1981, then in a cross-country regression of this ratio against log per capita GDP, its square, and an indicator for India, the India indicator should be positive and significant (see Table 2.4, Panel A, column 1). However, the coefficient is insignificant.

The coefficient on the India indicator is moderately negative when the dependent variable is the ratio of employment (see Table 2.4, Panel B, column 1). Finally, the India indicator is positive and significant when the dependent variable is the ratio of labour productivity in above-median labour-intensive industries to that in below median industries in 1981 (Table 2.4, Panel C, column 1).[9]

Let us now turn to skill intensity. The input–output matrix for South Africa contains data on forty-five sectors and five primary factors of production—capital plus four categories of labour: highly skilled, skilled, unskilled, and informal sector (see Alleyne and Subramanian, 2001). We use the share of remuneration of the highly skilled and skilled categories of workers in total value as a proxy for the skill intensity of an industry.[10] The categorization of industries according to skill is given in Table 2.3. The most skill-intensive industries are printing, other chemicals, and professional and scientific equipment. The least skill-intensive industries include textile, leather, footwear, and wood products. The correlation between an industry's labour intensity and its skill intensity is positive but small and not statistically significant (see Table 2.3), suggesting they capture different things.

The dependent variable in Table 2.4 (Panel A, column 2) is the ratio of the total value added by above-median-skill-intensity manufacturing industries to the total value added by below-median-skill-intensity

[9] In a number of places in this chapter, we use the median to divide industries. As a robustness check, we also grouped them into the top and bottom third, excluding the middle third to avoid possible misclassification of industries. Our results remained qualitatively unchanged using this alternative classification.

[10] The choice of South Africa was dictated primarily by data availability. Our results are robust to alternative definitions of skill intensity, including restricting the definition to the highly skilled category and defining skill intensity in terms of share of remuneration in output rather than value added. We also checked the correlation of our measures of skill intensity with that compiled for the United States by Rajan and Wulf (2004). It is 0.66, for the highly skilled category, and 0.5 when skill intensity includes highly skilled and skilled workers.

Table 2.4: India in the Cross-section, Labour Intensity, Skill Intensity, Scale, and Diversification, 1981

A.	Ratio of value added in above-median sectors to below median sectors			Concentration Index
	Labour intensity	Skill intensity	Scale	Based on valued added
Log GDP per capita	−0.77	−3.89***	0.33	−0.02***
	(1.13)	(1.35)	(1.39)	(0.01)
Log GDP per capita^2	0.04	0.26***	−0.01	0.001**
	(0.07)	(0.08)	(0.08)	(0.0004)
India dummy	0.17	1.28***	0.47***	−0.07***
	(0.13)	(0.2)	(0.14)	(0.02)
Control for size	Yes	Yes	Yes	Yes
Observations	80	80	80	80

B.	Ratio of employment in above-median sectors to below median sectors			Concentration Index
	Labour intensity	Skill intensity	Scale	Based on employment
Log GDP per capita	−0.60	−4.27***	−1.44	−0.02***
	(1.03)	(1.30)	(0.96)	(0.006)
Log GDP per capita^2	0.04	0.28***	0.1*	0.001***
	(0.06)	(0.08)	(0.06)	(0.0003)
India dummy	−0.18	0.25	0.31***	−0.06***
	(0.13)	(0.16)	(0.09)	(0.02)
Control for size	Yes	Yes	Yes	Yes
Observations	81	81	81	81

C.	Ratio of value added per worker in above-median sectors to below-median sectors		
	Labour intensity	Skill intensity	Scale
Log GDP per capita	−1.53***	0.48	4.06***
	(0.59)	(0.91)	(1.49)
Log GDP per capita²	0.09***	−0.04	−0.26***
	(0.03)	(0.05)	(0.09)
India dummy	0.17**	1.08***	−0.26
	(0.08)	(0.12)	(0.23)
Control for size	Yes	Yes	Yes
Observations	74	74	74

Notes: For the concentration indices, GDP per capita and area are not in log terms and GDP per capita2 is the square of GDP per capita
Area measured in sq. km. is used as measure of size
Concentration Index is measured by Herfindahl Index
Robust standard errors are reported in parentheses
***represents significance at 1 per cent, **represents significance at 5 per cent, *represents significance at 10 per cent.

industries. It is striking that even by 1981, India specialized in skill-intensive industries. Also, relative labour productivity in skilled industries was higher in India (Panel C, column 2).

Industry Scale and Firm Size

Next, we establish two facts about the 'scale' of Indian enterprise. First, manufacturing was unusually concentrated in industries that typically require large scale. Second, within industries however, the array of policies that discouraged large firms appear to have had their intended effect, with Indian firms unusually small relative to firms in the same industry in other countries.

It is not immediately obvious how we would approximate the typical scale of an industry. If the size of the domestic market matters, a larger country would have larger establishments [see the evidence in Kumar et. al. (1999), for example]. Also, as the coverage of manufacturing data varies across countries, the smallest firms may be covered in some countries but not in others.

For these reasons, we cannot simply take the value added per establishment (or employees per establishment) in an industry averaged across countries to get a measure of scale for the industry.[11] Instead, we focus on relative size, that is, we find the relative size of establishments in an industry in a country by dividing the value added (or employment) per establishment in the industry by the value added (or employment) per establishment in the country. It is this relative size that we average across countries for each industry to find a measure of the scale of establishments in that industry.

The industries with the largest scale across countries are petroleum refineries, tobacco, and iron and steel, while that with the smallest scale is furniture (Table 2.3). The ranking of industries differs only marginally across our two measures of establishment size, so we will use the measure based on value added per establishment. The results do not differ qualitatively if we use the other measure.

We find that the ratio of value added in above-median-scale industries to below-median-scale industries is significantly higher in India (Table 2.4, Panel A, column 3). Interestingly, relative employment shares in above-median-scale industries is also significantly higher in India relative to other countries (see Panel B, column 3). As a result, relative productivity is somewhat lower for above-median-scale industries in India, but not significantly so (Panel C, column 3).

The correlation between scale and labour intensity is strongly negative and significant (–0.59), while the correlation between scale and skill intensity is small (–0.01) and insignificant (see Table 2.3). This suggests that our measure of scale proxies for capital intensity, which in turn may explain why production is concentrated in the large-scale sectors in India; Indian planners laid emphasis on building capital-intensive, large-scale, heavy industries because of their belief that 'machines that made machines' would boost savings and hence long-run growth. They commandeered these sectors for the public sector, and many of the impediments to scale that were faced by the private sector simply did not apply to the public sector. Moreover, employment was an implicit objective in the public sector. As a result, a capital-scarce country was overrepresented, both in

[11] We would be mixing industries represented in large countries or countries with extensive coverage with industries represented in small countries or countries with little coverage, reducing comparability.

terms of value added and employment, in the capital-intensive/large-scale segments of industry.

The real impact of the discriminatory policy regime against private sector scale (industrial licensing, forced geographic distribution of production, reservation, and other incentives for small-scale sectors, and the anti-monopoly MRTP Act) may then have been felt within industry rather than between industries.[12] With the caveats about cross-country comparisons of establishment size noted above, and some attempt at correcting for them, we find that the average size of firms in India is substantially below that in other countries—this is true in the aggregate and in almost every industry. In Figure 2.1, we compare the average firm size in India with the average firm size in ten emerging market countries for

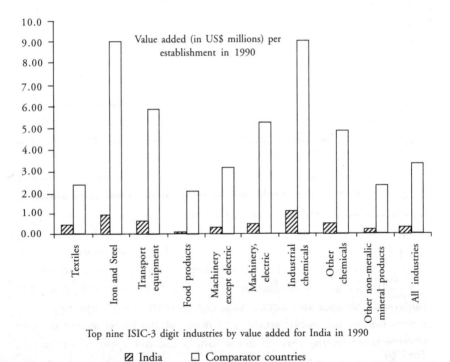

Top nine ISIC-3 digit industries by value added for India in 1990

▨ India   ☐ Comparator countries

Figure 2.1: Average firm size in India and comparator countries in 1990

[12] Even though some industries were reserved for the public sector, firms even there may have been inefficiently small because of the felt need to distribute production across the country. Moreover, our industries are broad enough that they typically include many private firms.

manufacturing as a whole and for the nine largest industries in India.[13] The contrast is striking: for example, the average firm size in manufacturing in India is about US$300,000 per firm, whereas it is about US$4 million in the comparator countries—a multiple exceeding 10. Parenthetically, note that in the figure, the pattern of size across industries in India matches the pattern in comparator countries (with, for example, iron and steel or industrial chemicals being large and food products small), albeit at a much lower level, verifying that relative size is a distinctive characteristic of an industry that holds across countries.

We have argued that regulations, especially those pertaining to labour, might partly account for why firms in India are typically small because they applied only to registered firms that exceeded a certain size. If labour laws matter, we should see relatively more activity in labour-intensive industries done by unregistered firms. Using data from unregistered manufacturing, we find the ratio of value added in above-median labour-intensive industries to that in below-median-labour-intensive industries in unregistered manufacturing (obtained from the Central Statistical Organization) is significantly higher (by about two times in 1980) than in registered manufacturing.[14] By contrast, labour laws were less applicable to non-unionized, highly skilled workers—for example, to professionals. So we should find the ratio of value added in above-median-skill-intensive industries to that in below-median-skill-intensive industries in unregistered manufacturing should not be significantly higher than in registered manufacturing. It is not—quite the opposite, the ratio of above- to below-median skill-intensive industries in the unregistered sector is about one-fourth of that in the registered sector.[15]

[13] In presenting this stylized fact, we attempt to avoid possible biases. We first compared manufacturing output from UNIDO and the World Bank's World Development Indicators (WDI). The UNIDO database only covers the registered manufacturing sector in India, defined as firms not using power and employing twenty or more people, or firms using power and employing ten or more people. Hence, the UNIDO data are biased toward larger firms in India. The UNIDO data cover about 60 per cent of the data reported in the WDI. For the purposes of comparison with other countries, we eliminated countries where the UNIDO data had a lower share of total value added in manufacturing than in India. This would bias our test towards finding that India had relatively larger firms.

[14] Recall that what we have reported thus far are figures from registered manufacturing using UNIDO data.

[15] The fact that the ratio is so much lower in the unregistered sector suggests that skill-intensive sectors might require a larger scale of operation for technological reasons.

Diversification

Before we discuss these findings, let us add one more fact, which follows from the facts on labour-intensity, skill, and scale. Imbs and Wacziarg (2003) show that in the course of development, countries first diversify within manufacturing, producing many things, and then after a certain level of income, start specializing, producing fewer things. Technically, the relationship between the concentration of value added across industries (the Gini coefficient or the Herfindahl index) and income is U-shaped, with the turning point occurring at about US$10,000 per capita.

Given that India has more of a presence in skill-intensive and large-scale industries, the presumption would be that it has specialized in more areas than the typical developing country, and hence it should exhibit a more diverse pattern of production. When we examine the concentration of Indian industry compared to the average country pattern, we find that India is significantly less concentrated (or more diversified), not just in terms of the distribution of value-added across industries, but also when concentration is measured in terms of employment (Table 2.4, panels A and B, column 4). The coefficient on the India indicator when the dependent variable is the concentration of value added is a significant -0.07, and it is -0.06 when the dependent variable is the concentration of employment. In other words, India has an output and employment profile across industries that is approximately one standard deviation less concentrated than that for the average country, suggesting a broader array of skills/capabilities in the labour force. [16]

The contrast with China is interesting. China's index which is close to that for India would suggest that China too is an outlier in terms of diversification. It turns out, however, that after controlling for size, China is not unusually diversified in the cross-section whereas India is.

The Effects of Pre-1980s Policies: Summary and Discussion

To summarize, compared with countries at a similar level of development and size, in 1981 India had approximately the normal share of output and employment in manufacturing. Output in services was below the norm, as

---

[16] It is possible that the highly restrictive and distorted trade regime was a key reason that the Indian economy was unusually diversified. To examine this possibility, we included various measures of trade openness in the cross-country comparisons. Although the measures of trade openness have some explanatory power, the finding that India is unusually diversified still stands—the coefficient on the India indicators is smaller in this case, but retains its statistical significance.

was employment in services. Manufacturing output and employment appeared to be above the norm in industries that typically are skill-intensive or have larger scale. Average establishment size within industries, though, was substantially smaller than in comparable countries. And finally, Indian manufacturing was significantly more diversified both in terms of output and employment than countries of comparable income and size.

One seemingly anomalous finding is the high relative labour productivity observed in the labour-intensive sectors in India. Why did this not, for example, translate into exports of labour-intensive goods? We offer three possible explanations. First, the high relative labour productivity could simply be the converse of the low labour productivity in the large-scale capital-intensive industries, which were probably dominated by state-owned firms where over-staffing was a common phenomenon and even an objective. Second, the stringent labour laws that make it hard to lay off labour and the consequent hesitancy to hire (and to drive down marginal labour productivity to the value maximizing level) could also explain why productivity is moderately higher in labour-intensive industries. Third, the discrimination against size that we have noted above may well have limited the labour-intensive sector's incentive and ability to exploit economies of scale and generate large volumes of exports.

The paradox of Indian manufacturing in the early 1980s is thus that of a labour-rich, capital-poor economy using too little of the former, and using the latter very inefficiently.[17] The reason, most likely, was perverse policy. Unlike the East Asian economies, which drew employment from agriculture into manufacturing at a rapid pace, India did not.

The one area where Indian manufacturing appears to have thrived is in the industries using highly skilled labour. The far greater investment in tertiary education for a country of its per capita income—of which the Indian Institutes of Technology and the Indian Institutes of Management are just the best-known examples—resulted in the plentiful availability of

---

[17] It may well be, of course, that India's labour-intensive production was concentrated in the unregistered sector, for which we do not have comparable data from other countries. To the extent that firms in the unregistered sector have inefficiently small scale, total production would still be smaller and less competitive than it could be without the spectrum of regulations. Also, unregistered labour-intensive production has been falling considerably over time, suggesting that this explanation for India's lack of concentration in labour-intensive manufacturing is less applicable today.

highly skilled, cheap labour. In addition, labour laws afforded much less protection to skilled labour. These factors are likely to have contributed to India generating relatively greater value added and employment in skill-intensive industries as compared to the typical poor country.

India was a significant negative outlier in services in 1981. In part, this may have been because the slow-moving public sector again dominated areas like telecommunications and business services where India's advantage in skills (as evidenced by the pattern of specialization in manufacturing) might have been used. By contrast, sectors like retail and construction were left to the private sector, where the limited access to finance (both for the service provider and the customer) kept businesses small and growth limited.

Finally, the greater diversification of Indian manufacturing could be explained as a consequence of all the policy distortions. The import substitution strategy, the skewed pattern of education, as well as the encouragement given to the public sector to invest in areas that are typically not a poor country's comparative advantage, may well have driven India into industries that other countries at comparable income levels shy away from.

HOW HAS INDIA CHANGED SINCE THE EARLY 1980S?

Policy Changes Since the 1980s

A number of observers (see, for example, Kohli, 2005, Rodrik and Subramanian, 2005; Virmani 2005) noted the tilt of the Indian economy, beginning in the early 1980s, away from controls and repression of the domestic private sector. The pace of reforms accelerated in earnest the early 1990s, in the wake of the external payments crisis. The reforms have been attributed to various causes ranging from a realization that the panoply of controls were self-defeating, to a realization by the Congress Party that given the growing challenges to its power, it had to woo business (see Kohli, 2005).

The key features of reforms in the 1980s were: (i) the liberalization of imports—especially of capital goods and intermediate inputs; (ii) the extension of export incentives through the tax system, and more liberal access to credit and foreign exchange; (iii) the significant relaxation of industrial licensing requirements through direct 'delicensing' of some industries and through 'broad banding', which permitted firms in some industries to switch production between similar product lines; (iv) the decontrol of administered prices of key intermediate inputs. Kohli (2005) and Rodrik and Subramanian (2005) characterized the reforms of the 1980s as 'pro-business' in orientation.

The reforms of the 1990s—which some have distinguished from the reforms of the 1980s as 'pro-market' in orientation—included: (i) the abolition of industrial licensing and the narrowing of the scope of public sector monopolies to a much smaller number of industries; (ii) the liberalization of inward foreign direct and portfolio investment; (iii) the sweeping liberalization of trade which included the elimination of import licensing and the progressive reduction of non-tariff barriers; (iv) financial sector liberalization, including the removal of controls on capital issues, free entry for domestic, and foreign, private banks and the opening up of the insurance sector; (v) and the liberalization of investment in important services, such as telecommunications. Areas that remained largely untouched by reforms in the 1990s were the labour market; small-scale reservations (where there has been some movement only in the last four to five years); privatization both of non-financial enterprises and of banks; and further agricultural sector reforms.

How have these twenty years of slow but steady reforms affected the pattern of development, if at all? We first look at the evolution in the variables discussed above—sectoral shares, factor intensities, size and diversification, between the early 1980s and early 2000s. Our point is that given the distinct turn towards business and markets and away from controls, any anomalies in the pattern of development or in their underlying trend should have been corrected or at least arrested. The data, as we will see, do not support this hypothesis.

Manufacturing Versus Services in the Cross-Section

The traditional perspective of Kuznets or Chenery would predict a rapid increase in the share of manufacturing, a decline in agriculture, and an uncertain or modest effect on services. However, between 1980 and 2002, India's share of services in value added exploded from 37 per cent to 49 per cent. Its share of manufacturing in value added remained broadly unchanged at 16 per cent, while the decline in agriculture mirrored the performance of services.[18] The corresponding numbers for employment were 19 per cent to 22 per cent and 14 per cent to 18 per cent (Table 2.1).

---

[18] This development contradicts the Kuznets–Chenery hypothesis. Kongsamut et al. (2001), however, argued based on an analysis of 123 countries over the period 1970–89 that the share of services rises with development more than anticipated by the Kuznets–Chenery view.

Table 2.5: India in the Cross-section: Shares of Manufacturing and Services, 2000

Panel A

	Share of output				Share of employment			
	Manufacturing		Services		Industry			Services
	(1)	(2)	(3)	(4)	(5)	(6)	(7)	(8)
Log GDP per capita	13.18**	15.41**	10.88	8.01	51.79***	52.4***	38.99	39.69*
	(6.41)	(6.38)	(10.34)	(10.3)	(11.28)	(11.23)	(23.91)	(23.83)
Log GDP per capita	−0.610	−0.72*	−0.19	−0.040	−2.67***	−2.71***	−1.49	−1.54
	(0.12)	(0.38)	(0.6)	(0.6)	(0.62)	(0.63)	(1.31)	(1.3)
India indicator	2.4***	0.26	−0.05	3.77**	0.56	1.13	−17.22***	−16.57***
	(0.73)	(1.11)	(1.17)	(1.46)	(1.17)	(1.36)	(3.03)	(3.78)
Control for size	No	Yes	No	Yes	No	Yes	No	Yes
Observations	149	149	156	156	76	76	74	74

Panel B

	Change in share of output (1981–2000)		Change in share of employment (1983–2000)	
	Manufacturing	Services	Industry	Services
	(1)	(2)	(3)	(4)
Log initial GDP per capita	−1.91***	3.96***	−3.37***	2.91**
	(0.66)	(0.77)	(0.92)	(1.39)
Average annual growth rate	0.7**	0.41	0.47	−0.18
	(0.33)	(0.53)	(0.6)	(0.64)
India indicator	−2.57*	9.87***	1.70	0.94
	(1.37)	(1.63)	(2.05)	(3.59)
Observations	93	116	39	38

Notes: Robust standard errors are reported in parentheses

***represents significance at 1 per cent , **represents significance at 5 per cent , *represents significance at 10 per cent

Country size is measured by area in sq. km.

Is this evolution in sectoral shares unusual when compared with that of other countries? In the level regressions for 2000 (Table 2.5, columns 1 and 2, Panel A), the coefficient of the India indicator is still positive but smaller than in the corresponding specification for 1981.[19] Furthermore, in the regressions using the change in the share of manufacturing value added to overall growth (column 1, Panel B), the India indicator is negative. Thus, the data suggest a relative slowing in manufacturing growth.

What is indisputable is the performance of services over this period. India has been unusual in this regard. India's share in services is a significant 3.8 per cent higher than in other countries in 2000 (Table 2.5, Panel A, column 4). This is broadly confirmed in the change regressions (Panel B), where India records an increase in the size of the services sector that is 10 percentage points of GDP *greater* than that of the average country.

Finally, note in Table 2.5 (column 8, Panel A) that India is again a negative outlier in terms of the employment share in services, falling below other countries by a huge 17 percentage points in 2000. Gordon and Gupta (2004) have also observed that, unlike other countries, Indian labour's share in services employment has been flat rather than growing with income. The huge increase in value added in services without a commensurate increase in employment, must have come from tremendous gains in labour productivity in services.[20]

Labour and Skill Intensity in the Cross-Section

Recall that around 1980 India specialized in skill-intensive industries and in industries where establishments were relatively large in scale. India did not produce an unusually high share of labour-intensive products. What happened to this pattern after the 1980s?

In Figure 2.2, we plot the evolution in the share of output generated in labour-intensive relative to non labour-intensive industries for India and a selected group of comparator countries. India's share is decreasing, when that of many of the other countries is either increasing, or decreasing but at much higher levels of income. Figure 2.3 complements this picture by

[19] However, we find that industry (i.e., manufacturing, mining and core infrastructure industries) was a significant negative outlier in 2000, possibly related to the much worse than average performance of India's infrastructure sector.

[20] Gordon and Gupta (2004) argue that the increase in labour productivity in India was caused by a greater emphasis on skill-intensive services, rather than an increase in capital intensity.

Ratio of value added in above median labour intensive sectors by to below median sectors

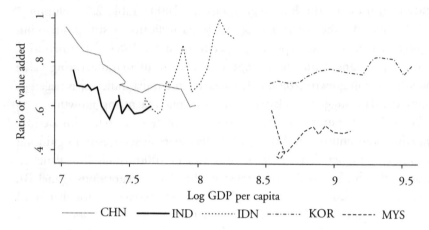

Figure 2.2: Value-added share of labour-intensive industries

Sources: Authors' calculations; UNIDO 3-digit industrial statistics database (2003).
Notes: The sample for all countries includes observations from 1981 to 1996. The classification
of above- and below-median labour-intensive sectors is given in Table 2.2. CHN stands for
China, IND for India, IDN for Indonesia, KOR for Korea, and MYS for Malaysia.

Ratio of value added in above median sectors by relative size to below median sectors

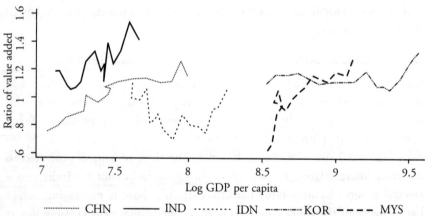

Figure 2.3: Value-added share of industries with large scale.

Sources: Authors' calculations; UNIDO 3-digit industrial statistics database (2003).
Notes: The sample for all countries includes observations from 1981 to 1996. Relative size is as
defined in the text. The classification of above- and below-median sectors by relative size is given
in Table 2.3. CHN stands for China, IND for India, IDN for Indonesia, KOR for Korea, and
MYS for Malaysia.

showing that the relative share of output generated in large-scale (typically, capital-intensive) industries has been rising sharply in India.

In Figure 2.4, we plot the evolution in the relative share of output generated in skill-intensive industries for India and a selected group of comparator countries. Again, it is striking that India's share in skill-intensive manufacturing, which was already high in 1980 despite its lower level of per capita income, has been increasing; it is at levels reached by Malaysia or Korea at much higher levels of per capita income. These developments are not affected by the fact that our data so far have been limited to the registered manufacturing sector in India. Indeed, when we trace the evolution of labour- and skill-intensive products in the informal sector, we see the same pattern (Figure 2.5).

These developments are more formally captured in the regressions reported in Table 2.6 for 2000. They show that India is not an outlier in terms of the share of manufacturing output or employment generated in labour-intensive industries, but continues to be strongly so for the share of value added in skill-intensive industries and large-scale industries.

In terms of labour productivity too, skill-intensive industries stand out

Ratio of value added in above median skill-intensive sectors to below median sectors

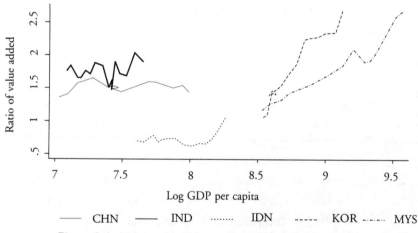

Figure 2.4: Value-added share of skill-intensive industries.

Sources: Authors' calculations; UNIDO 3-digit industrial statistics database (2003).

Notes: The sample for all countries includes observations from 1981 to 1996. The classification of above- and below-median skill intensive sectors is given in Table 2.4. CHN stands for China, IND for India, IDN for Indonesia, KOR for Korea, and MYS for Malaysia.

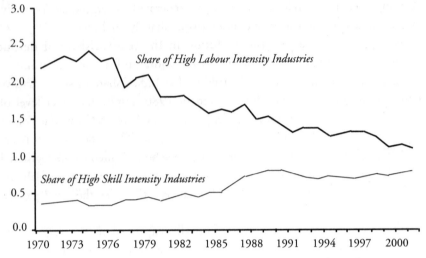

Figure 2.5: Value-added share in unregistered manufacturing.

Source: Authors' calculations; data on unregistered manufacturing are from the Central Statistical Organization, Government of India.

Notes: The share of high labour (skill) intensity industries is the ratio of value added in sectors with above-median labour (skill) intensity to that in sectors with below-median labour (skill) intensity. The relevant sector classification is given in Table 2.3.

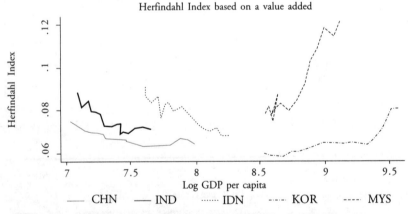

Figure 2.6: Diversification in Indian manufacturing.

Sources: Authors' calculations; UNIDO 3-digit industrial statistics database (2003).

Notes: The sample for all countries includes observations from 1981 to 1996. CHN stands for China, IND for India, IDN for Indonesia, KOR for Korea, and MYS for Malaysia. For each country, the Herfindahl Index measures concentration in the value added across sectors; the lower the index, the lower the concentration, or the higher the diversification.

while the relative productivity of large-scale industries is strongly negative. Relative labour productivity in labour-intensive industries has remained approximately similar to 1981 (Tables 2.4 and 2.6, Panel C).

Finally, we find that India continues to be an outlier in 2000 on both measures of diversification. Indeed, when we compare the change in diversification between 1980 and 2000, we find that India is again an

Table 2.6: India in the Cross-section, Labour Intensity, Skill Intensity, Scale, and Diversification, 2000

A.	Ratio of value added in above-median sectors to below-median sectors			Concentration Index
	Labour intensity	Skill intensity	Scale	Based on valued added
Log GDP per capita	−1.87	−1.14	0.79	−0.003
	(1.60)	(1.70)	(0.84)	(0.003)
Log GDP per capita^2	0.12	0.11	−0.04	0.0001
	(0.09)	(0.10)	(0.05)	(0.0001)
India dummy	0.69	0.88***	0.32***	−0.05***
	(0.46)	(0.21)	(0.11)	(0.01)
Control for size	Yes	Yes	Yes	Yes
Observations	47	47	47	47
B.	Ratio of employment in above-median sectors to below-median sectors			Concentration index
	Labour intensity	Skill intensity	Scale	Based on employment
Log GDP per capita	2.49	−1.22	−0.17	−0.01**
	(4.99)	(0.85)	(0.47)	(0.004)
Log GDP per capita^2	−0.14	0.10**	0.02	0.0003**
	(0.30)	(0.05)	(0.03)	(0.001)
India dummy	−0.06	−0.01	0.21***	−0.09***
	(1.04)	(0.12)	(0.07)	(0.02)
Control for size	Yes	Yes	Yes	Yes
Observations	61	60	60	61

C.	Ratio of value added per worker in above-median sectors to below-median sectors		
	Labour intensity	Skill intensity	Scale
Log GDP per capita	−1.05*	1.12	2.70*
	(0.58)	(0.77)	(1.40)
Log GDP per capita^2	0.07**	−0.07	−0.17**
	(0.03)	(0.05)	(0.08)
India dummy	0.21***	0.95***	−0.62***
	(0.07)	(0.13)	(0.19)
Control for size	Yes	Yes	Yes
Observations	47	47	47

Notes: For the concentration indices, GDP per capita and area are not in log terms and GDP per capita^2 is the square of GDP per capita.
Area measured in sq. km. is used as measure of size.
Concentration Index is measured by Herfindahl Index.
Robust standard errors are reported in parentheses.
***represents significance at 1per cent, **represents significance at 5 per cent, *represents significance at 10 per cent.

outlier, implying that the pace of diversification in India after 1980 has been greater than that for the average country (see Figure 2.6).

In sum, the evidence suggests that many of the unique features of India's development that were apparent in 1981 have not changed, despite the reforms. This continuity of trends may be explained partly by the fact that the reforms have not been completed. For example, labour markets remain untouched and education expenditure is still skewed. But part of the explanation may well rest with the fact that in India, the policy distortions created organizational capabilities and human capital that led to hysteresis in growth paths. The growth experience of the Indian states offers some support to this view.

THE STATES' STORY

Manufacturing Versus Services at the Level of the States

In the fast-growing Indian states, the share of manufacturing has remained constant or declined (Figure 2.7). Where there has been an increase—in

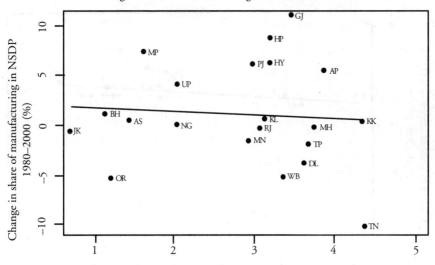

Figure 2.7: Manufacturing and states' growth.

Sources: Authors' calculations; EPW Research Foundation, Domestic Product of States of India: 1960–1 to 2000–1.

Notes: NSDP is net state domestic product.

Code	State	Code	State	Code	State
AP	Andhra Pradesh	JK	Jammu & Kashmir	OR	Orissa
AS	Assam	KK	Karnataka	PJ	Punjab
BH	Bihar	KL	Kerala	RJ	Rajasthan
DL	Delhi	MH	Maharashtra	TN	Tamil Nadu
GJ	Gujarat	MN	Manipur	TP	Tripura
HP	Himachal Pradesh	MP	Madhya Pradesh	UP	Uttar Pradesh
HY	Haryana	NG	Nagaland	WB	West Bengal

Andhra Pradesh, Gujarat, and Haryana—it has occurred in capital- and skill-intensive industries. (In Gujarat, the share of the textiles industry declined a lot, while that of the petrochemical industry rose substantially; similarly, in Andhra Pradesh the decline in the share of food, beverages, tobacco, textiles, and paper-related industries was matched by a significant increase in the share of basic metals and alloys.) Interestingly, there is little correlation between the change in share of value added in labour-intensive industries and growth. The fast-growing states, are not uniformly increasing

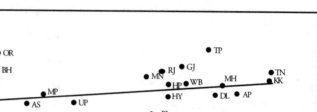

Figure 2.8: Services and states' growth.

Source: Authors' calculations; EPW Research Foundation, Domestic Product of States of India: 1960–1 to 2000–1.

Notes: NSDP is net state domestic product. Codes same as Figure 2.7.

their share to labour-intensive industries, nor are the slow-growing states; on average there seems to be a slight decline in share.

By contrast, nearly all states in India—regardless of their growth performance—have seen a uniform shift toward services (see Figure 2.8 where the increase in share of all states in services is uniformly high, with the fastest growing states having the highest increase in share). There does seem to be a noteworthy difference between services that are predominantly in the public sector and those that are in the private sector. In Figure 2.9, we find a negative correlation between the change in share of services that are performed mostly by the public sector (such as electricity, public administration, railways, and other community services) and the average annual state growth.[21] In other words, the share of public sector services

---

[21] Acharya (2002) argued that the growth of the services sector is artificially inflated by the large wage increase awarded to public sector employees in 1998 by the Fifth Pay Commission. Our findings suggest that the growth in services in the fast-moving states has been outside the public sector.

Change in Share of Public Services in NSDP 1980–2000

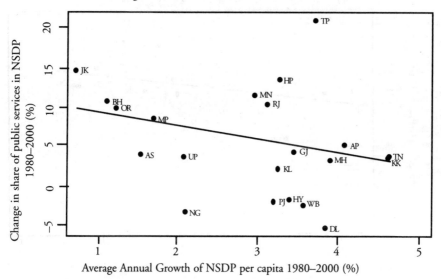

Average Annual Growth of NSDP per capita 1980–2000 (%)

Figure 2.9: Public services and states' growth.

Source: Authors' calculations; EPW Research Foundation, Domestic Product of States of India: 1960–1 to 2000–1.

Notes: NSDP is net state domestic product; selected public sector services include electricity, public administration, railways, and other public sector services. Codes same as Figure 2.7.

including administration is growing in the laggard states, while the share of private sector services is growing in the fast-moving states.

Diversification

Let us now turn to diversification. Figure 2.10 suggests that there is hardly relationship between a state's growth in the period 1980–2000 and the increase in its concentration, though if anything, it is mildly positive. The majority of states, however, continue to become more diversified (i.e., the change in their Herfindahl index is negative).

Recall that Imbs and Wacziarg (2003) find that the relationship between diversification and income turns negative beyond a threshold level of income. This may well be what has been happening in India. While states in general continue to become more diversified, a number of fast-growing states—Tamil Nadu, Karnataka, West Bengal, Delhi, and Maharashtra—saw stagnation or declines in their share of manufacturing and a sharp rise in the share of services. These states have also been those that have seen no significant increase in

Change in Share of Public Services in NSDP 1980–2000

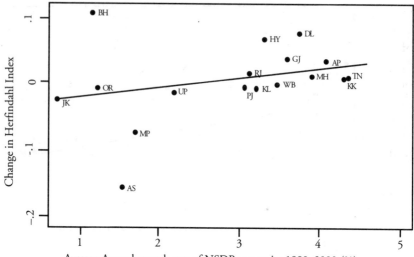

Average Annual growth rate of NSDP per capita 1980–2000 (%)

Figure 2.10: Change in diversification and states' growth

Source: Authors' calculations; EPW Research Foundation, Domestic Product of States of India: 1960–1 to 2000–1; 3-digit industry level data at the state level from Circon India Data Center. *Notes*: NSDP is net state domestic product. For each state, the Herfindahl Index (HI) measures the concentration of value added across 3-digit industries; the change in the Index is the difference between its average value for 1982, 1984, and 1985, and its average value for 1995–7. Codes same as Figure 2.7.

diversification. In other words, some of the richer states have started to behave like rich countries in starting to specialize in manufacturing even as, or because, they are doing less manufacturing and more services. But these states are becoming less diversified not because they are reverting to the pattern followed by less developed, labour-abundant countries [hence moving left and up the quadratic relationship documented by Imbs and Wacziarg (2003)] but more likely because they are behaving more like advanced skill intensive countries (hence moving right and up the quadratic relationship).

UNDERSTANDING POST-1980 PERFORMANCE

Instead of reverting to labour-intensive manufacturing growth, which was the specialization undertaken by many Asian countries at India's stage of development, India and its fast-growing states appear to be skipping a stage—specializing in skill-intensive and large-scale industries and services.

Liberalization has allowed states to achieve their potential, instead of being held down by a centralized 'convoy' system that forced each state to move at a common but mediocre growth rate. We now show that the performance of the fastest moving states seems to be driven in part by the *specific* capabilities they acquired by adaptation to the policy environment during the era of controls. In part their performance may have resulted from *general* capabilities they may have acquired or that were latent during that period.

State Capabilities

In the conventional view of the Indian development process, there was a long and dark period—the period of controls and import substitution—followed by a burst of sunlight and reforms since 1991. The boom in the IT industry first awakened observers to the fact that the dark age was not all dark, that important capabilities such as skilled human capital were being built that yielded rewards with a lag, and that these capabilities were as important as the (largely external) opportunities that sparked the IT boom.

One form of capability is *specialized human or organizational capital*— trained personnel or incumbent firms in specific industries. This kind of capability could have been acquired by the states during the period of controls. For example, engineers who originally were employed by the state-owned Computer Maintenance Corporation or Electronic Corporation of India Ltd (ECIL) provided the backbone for many of the computer firms that started up in Bangalore. Similarly, many of the key players in the explosive growth of the financial sector in Mumbai were alumni of the State Bank of India. Bharat Heavy Electricals Limited (BHEL) was a substantial supplier of managerial talent for many private sector firms. Even the much-derided Indian Airlines supplied the private sector with highly qualified pilots.

Another form of capability is more *general human capital and entrepreneurial spirit*, or even an entrepreneurial environment. Some states may have trained substantial numbers of skilled personnel who could move into new sunrise industries, regardless of what their initial training was in. Alternatively, they may have had vibrant entrepreneurial communities that could take advantage of opportunities once the economy opened up. These capabilities may have been acquired during the period of controls or may have remained latent even as controls crushed initiative.

One proxy for both capabilities could be the extent to which states were diversified across manufacturing. Clearly, states that diversified the most

Diversification Index

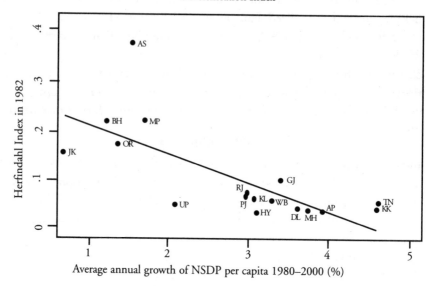

Average annual growth of NSDP per capita 1980–2000 (%)

Figure 2.11: Initial diversification and states' growth.

Source: Authors' calculations; EPW Research Foundation, Domestic Product of States of India: 1960–1 to 2000–1; 3-digit industry level data at the state level from Circon India Data Center. *Notes*: NSDP is net state domestic product. For each state, the Herfindahl Index measures the concentration of value added across 3-digit industries in 1982; the lower the index, the lower the concentration, or the higher the diversification. Codes same as Figure 2.7.

were more likely to have a presence in the industries that subsequently grew the most, and thus could have possessed the relevant specific human capital. Also, one could argue that those states with a vibrant entrepreneurial community should have diversified the most in response to the pre-1980 distortions (e.g., into areas that were not dominated by the public sector).

In Figure 2.11, we plot the Herfindahl coefficient of concentration within manufacturing in the different states in the early 1980s against the subsequent overall growth rates. The figure shows a very strong correlation between the initial level of diversification of manufacturing in a state and the state's subsequent economic performance.[22]

---

[22] This is consistent with the findings in Aghion et al. (2005) who show that states that were closest to the technological frontier were the ones that benefited most from the reforms of the early 1990s. It is also consistent with Rodrik and Subramanian (2005) who show that states with the greatest manufacturing capability pre-1980s were the ones that benefited most post-1980s.

Using state-level data for the period 1960–2000 compiled and recently released by the EPW Research Foundation, we put the correlation observed in Figure 2.11 on firmer ground. We create a panel data set with variables defined for four decades—1960s, 1970s, 1980s, and 1990s. We run standard growth regressions with a measure of each state's economic performance in each decade as the left-hand side variable. Since we are interested in the differential effect of manufacturing concentration across decades, we interact the explanatory variables with the appropriate decadal dummies. We include state fixed effects. In the first six columns of Table 2.7, the left hand side variable is measured over decades, while in the last six it is an average over

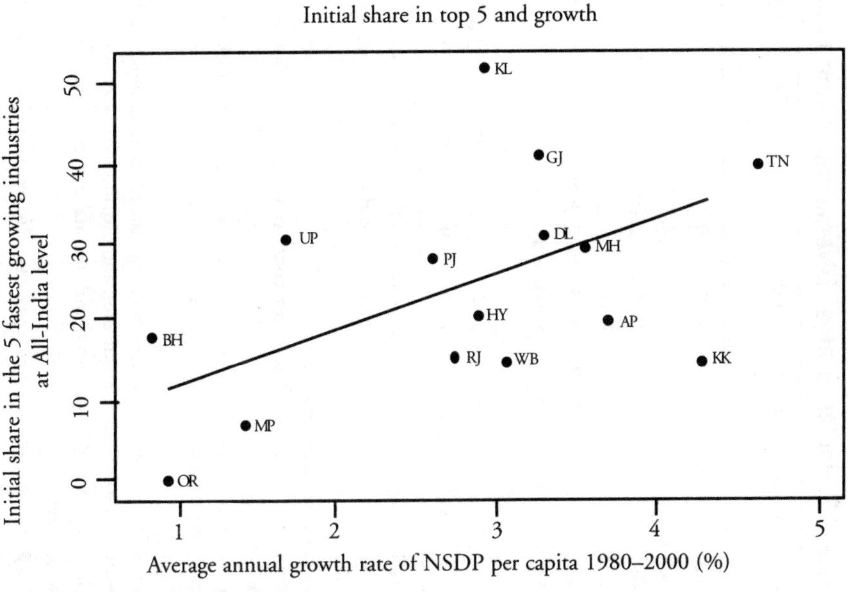

Initial share in top 5 and growth

Figure 2.12: Initial shares in manufacturing and states' growth

Source: Authors' calculations; EPW Research Foundation, Domestic Product of States of India: 1960–1 to 2000–1 and Annual Survey of Industries for 2-digit industry level.

Notes: NSDP is the net state domestic product. The vertical axis measures the share of the five fastest growing industries (in India) in total value added for the state in 1982. The five fastest growing industries are: Manufacture of textile products (26), Other Manufacturing Industries (including Manufacture of Scientific Equipment, Photographic/Cinematographic Equipment and Watches & Clocks) (38), Manufacture of Leather and Leather Products, Fur & Leather Substitutes (29), Manufacture of Basic Chemicals and Chemical Products (Except Products of Petroleum and Coal) (30), Manufacture of Rubber, Plastic, Petroleum and Coal Products; Processing of Nuclear Fuels (31). Codes same as Figure 2.7.

Table 2.7: Indian States: Diversification and Growth

	Ten-year state growth rates (1960–2000)						Twenty-year growth rates (1960–2000)					
	(1)	(2)	(3)	(4)	(5)	(6)	(7)	(8)	(9)	(10)	(11)	(12)
HI* dummy for 1970s	4.77*	5.31*	4.01	0.83	0.80	0.79						
	(2.57)	(2.77)	(2.56)	(2.98)	(2.39)	(2.20)						
HI* dummy for 1980s	–2.14	–2.17	–0.42	–4.59	–3.28	–2.49						
	(2.96)	(3.10)	(3.07)	(3.09)	(2.68)	(2.27)						
HI* dummy for 1990s	–8.73**	–8.26**	–7.3*	–16.29***	–14.65***	–11.29**						
	(3.44)	(3.69)	(4.10)	(5.63)	(5.04)	(4.76)						
HI* dummy for 1980–2000							–7.81***	–7.97**	–5.47*	–8.72**	–6.75***	–5.77**
							(2.41)	(2.65)	(2.57)	(3.48)	(2.55)	(2.38)
Observations	67	63	63	63	63	59	33	31	31	31	31	29

Notes: In columns 1–5, the dependent variable is average per capita state growth calculated over the four ten-year periods, 1960–70, 1970–80, 1980–90, 1990–2000. In columns 6–10, the average per capita state growth is calculated over the two twenty-year periods, 1960–80 and 1980–2000. All regressions include state and period effects.

The Herfindahl Index (HI) of value added is the measure of concentration.

Columns 2 and 8 include the Besley Burgess Index (2004). The index codes states as pro-worker, pro-employer or neutral based on state-level amendments to the Industrial Disputes Act of 1947.

Columns 3 and 9 include the Besley Burgess Index (2004), its interaction with the decadal dummies and twenty-year period dummies, respectively.

Columns 4 and 10 include the Besley Burgess Index (2004), its interaction with the decadal dummies, and twenty-year period dummies, respectively; and the log of initial per capita income.

Columns 5 and 11 include the Besley Burgess Index (2004), its interaction with the decadal dummies and twenty-year period dummies, respectively; log of initial per capita income and a measure of institutions (transmission and distribution losses) interacted with decadal dummies and twenty-year period dummies, respectively; and initial literacy (in 1980) interacted with decadal dummies and twenty-year period dummies, respectively. Robust standard errors are reported in parentheses.

***represents significance at 1 per cent, **represents significance at 5 per cent, *represents significance at 10 per cent twenty years. In all cases, we find that the initial level of concentration in manufacturing is strongly negatively correlated with subsequent economic performance especially in 1990 but not in 1980 or the decades prior to the onset of reforms. This suggests that the capabilities proxied for by diversification came into their own when the shackles on state growth were removed, but did not matter before.

Which capability mattered? Perhaps both kinds. In Figure 2.12, we plot the correlation between each state's 1980 share of the five manufacturing sectors that grew fastest during the period 1980–2000 against subsequent overall state GDP growth. The correlation is strongly positive, suggesting that initial manufacturing patterns, and specific human capital thus acquired, did matter for subsequent growth.

However, general human capital may also have mattered. Figure 2.13 suggests that initial diversification in manufacturing is also strongly

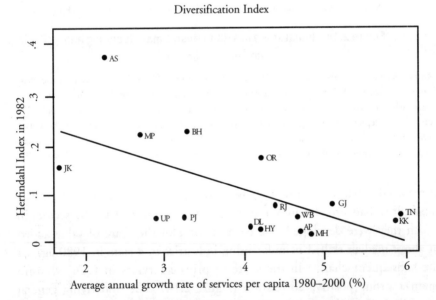

Figure 2.13: Initial diversification and services.

Sources: Authors' calculations; EPW Research Foundation CD-ROMs, Domestic Product of States of India: 1960–1 to 2000–1; 3-digit industry level data at the state level from Circon India Data Center.

Notes: For each state, the Herfindahl Index measures concentration of value added across 3-digit industries in 1982; the lower the index the lower the concentration, or the higher the diversification. Codes same as Figure 2.7.

Growth in private services per capita and initial share of skill-intensive manufacturing

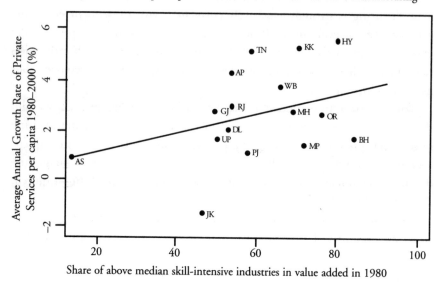

Figure 2.14: Initial share in skill-intensive manufacturing and
private services growth

Sources: Authors' calculations; EPW Research Foundation CD-ROMs, Domestic Product of States of India: 1960–1 to 2000-1 and Annual Survey of Industries for 2-digit industry level. *Notes*: Selected private sector services include business services, real estate, and retail trade. The vertical axis depicts the average annual growth of private services per capita over the period 1980-2000. On the horizontal axis is the share of the value added by the above median skill intensive industries in 1980 in each state at 2-digit industry level. Codes same as Figure 2.7.

correlated with subsequent growth in services, suggesting that the capabilities had broader uses and were not just confined to the sectors in which they were developed. Moreover, if we plot the share of value added in above-median skilled manufacturing industries in a state in 1980 against the subsequent change in the share of private services in GDP, we find again a strong positive correlation (Figure 2.14). The underlying general capabilities—such as the presence of skilled labour—that fed skilled manufacturing prior to the reforms were also available to feed the skill-reliant private services when they took off post-reforms.

Finally, there is evidence of a dynamic entrepreneurial process at work in the fast-moving states. We determine the correlations, state by state, of the value added in each industry in 1982 with the value added in 1997. If fast-

Correlation between share of value added in 1982 and 1997

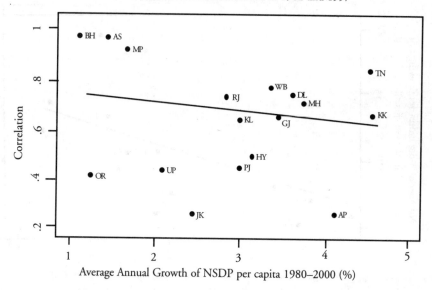

Figure 2.15: Persistence in industry share and states' growth.

Sources: Authors' calculations; EPW Research Foundation , Domestic Product of States of India: 1960–1 to 2000–1; 3-digit industry level data (NIC-1987) at the state level from Circon India Data Center.

Notes: NSDP is the net state domestic product. The vertical axis depicts the correlation between the share of value added in 1982 and 1997 at the 3-digit industry level data (NIC-1987). Codes same as Figure 2.7

moving states were simply doing what they did before, the correlation should be strongest for those states. In fact, as Figure 2.15 suggests, the faster growing states show lower correlation, or greater dynamism, across time.

Data on number of establishments in each industry provide additional evidence of dynamism. We rank manufacturing industries by their value-added growth rates over the period 1980–2000 and determine industries that fall in the fastest and slowest growing quartiles. For each state, we determine the number of industries in the fastest growing quartile in which there was a net addition of establishments as well the number of industries in the slowest growing quartile in which there was a net reduction in establishments. (Figure 2.16). We find that the fastest growing states did have larger numbers of high growth manufacturing industries with net growth in number of firms as well as larger numbers of slow growth manufacturing

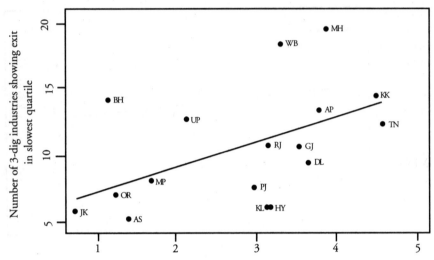

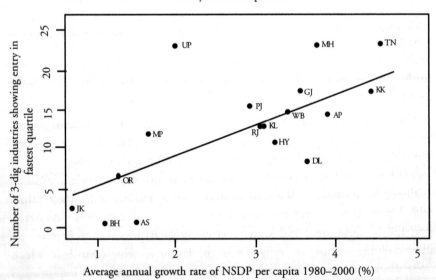

Figure 2.16: Manufacturing sector growth and entry and exit

Sources: Authors' calculations; EPW Research Foundation , Domestic Product of States of India: 1960–1 to 2000–1; 3-digit industry level data at the state level from Circon India Data Center.

Notes: NSDP is the net state domestic product. In the top panel, the vertical axis depicts, for each state, the number of industries at the 3-digit level, with an average value added growth between 1980-2000 in the slowest quartile, that record a net reduction in the number of establishments. In the bottom panel, the vertical axis depicts, for each state, the number of industries at the 3-digit level, with an average value added growth in the fastest quartile, that record a net addition in the number of establishments. Codes same as Figure 2.7.

sectors with net reduction in number of firms, suggesting that the process was not just passive growth by incumbents and purely history dependent.[23]

Decentralization, Infrastructure, and Institutions

While the formal reforms at the centre received tremendous publicity, perhaps less noticed was the growing decentralization of policy. The Congress Party had held power without a break at the centre since independence, but the aura of invincibility surrounding it started waning soon after Indira Gandhi lost the post-Emergency election in 1977. Also, even though the Congress Party was returned to power at the center through much of the 1980s, a number of states were captured by the opposition, often by regional or even single-state parties.

No longer could a regional leader be confident that the centre—especially if the party in power was different from that running the state—would dole out its bounty fairly across states, and over time. Also, the parties in power could change, so that implicit agreements reached by prior governments might not be honoured by subsequent governments. Simply put, the centrifugal forces created by the dispersion of political power in India did not sit well with the enormous centralization of economic power, and the inter-state cross-subsidies the centre effected through its investment strategy. Something had to give, and it was the centralization of economic power.

Greater economic decentralization meant states could differentiate themselves, not least in their ability to attract private sector investment. This was, of course, facilitated by the gradual dismantling of the industrial licensing system that used regional equity as one of the primary criterion guiding industrial investments. Further contributing to differentiation over this period was the rising trend in private investment, as well as the falling trend in public investment, with private investment likely to be more sensitive to differences in policies across states.

[23] By contrast, Topalova (2004) suggests that Indian manufacturing has witnessed little exit, although there have been improvements in the more recent past.

Table 2.8: Indian States: Convergence and Divergence, 1960–2000

	Unconditional		Conditional	
	1960–2000	*1960–2000*	*1960–2000*	*1960–2000*
	(1)	(2)	(3)	(4)
			System	*Difference*
	OLS	*OLS*	*GMM*	*GMM*
Log Initial NSDP per capita	0.94**	−6.99***	0.51	−8.37
	(0.37)	(2.22)	(0.76)	(6.42)
Log Initial NSDP per capita* 1970s dummy	−0.03	−0.16	−0.03	0.11
	(0.04)	(0.71)	(0.04)	(0.09)
Log Initial NSDP per capita* 1980s dummy	0.16***	0.43	0.17***	0.4**
	(0.04)	(0.78)	(0.04)	(0.17)
Log Initial NSDP per capita* 1990s dummy	0.17***	2.3**	0.19***	0.69**
	(0.06)	(1.05)	(0.07)	(0.34)
Observations	79	79	79	58

Notes: The dependent variable in all regressions is the annual average decadal rate of growth in per capita state domestic product.

The regressions for conditional convergence in columns 2–4 include state and time-fixed effects. The system GMM estimator is based on Blundell and Bond (1998) and the difference estimator is based on Arellano and Bond (1991).

The Hansen test of overidentification and the test of no second order autocorrelation are satisfied for the system and difference GMM estimations.

Robust standard errors are reported in parentheses.

***represents significance at 1 per cent, **represents significance at 5 per cent, *represents significance at 10 per cent

To see the decentralization dynamic at work, let us examine the comparative growth performance across states. In Table 2.8, column 1, we regress state growth against beginning-of-period per capita gross domestic product (GDP) interacted with decadal dummies. Since there are no other covariates, this specification addresses the question of unconditional convergence. In columns 2–4, we add time-and-state fixed effects to answer the question of whether there is conditional convergence. In columns 1 and 2, the ordinary least squares estimator is used, while the estimations in columns 3 and 4 are based on the Generalized Method of Moments (GMM) procedure.[24] For our purposes, the important point is not whether there is convergence or divergence on average (which seems to depend on the procedure used) but that regardless of estimation procedure, divergences accelerated in the 1990s (also see Aiyar, 2001). The coefficient on the beginning-of-period state income term interacted with an indicator for the 1990s is positive and significant, suggesting richer states grew faster in the 1990s (and the coefficient of the interaction term is greater in magnitude than in previous decades).

We can see the decentralization dynamic in yet another way: if decentralization was indeed important then states' economic performance should be more closely tied to state-level policies and institutions in the post-1980s period than before. After all, if the pre-1980s era was about the centre deciding, for example, where and how much electricity capacity to install, there is little that the states could have done to affect economic performance within their borders.

In terms of analysis, this suggests that state-level explanatory variables should be more meaningful in state-level growth regressions for the post-1980s period than before. The explanatory variables we focus on are measures of state-level infrastructure and institutions. We could hope to pick up their effects in two kinds of regressions. In the first, we use the Rajan–Zingales (1998) methodology to ascertain the specific impact of infrastructure development: if the quality of infrastructure were a constraint, in states that have better infrastructure, industries that are more infrastructure-intensive should grow faster. Moreover, to the extent that state policies began to matter with some lag, after initial reforms in the 1980s and accelerating decentralization in the coalition governments of the 1990s, we should see the effects most pronounced in the later decade.

For the 1980s and 1990s, we have two–digit industry growth data. Next, we need a measure of state-level infrastructure development. Such measures of infrastructure development could include electricity generation capacity per capita or the extent of road and rail networks. There are three problems with these measures. First, they were largely central government

---

[24] The ordinary least squares estimation is inconsistent in the presence of a lagged dependent variable and fixed effects, but the GMM procedures do not suffer from this shortcoming.

determined, often a legacy of the pre-reform era. Second, capacity creation could have been related to prospects of growth. Third, infrastructure capacity could be quite different from infrastructure quality.

Instead, as a joint measure of infrastructure capability as well as state policies affecting the quality of infrastructure and the business environment, we use the transmission and distribution losses (T&D losses) of state-level electricity boards (as a fraction of generating capacity). T&D losses refer to power that is generated but not paid for—in part because some of it is lost naturally along power lines in the process of transmission and distribution, but also in part because it is stolen. In areas where T&D losses are high, the quality of power, as reflected in the voltage as well as reliability, is low. Thus T&D losses are not directly related to capacity, but are determined by state-level political decisions. They broadly reflect the quality of both infrastructure and institutions (politicians turning a blind eye to power theft by their constituencies, or politicians' unwillingness to enforce laws, as well as viability and level of corruption in state electricity boards).

As a measure of infrastructure intensity of an industry, we use the amount of electricity consumed per unit of value added in that industry, obtained from Indian input–output tables

In Panel A of Table 2.9, we report regressions in which the growth rate of industry i in state s is regressed on industry and state fixed effects and interactions between our infrastructure development and infrastructure intensity measures. In column 1 we present the results for the 1980s and in column 2 for 1990s.[25] We find that the coefficient on the interaction is negative and significant for the 1990s but not for the 1980s. That is, for the 1990s, we find that in states that have more T&D losses (worse infrastructure and institutions), industries that are intensive in the use of electricity grow slower. These results suggest that decentralization is affecting the growth dynamic because a state-level policy variable has started influencing a state-level outcome.

More generally, state-level institutions do appear to have had a greater impact on state growth, not just on infrastructure intensive industries. As Figure 2.17 shows, there is a negative correlation between the average T&D losses in 1980–2000 in a state and its growth during that period.

[25] We cannot run these regressions for the 1970s because we do not have state- and sector-level manufacturing data.

Table 2.9: Decentralization: State Characteristics and Growth

Panel A: Sectoral growth rates

| | Electricity Intensity | |
| | (1) | (2) |
	1982–90	1990–7
TD* Intensity	0.06	−0.19**
	(0.13)	(0.09)
Initial share of sector i in state s	−0.9	−1.23
	(0.59)	(0.84)
Observations	269	266

Panel B: 10 year state growth rates (1960–2000)

	(1)	(2)	(3)	(4)	(5)	(6)	(7)	(8)
	Transmission and distribution losses			Investment climate	Infrastructure penetration	Financial sector strength	Mass media penetration	Primary schooling in English
I* dummy for 1970s	−0.01	0.0002	0.01	−0.11	0.43	0.41	−0.1	0.05
	(0.03)	(0.03)	(0.01)	(0.69)	(0.77)	(0.6)	(0.69)	(0.04)
I* dummy for 1980s	−0.05*	−0.06*	−0.06**	−0.1	1.08	0.87	0.52	0.04
	(0.03)	(0.03)	(0.03)	(0.57)	(0.68)	(0.65)	(0.64)	(0.05)

	(1)	(2)	(3)	(4)	(5)	(6)	(7)	(8)
	Transmission and distribution losses			Investment climate	Infrastructure penetration	Financial sector strength	Mass media penetration	Primary schooling in English
I* dummy for 1990s	−0.08***	−0.11***	−0.11***	3.52***	3.85***	2.63***	2.75***	0.21***
	(0.03)	(0.02)	(0.02)	(0.83)	(0.69)	(0.93)	(0.76)	(0.06)
Observations	67	63	63	59	63	63	63	55

Notes: Panel A: The dependent variable is the annual average rate of growth of industry (i) in state (s). All regressions include state and industry effects. Transmission and distribution losses (TD) is the fraction of electrical power generated but not paid for, measured as a percent of availability in 1980. Electricity intensity is the share of electricity input in the value added of the sector. Overall infrastructure intensity is the share of the sum of electricity, transportations and communications inputs in the value added of the sector. Both these indices are measured in percent.

Panel B: The dependent variable is the decadal average of annual state growth rates. All regressions include state and period fixed effects, initial income in teracted with tim e effects (not reported), and a measure of state-level institution (I) interacted with time effects as follows: (I) as defined at the top of each column, is transmission and distribution losses in columns (1) to (3); investment climate, reflecting the overall investment attractive of the state, in column (4); a measure of the spread of infrastructure throughout the state in column (5); a measure of the strength of the financial sector in column (6); a measure of the outreach of mass media within each state in column (7); and the enrolment in classes instructed in English as a percent of total enrollment at the primary and upper primary level in column (8).

Column (2) includes the Besley Burgess Index (2004). Columns(3) to (8) include the Besley Burgess Index (2004), and its interaction with the decadal dummies. Robust standard errors are reported in parentheses.

***represents significance at 1%, **represents significance at 5%, *represents significance at 10%

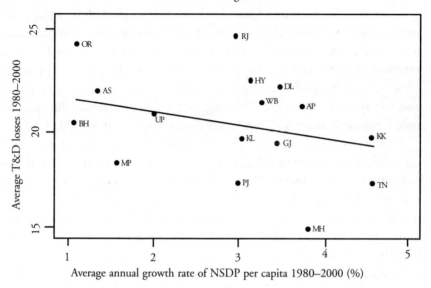

Figure 2.17: Transmission and distribution losses and states' growth

Sources: Authors' calculations; EPW Research Foundation, Domestic Product of States of India: 1960–1 to 2000–1.

Notes: NSDP is the net state domestic product. Transmission and distribution losses (T&D) is the fraction of electrical power generated but not paid for, measured as a per cent of availability. Codes same as Figure 2.7.

In Table 2.9, Panel B, we explore this further. We estimate regressions where the dependent variable is the decadal average of annual state growth rates. All regressions include state and period fixed effects, initial income interacted with time effects (not reported), and a measure of state-level institution (I) interacted with time effects as explanatory variables. Institutions should not yield significant coefficients for the pre-1990s period if decentralization really took hold in the latter period of reforms.[26] In columns 1–3 we report the coefficient estimates for different combinations

[26] In these regressions, the measure of institutions is time-invariant, measured either as the average for the 1980–2000 period or for 2000. This raises concerns about endogeneity. Our assumption, however, is that institutional quality is fairly persistent. This is consistent with the high correlation between the historically determined Banerjee and Iyer (2005) measure of the non-landlord holdings in colonial India, which could be interpreted as a measure of the historical determinants of current institutions, and contemporary institutions. For example, the correlation between the Banerjee–Iyer measure and the measure of current investment climate is 0.77.

of the controls when the measure of institutions is T&D losses. In columns 4–8, we vary the measure of state-level institutions (including, successively, measures of investment climate, infrastructure penetration, financial sector, mass media, and primary school education). In all cases, we find that the interaction coefficient for the 1970s and for the 1980s (in seven out of eight cases) is insignificant while the coefficient for the 1990s is significant and has the expected sign. This suggests a tighter relationship between state-level institutions and state-level performance in the 1990s.[27]

Finally, we check whether diversification (our measure of state-level capabilities) and institutional quality proxy for the same thing. In columns 5–6 and 11–12 of Table 2.7, the coefficient on diversification interacted with the 1990s dummy is significant even after controlling for the quality of the institutions in the states (columns 5 and 11) and for literacy levels (columns 6 and 12). Thus, the diversification measure is picking up something beyond the institutional quality in these states.

In sum, both state-level capabilities and state-level policies and institutions seem to start mattering in the 1990s. With the centre no longer enforcing inter-state equity, divergences in growth rates between states increased. These divergences raise a number of questions that we now turn to.

LOOKING AHEAD

Where is India headed? Comparing the level of income at which the average country in the cross-section exhibits a declining share of manufacturing and increasing diversification with that at which the fast-growing states exhibit the same characteristic or 'pathology' shows that the Indian states have started behaving like industrial countries at nearly a quarter or one-fifth of their income levels. For example, manufacturing should normally start declining at about US$14,700 per capita: yet, Karnataka and Maharashtra have seen a decline in the share of manufacturing at an income per capita of about US$2,700 and US$3,400, respectively. A similar pattern is evident with respect to diversification.

With the caveat that Indian states are vast entities, internally very diverse, it would appear that the fast-growing peninsular states are starting to

---

[27] These results on the impact of institutions (in Table 2.9) broadly hold even after controlling for the initial level of capability, for which we use the initial value of the Herfindahl index as a proxy.

resemble more developed countries in their specialization, while the slow-growing hinterland states, with their still rapidly growing, less well-educated populations are falling behind.

Indeed, there are additional reasons for concern. Visaria and Visaria (2003), projecting on current fertility rates in different states, suggest that 60 per cent of the expected 620 million addition to the Indian population between now and 2051 will be in Bihar, Madhya Pradesh, Rajasthan, and Uttar Pradesh; only 22 per cent will be in the fast-growing states of Kerala, Tamil Nadu, Andhra Pradesh, Karnataka, and Maharashtra. With populous laggard states like Uttar Pradesh and Bihar having substantial political power because of their numbers, the demands for redistribution will increase, as will migration. Such trends will create immense political strains between Indian states and the potential for serious differences.

It may well be that these hinterland states (as well as backward areas in the fast-growing states) will have to follow a more traditional path of growth, focusing on labour-intensive manufacturing. But they have not thus far.[28] That they have not may be because further reform is needed—in particular, more flexible labour laws and an improvement of infrastructure, especially vis-à-vis the states in the hinterland so that these industries can be internationally cost-competitive—to revitalize labour-intensive manufacturing.

Here again the weight of history may be telling. The archaic labour laws have strong organized constituencies, in particular, labour unions tied to political parties, backing them. Given the way Indian industry has specialized, the costs of these laws are not experienced by incumbents, and the political leadership, or will, to amend them has not emerged.[29] Furthermore, given that poor governance, which tends to be persistent (see footnote 28), in part, explains the slow growth of the hinterland states, the needed changes will be more difficult there.

Even if serious reforms were undertaken in the laggard states, competition from the more advanced states will not make it easy for them to grow. First,

[28] For example, Figure 2.9 illustrates that, between 1980 and 2000, the share of labour-intensive industries in total value added declined in Uttar Pradesh and Madhya Pradesh, and remained unchanged in Orissa and Bihar.

[29] In other words, most commentators look to existing firms to see if labour laws are a problem. But existing firms have adapted to these laws, as suggested both by their pattern of specialization and their scale. The more pertinent question is whether new firms are kept from entering because of the laws. The pattern of specialization in India suggest they are.

consider the output side. The laggard states are typically distant from ports and airports. Transportation costs will come down as infrastructure is built up, but it is unclear whether the improvements will help them out-compete the fast-growing peninsular states where many of the initial large-scale infrastructure projects are being undertaken, and where ancillary infrastructure exists. Even if India moves to using its unskilled labour, one might expect the effects to be seen first in the fast-growing states (which have their own share of surplus labour in agriculture) before trickling down to the laggard states.

On the input side, even labour-intensive unskilled manufacturing requires a skilled supervisory and managerial force. Despite the large numbers of graduates emerging from universities in India, the number of graduates with the skills to work in industry or the service sector is relatively limited. With the immense demand for skilled workers in the export-oriented services industry, wages of skilled workers have been going up very fast.[30] Given the extremely competitive situation in (typically tradable) labour-intensive industries, highly paid supervisory skilled workers are affordable only if they are used very economically relative to the use of unskilled labour—if, for example, firms have scale.[31] Here again, the fast-moving states where the business and political climate is more conducive to scale have an advantage. In sum, the fast-growing states could absorb the more mobile skilled labour from the slow-moving states leading to a further hollowing out of prospects there.

The obvious solution is not to impede the growth of the fast-movers but to enhance the availability of the resource in scarce supply. While the earlier emphasis on funding tertiary education at the expense of primary education may well have been an aberration, India may now have too little tertiary

[30] A recent issue of *Business Week* notes that: 'As India's domestic economy expands, the shortfalls are spreading beyond tech. Wages for semi-skilled workers in the textile factories of Coimbatore, for example, are up 10 per cent this year, while supervisors' salaries have risen by 20 per cent. Pay in the banking industry is up 25 per cent in the past year and has more than doubled in hot areas such as private equity. Airline pilots have seen wages rise 25 per cent. Overall, Indian salaries will rise by 12.8 per cent, compared with inflation of 5.5 per cent, according to human resources consultancy Mercer, which warns that continued increases could hurt India's economic revival.'

[31] Alternatively, the wages on unskilled labour may fall, but wages in agriculture may place a floor here.

education of the right kind at this juncture. India does produce an immense number of degree holders, but there are serious doubts about the quality of education many of them receive. The number of high-quality institutions is still very small, witness the extraordinary competition to get into them. In the same way as industry was delicensed, India needs to 'delicense' higher education, remove the barriers to starting new institutions, as well as encourage foreign direct investment here.[32] In short, from a policy perspective, the irony is that in order to promote unskilled labour-intensive activities in the future, a great deal of attention may need to be paid in fostering the supply of skilled labour. [33]

It may well be that new institutions of higher education are easier to start in the fast-growing states. If so, limits on access to out-of-state students (or a refusal to recognize results from other state examinations) need to be reduced, and educational standards harmonized across states, so that a truly all-India market for higher education can be created. This will then create a pool of skilled workers who will be essential to enhance the growth of the now-laggard states.

In summary, then, changes since the early 1980s—the move toward pro-business and pro-market economic policies and economic and political decentralization—have unleashed tremendous economic opportunities; at the same time, thanks to pre-existing patterns of specialization in favour of skill-based production, they have also unleashed the gale winds of divergence, big time. A unitary India, centralized politically and uniformly mediocre in economic performance, has given way to multiple Indias with performance more related to the capabilities of individual states and the opportunities they create.

Ideally, of course, the laggard states would reform on their own—push for scrapping archaic labour laws, improve infrastructure and the business climate —and utilize their vast pools of underemployed low-cost labour to

---

[32] Here the government has an obvious role in setting standards and assessing quality, but there is also the danger that the public sector education constituency will turn this function into barriers to entry.

[33] To some extent, there has been an encouraging endogenous response in terms of the increased demand for education throughout India triggered by the prospect of better income opportunities (see Rodrik and Subramanian, 2004). In fact, using Mincerian wage regressions, Desai et al. (2005) show that the returns to education have increased substantially for the two highest levels of educational attainment between 1994 and 1999.

attract investment in labour-intensive manufacturing and agri-business. They would thereby catch up with the leading states in India.[34]

In this scenario, the pattern of convergence that we observed in the post-war period between industrial countries and the East Asian economies would play itself out within India in the future. The recent revival of manufacturing growth (we do not have complete data on the most recent years, hence this revival is not captured by our study), albeit seemingly heavily concentrated in skill-intensive and capital-intensive industries, offers some hope for this scenario.

However, even if the needed reforms were to occur, there is a possibility that powerful forces emanating from the common market for resources could slow convergence. If they were to do so, India will have to brace itself for a lot of social churning as people move not just in search of jobs but also in search of acquiring the human capital to become employable. How India reacts to, and shapes, these forces may well be the biggest economic question India faces over the next few decade.

REFERENCES

Acharya, S. (2002), Macroeconomic management in the 1990s', *Economic and Political Weekly*, 37(16) 20 April, pp. 1515–38

———— (2006), *Essays on Macroeconomic Policies and Growth in India*, Oxford University Press, New Delhi.

Aghion, P., R. Burgess, S. Redding, and F. Zilibotti (2005), Entry liberalization and inequality in industrial performance, *Journal of the European Economic Association*, 3(2–3), pp. 291–302, April–May.

Ahluwalia, M. (2000), Economic performance of states in the post reforms period, *Economic and Political Weekly*,6 May, pp. 1637–48.

Aiyar, S. (2001), 'Growth theory and convergence across Indian states: A panel study', in T. Callen, P. Reynolds, and C. Towe (eds), *India at the Crossroads*, International Monetary Fund, Washington.

Alleyne, T., and A. Subramanian (2001), 'What does South Africa's pattern of trade say about its labour markets?' *IMF Working Paper 01/148*, International Monetary Fund, Washington.

---

[34] Convergence could also come about if labour moves across states but labour mobility, especially for the low-skilled, seems limited in India; low mobility stems from the lack of a portable safety net as well as antiquated land laws that reduce the availability of low-cost housing for migrants.

Arellano, M., and S. Bond (1991), 'Some tests of specification for panel data: Monte Carlo evidence and an application to employment equations', *Review of Economic Studies* 58(2), pp. 277–97.

Besley, T. and R. Burgess (2004),' Can labor regulation hinder economic performance? evidence from India?', *The Quarterly Journal of Economics*, 119(1), pp. 91–134.

Bhagwati, J., and P. Desai (1970), *Planning for Industrialization*, Oxford University Press, London.

Bhagwati, J., and T. N. Srinivasan (1993), *India's Economic Reforms*, paper prepared for the Ministry of Finance, Government of India.

Banerjee, A., and L. Iyer (2005), 'History, institutions and economic performance: the legacy of colonial land tenure systems in India,' *American Economic Review*, 95(4), pp. 1190–213.

Blundell, R., and S. Bond (1998), Initial conditions and moment restrictions in dynamic panel data models, *Journal of Econometrics*, 87, pp. 115–43.

Chenery, H. B. (1960), Patterns of industrial growth, *American Economic Review*, 57, pp. 415–26.

———, and L. J. Taylor (1968), Development patterns: among countries and over time, *Review of Economics and Statistics*, 50, pp. 391–416.

Desai, M., D. Kapur, and J. Mchale (2005), *The Fiscal Impact of High-skilled Emigration: Flows of Indians to the US*, mimeo, Harvard University.

Gordon, J., and P. Gupta (2004), Understanding India's services revolution, *IMF Working Paper No. 171*, International Monetary Fund, Washington.

Imbs, J., and R. Wacziarg (2003), 'Stages of development', *The American Economic Review*, 93(1), pp. 63–86.

Joshi, V., and I. M. D. Little (1994), *India: Macroeconomics and Political Economy 1964–1991*, The World Bank, Washington.

——— (1996), *India's Economic Reforms, 1991–2001*, Clarendon Press, Oxford.

Kelkar, V. (2004), 'India: on the growth turnpike', *K.R. Narayanan Memorial Lecture*, Australian National University, http://ecocomm.anu.edu.au/nieb/KRNarayanan Oration2004.htm

Krueger, A. O. (1975), *The Benefits and Costs of Import Substitution in India: A Microeconomic Study*, University of Minnesota Press, Minneapolis.

Kohli, A. (2005), *Politics of Economic Growth in India, 1980–2005, Economic and Political Weekly*, 1 April 2006.

Kongsamut, P., S. Rebelo, and D. Xie (2001), Beyond balanced growth', *IMF Working Paper 01/85*, International Monetary Fund, Washington.

Kumar, K., R. Rajan, and L. Zingales (1999), 'What determines firm size?' *NBER Working Paper 7208*, National Bureau of Economic Research, Cambridge, Massachusetts.

Mehta, B. P. (2005), 'How India lost the will to reform', *Financial Times*, 1 November.

Mohan, R. (2002), 'Small scale industry policy in India: A critical evaluation', in A.O. Krueger (ed.), *Economic Policy Reforms and the Indian Economy*, University of Chicago Press, Chicago.

Rajan, R., and A. Subramanian (2005), 'What undermines aid's impact on growth?' *IMF Working Paper 05/126*, International Monetary Fund, Washington.

Rajan, R., and J. Wulf (2004), 'Are perks purely managerial excess?' *NBER Working Paper No. 10494* National Bureau of Economic Research, Cambridge, Massachusetts.

Rajan, R., and L. Zingales (1998), 'Financial dependence and growth', *American Economic Review*, 88(3), pp. 559–86.

Rodrik, D., and A. Subramanian (2004), 'Why India can grow at seven per cent a year or more? Projections and reflections', *Economic and Political Weekly*, 39(16), 17 April, pp. 1591–6.

——— (2005), 'From "Hindu growth" to productivity surge: The mystery of the Indian growth transition', *IMF Staff Papers*, 52(2), pp. 193–228.

Srinivasan, T.N. (2003), 'India's statistical system: critiquing the report of the National Statistical Commission', *Economic and Political Weekly*, 38(4), 25 January, pp. 303–6.

Topalova, P. (2004), *Factor Immobility and Regional Impacts of Trade Liberalization: Evidence on Poverty and Inequality from India*, unpublished manuscript, Department of Economics, Massachusetts Institute of Technology, Massachusetts.

Virmani, A. (2005), 'Policy regimes, growth and poverty in India: lessons of government failure and entrepreneurial success', *ICRIER Working Paper No. 170*, Indian Council for Research on International Economic Relations, New Delhi.

Visaria, L., and P. Visaria (2003), 'Long term population projections for major states, 1991–2101', *Economic and Political Weekly*, 38(45), 8 November, pp. 4763–75.

Wiener, M. (1991), *The Child and the State in India*, Princeton University Press, Princeton.

SUMMARIES

India Needs Skill to Solve the 'Bangalore Bug'

The market for skilled labour is scorching hot in India. A McKinsey report indicates that wages for project managers have risen by a compound annual growth rate of 23 per cent since 2000 (albeit from a low level). These are indeed the wages of success. But should India worry?

Rising wages reflect, in no small measure, productivity increases as Indian manufacturing and services become globally competitive. Short-term concerns about inflation are thus mitigated. But the wage increases also reflect India's unique pattern of development, which has created a relative scarcity of skilled labour. This prompts concerns about the medium term: the rising fortunes of the skilled sector may limit the vitality of industries that employ the unskilled and uneducated. It is a conundrum that one might term the 'Bangalore bug', after the country's high-technology centre.

Since the 1980s, a unitary India—centralized politically and uniformly mediocre in economic performance—has given way to multiple Indias with performance more related to the capabilities of individual states. Peninsular India, including states such as Karnataka, Maharashtra, Gujarat, and Tamil Nadu, has grown rapidly. The hinterland, with states such as Uttar Pradesh, Bihar, Madhya Pradesh, and Rajasthan, has lagged behind.

The divergence relates not just to growth but to patterns of specialization. Policy choices emphasizing university education over basic education and capital-intensive manufacturing over labour-intensive manufacturing have bequeathed a strange legacy. The fast-growing states are increasingly specializing in skill-based services (information technology, finance and telecommunications) and skill-based manufacturing (petrochemicals and pharmaceuticals).

A big question is how the lagging states, with their large populations and attendant political power, can catch up. India's primary and secondary education system, as well as its labour laws, needs serious attention if the benefits of the recent dynamism are to be widely shared. Reforms in these areas, along with improvements in governance and infrastructure, are necessary to attract investment and create jobs.

However, even if all these reforms—on the need for which there is consensus among Indian policy economists, although not politicians—are implemented, there is another concern. Recall Dutch disease, which is about the competitive squeeze exerted on one tradable sector (manufacturing) as a result of wage increases stemming from the rising fortunes of another (typically oil). The Bangalore bug is the contemporary Indian variant, with skill-based services substituting for oil.

Textile plants need supervisors. Bicycle factories need designers. They both require managers. Yet these are the very people whose wages are being bid up sharply, squeezing the profitability of labour-intensive and tradable manufacturing, with its wafer-thin profit margins in an era of global competition. Thus, highly productive skill-based development in the fast-growing states, while beneficial for the nation, may indirectly undermine the profitability and growth of labour-intensive manufacturing in the others. Moreover, the rise in skilled wages also leads to an exodus of scarce skilled labour from the states lagging behind to the fast-growing ones.

What is the remedy? The obvious solution is not to impede the growth of the fast movers but to enhance the availability of the resource in scarce supply. The strong growth in particular sectors requires India to continue to foster the supply of skilled labour, even while redressing the past neglect of primary and secondary education.

Fortunately, tertiary education does not require more government resources. Instead, the government needs to remove the barriers that prevent foreigners and locals from starting new institutions, while improving accreditation procedures and disclosure standards. It should not encumber private institutions with onerous conditions and it should allow government-aided institutions to raise resources by charging students a reasonable fee. This means overcoming a number of vested interests.

The irony of the Bangalore bug is that to create opportunities to benefit the poor and the unskilled, India may in fact have to produce more skilled workers.

From Bharat to India

Thirty years ago, when India Today was launched, it was a miracle if one was allotted a phone, and after that it took a further act of God and the benevolence of the P&T worker for the phone to work. Thirty years ago, we had black-and-white TVs and that too only in a few cities. Urban schoolboys like us had to watch Krishi Darshan for entertainment on Doordarshan, where farmer's responded to penetrating questions like, 'Kya aap khet ko pani dete hain (Do you water your fields)?' Of course, most of the intended audience, villagers, did not have access to TV or the electricity to power it with.

Within a few years of India Today's launch, the Indian economy became a veritable dynamo (we are not suggesting cause and effect here), posting an average growth of nearly 6 per cent per year over the past twenty-five years. Despite the inevitable, unfavourable comparisons with China, very few countries have grown so fast over such a prolonged period of time or reduced poverty so sharply. We should indeed be proud of what India has achieved, and clearly, many Indians are. There is a buzz today in India, a sense of limitless optimism. But is it justified?

To answer this question, let us start by asking how we got here. The economic policies that our founding fathers conceived defy easy characterization. They were an exasperating combination of simultaneously supporting and stifling private entrepreneurship. The barriers erected against foreign competition served to coddle domestic enterprise. But the private sector was kept out of large areas of economic activity. The overarching principle was to prevent wealth concentration in a few hands. So, licensing regulated the scale of operations of every firm; reservations and other carrots favoured small-scale industries; strict labour laws penalized large enterprises; and the MRTP Act was the final bulwark against expansion. In short, private initiative and growth, except for a favoured few, were stymied.

So what were the consequences of this jumble of policies for India's pattern of development, circa 1980? First and foremost, these policies held India's growth to a low, but not disastrous, level, famously dubbed the Hindu rate of growth. Surprisingly, these policies did not mean that India produced less manufacturing goods as a whole. It did mean, however, that the composition of its manufacturing activity was unusual: India produced more than its share of capital- and skill-intensive goods (think public-sector petrochemical plant), while underutilizing what it had in plentiful supply—its abundant labour. Constrained by regulations and protected from external competition, Indian industry was inefficient and exported very little. There was a silver lining though. India was highly diversified in its manufacturing even in 1980. And a portion of its labour force was highly skilled, a clear legacy of Jawaharlal Nehru's emphasis on science, higher education, and leading-edge technologies for the public sector. How many nations, at India's stage of development at the time, could boast of a space programme?

Around 1980, two major changes began to transform the Indian economic landscape. First, attitudes towards the economy, and the private sector in particular, started to change. Under Indira Gandhi and then Rajiv Gandhi, pro-business reforms were set in motion, with liberalized access for domestic firms to capital imports, technology, and foreign exchange, and the gradual relaxation of industrial licensing. Later, in the aftermath of the forex crisis in 1990, broader reforms that were more pro-competition were introduced. Second, India started becoming more decentralized politically. The decline of the Congress' power and the rise of regional parties conferred greater political autonomy on the states, translating into autonomy even in the economic sphere. States increasingly prospered, or not, based on what they did, rather than because of the actions at the centre.

What did these changes accomplish? Many things. Above all, the economy responded with the vigour of an uncaged tiger as per capita growth surged from less than 1 per cent a year to over 3.5 per cent, not so much by employing more workers and capital but by using them more efficiently. Surprisingly, neither the reforms nor the pick-up in growth has altered India's specialization in capital- and skill-intensive industries. In fact, the fastest growing services—finance, telecommunications, and business services—are also skill-intensive. In many ways, India is building on the capabilities created before the 1980s, with veterans from the state-owned CMC or ECIL seeding the firms that were in the vanguard of the software boom, and the State Bank of India alumni permeating the financial sector to launch the boom in finance.

These developments are mirrored at the state level. With greater decentralization, better run states such as Delhi, Gujarat, and Tamil Nadu have improved the quality of infrastructure and business climate, attracted more investment, and surged ahead. The pattern of development in these states has been unusual. They seem to have skipped a phase that most high-growth countries in East Asia went through-of specializing in labour-intensive activities. Instead, these states are behaving more like the United States and Europe, exploiting their diversified skills, emphasizing on skill-based manufacturing (pharmaceuticals, petrochemicals, and auto parts) and services.

So what does this mean for the future? Fast-growing states will need more capital, skilled workers, and necessary infrastructure, on which there is a consensus in the country. India has a vibrant financial sector and it should have no problem raising and allocating capital, but for one impediment. The government appropriates significant amounts of savings to finance its deficit. Not only does this leave less to allocate to private investment or infrastructure, it is also a source of vulnerability if the country were to rely more on foreign capital. The need to force-feed the fiscal deficit to domestic banks also makes it hard for the country to open the capital account or to privatize banks, a must if India is to achieve its legitimate aspirations of becoming a world-class financial centre.

The greater bottleneck is likely to be skilled workers. India's universities have not expanded in a way that is commensurate with the growing skill intensity of its production. Even as India redresses its previous neglect of primary education, it needs to multiply institutions like the IITs and regional engineering colleges on which its current success is based. Unfortunately, higher education remains one of the last bastions of the license-permit raj.

Despite these concerns, India's fast-growing states have a certain success-breeds-success dynamic which will be difficult to derail. More worrisome is job creation for India's growing unskilled labour force and the related problem of laggard states, where the majority of low-skilled, under-educated Indians still reside. Ideally, of course, such states would reform on their own—scrap archaic labour laws, improve infrastructure and business climate—and utilize their vast pools of under-employed, low-cost labour to attract investment in labour-intensive fields. They would then catch up with the leading states in India. Unfortunately, there is a reason these reforms have not been undertaken so far—few things are more persistent than bad governance.

Is India then likely to face increasing political strife as the politically powerful but laggard states hold back the economically powerful, fast-growing ones? There is a more hopeful scenario—Europe had similar disparities but through various initiatives, prosperous Western Europe offered incentives for laggard nations to reform. If a loosely knit community of nations can do it, why can not a united nation of states? A reformist centre—India can not afford to not have one—could play the role of the European Commission and offer laggard states incentives to reform.

For India to pull together better, though, the country has to become more of a common market, with easy cross-state flow of people, goods, and capital. Harmonization of taxes, standards and access is necessary. One area where this is critical is education—so that a student from a laggard state can find a place in a Mumbai college as easily as a student from Nagpur—for returning skilled workers can provide these states both the capabilities and the enthusiasm that has been so instrumental in India's growth.

Perhaps the defining metaphor for India today is churning, as entrenched interests lose power, as new jobs are created, as people move across states, as yesterday's Bharat becomes today's India, which becomes tomorrow's Bharat again.

Precocious India

Sixty years usually signals the onset of dotage in humans. But it is in fact a relatively young age for nations. So, what kind of infant is the Indian economy? A decade or two ago, against the background of unsuccessful performance, this question would probably have elicited the caustic comparison: 'Indian industry and the Indian economy are like Peter Pan: They never grow up.' Today, however, the infant seems more precocious than immature. The Indian economy has been doing many things well ahead of what countries usually do at this stage of their development.

No account of Indian precociousness can begin, of course, without mentioning the mother of all precocious feats, namely, sustaining a democracy in the inhospitable terrain of low levels of income and literacy, and a highly fractured society. In the post-war period, only a few other developing countries (e.g., Mauritius, Botswana, and Cost Rica) have sustained uninterrupted democracies, but they have been much smaller than India. The more common chronology has been growth first and democracy (maybe) later as the experience of East Asia has shown.

Moving on to economics, start with the most-cited anomaly of India relying on services rather than manufacturing as the basis for its growth. A slightly different way of characterizing this is the following. Historically, no country has escaped from underdevelopment using relatively skill-intensive activities as the launching pad for sustained growth as India has done. The most common mode of escape has been jeans, geology, or geography.

East Asian countries relied on relatively low-skilled manufacturing, typically textiles and clothing. Countries in West Asia today, and Australia and Canada further back in time, exploited their natural resources. And some of the island successes (Barbados and Mauritius) have exploited their geography by developing tourism.

Put differently, India seems to have defied its 'natural' comparative advantage, which probably lay in the jeans mode of escape because of its abundant unskilled and low-skilled labor. Instead, it found or created—thanks to historical policy choices and technological accidents—such advantage in relatively skilled activities. That the relevant distinction is skill-based rather than sectoral is reflected in the fact that even within manufacturing, India has an atypically high share of skilled-intensive sectors.

India's anomalous pattern of development on another score is less well known. Development involves countries diversifying their economic base and only later—after an income level of about $15,000 per capita—specializing in fewer activities. India has diversified to a greater extent and faster than usual for a country of its income level and has also started specializing much earlier than the typical country. This early and precocious diversification proved to be an asset because it equipped Indian industry to exploit some of the subsequent opportunities created by the IT and software revolution.

But in some ways, the most astonishing sign of precociousness has related to capital. Development theory's version of gravitational pull asserts that capital should flow downhill: from rich countries (where the risk-adjusted returns to capital are much lower because of diminished returns to capital) to poorer ones (where these returns are greater). But capital flowing uphill has been one of the anomalies of recent times: Many East Asian countries, especially China, and more recently, the oil-rich countries of West Asia, have run current account surpluses, whose mirror image is the export of financial capital. India has only rarely exported financial capital.

But India is the one country that seems to be defying a stronger version of the gravitational law of development, which says that managerial and entrepreneurial capital—foreign direct investment (FDI)—will always flow downhill. Empirical validation for this 'law' can be found in a paper that I coauthored with Eswar Prasad and Raghuram Rajan, *Foreign Capital and Economic Growth*: Whereas overall capital had occasionally flowed uphill, FDI never did. In the post-war period, the average income of countries that have been net exporters of FDI has been about $45,000 per capita. If only exports of FDI going to the rich countries had been considered, the number would have been higher still.

In 2006–7, India's net imports of FDI were 0.9 per cent of GDP. So, India is still not a net exporter (it could have been had some transactions been recorded differently) but the really striking fact is that India's gross exports of FDI were a whopping 1.2 per cent of GDP, and much of this was destined for the OECD countries. In other words, India has become a large exporter of FDI to rich countries at a per capita GDP of about $900 per capita, when the average country has done so closer to a per capita GDP in excess of $50,000. How precocious is that? As impressive is the range and sophistication of industries that Indian managers and entrepreneurs are moving into: oil, automotives, information technology, pharmaceuticals, steels, and even wind energy. In contrast, a lot of Chinese FDI is in Africa and is resource-related.

For a country that shunned global capitalism until very recently—IBM and Coca Cola were asked to leave in the late 1970s—and was seen as a paragon of inefficiency, it is a remarkable, ironic turnaround. Indians are engaged in global capitalism not just as workers but as 'bosses', taking over and efficiently managing global capital!

In some ways, all this precociousness should be no surprise at all. The fact is that there are many Indian economies within geographic India and some of them do resemble developed economies: in being endowed with educated and entrepreneurial people, in being well-connected with the outside world, and in having access to capital. They are probably also too well 'connected' within India. It would be more anomalous if these Indias had not recorded some of these precocious achievements.

But there are enough other Indias that should temper any triumphalism that the achievements of the precocious Indias might tempt us into. For one, poor India rather than precocious India is still the rule. And the very fact of defying comparative advantage means that India's abundant resource—its unskilled labour—has been afforded limited opportunities for economic and social advancement.

So, at sixty, let us savour the achievements by all means, but always remembering that precocious infants can be maladapted ones, and also that they do not always grow into successful, happy, or even, normal adults.

CHAPTER 3

THE EVOLUTION OF INSTITUTIONS IN INDIA AND ITS RELATIONSHIP WITH ECONOMIC GROWTH

Fish do not know that they are in water.
—Venezualan proverb

The tepid-to-torrid transformation in India's economic growth since the early 1980s is one of the big stories of recent times. Whereas 'Midnight's children' saw their standard of living double over forty years, Midnight's grandchildren—the 'India Shining' generation—can expect a five- or six-fold improvement in their lifetimes. But how have India's public economic institutions fared over this period? And what is their relationship with this growth transformation? This chapter represents a modest and preliminary attempt at answering these questions.

On the first, this chapter presents some stylized facts and new empirical evidence on the evolution in selected public institutions in India. The main finding is that, at least based on the limited number of institutions explored in this chapter—the bureaucracy and judiciary— there does not seem to be evidence of improvements in the average quality of institutions over time; if anything, the evidence leans in the other direction.

The second question that this chapter addresses is the two-way relationship between economic growth and institutions in India. It does so in terms of two apparent paradoxes. First, why has growth taken off despite institutional stagnation (see Aiyar, 2006)? And the second, which is the mirror image of the first, why despite nearly thirty years of rapid growth there has been no perceptible improvement in India's institutions? The central message of this chapter is the following.

India's founding fathers bequeathed a strong set of institutions, much stronger than for the average country. These institutions have played a key role in the turnaround in India's recent economic performance, a fact that has been overshadowed by, and because of, the more dramatic and necessary reduction in the ownership/regulatory functions of public institutions (a process that is usually described as policy reforms). Indians, above, have not sufficiently realized the importance of the legacy of good institutions (as the Venezuelan proverb indicates).

Over time, though, it is not obvious that India's public institutions are keeping up with the demands of a rapidly evolving economy. Thus, contrary to the near-universal views that the binding constraints to sustained Chinese-style rates of growth is the need to finish the unfinished task of rolling back the frontiers of the state, giving full play to the energies of the private sector, this chapter implies that a future reform agenda should focus equally on strengthening, or reversing the decline in, public institutions.

This chapter is organized as follows. Section 'The Role of Public Institutions' describes briefly the role of institutions in a market economy. Section 'How are Indian Institutions Faring?' presents empirical evidence that sheds some light on the evolution in Indian institutions over time and across states. In the section 'From Institutions to Growth', we focus on the effects of institutions on India's growth performance. In the section 'From Growth to Institutions: Disconnect between Growth and Institutions', we look at the impact (or lack thereof) of growth on institutions. The last section offers some concluding remarks.

THE ROLE OF PUBLIC INSTITUTIONS

Recent economic research gives centre stage to the role of public institutions in promoting and sustaining long-run development (see North, 1990; Hall and Jones, 1999; Acemoglu et al., 2001; Rodrik et al., 2004). Institutions perform a number of economic functions in a market system that affect efficiency and equity objectives.

First, institutions *create* markets. By protecting property rights, guaranteeing sanctity of contract, and providing law and order, they create an environment in which business and private investment can flourish. Thus, the judiciary, bureaucracy, and police are key institutions in facilitating the development of markets.

Second, institutions *regulate and/or substitute for* markets. The need for these functions arises from some kind of market failure and/or other social objectives such as income distribution that societies wish to fulfill. That is, markets do not deliver what is socially desirable. For example, banks and other financial institutions need to be regulated to ensure that they do not take on excessive risk, which can lead to socially costly bank runs or collapses. The private sector may not deliver education and water to the most needy because they cannot afford to pay for these services.

Third, institutions, such as the central banks or fiscal rules, *stabilize* markets by ensuring low inflation and macroeconomic stability and helping to avoid financial crises. Finally, institutions *legitimize* markets through mechanisms of social protection and insurance, and importantly, through mechanisms for redistribution and managing conflict. Democracy is, of course, the institution par excellence for legitimizing markets.

The most interesting evolution has been the market-regulating/ownership role of institutions. For much of the post-war period up to the 1980s, most countries sought to address market failures by the state substituting for markets; hence power, education, telecommunications, and water were provided by the public sector. In the case of India, the reach of the state was especially pervasive. Not only in these areas but also in others, including the bulk of manufacturing, public sector ownership was the norm. And where the private sector was allowed, extensive restrictions of Kafkaesque proportions were placed on the terms it could operate under, including the scale of operation, what products could be produced, how much labour could be hired, where plants could be located, etc.

The great ideological revolution of the last few decades has, of course, been the recognition that the state should cede much of this ground—and not just the old 'commanding heights'—to the private sector.[1] But even while ceding the function of providing these economic goods and services, the state still has an important regulatory function. And India too, albeit more slowly than most countries, has followed this path of less provision and more regulation, creating institutions such as the Securities and Exchange Board of India (SEBI), Telecommunications Authority of India (TRAI), Insurance Regulatory and Development Authority (IRDA), Central Electricity Regulatory Commission (CERC), etc. to undertake the regulatory role.

---

[1] The distinction between policies and institutions is not always easy to draw. In the schema described above, policies can be seen as actions that affect the scope of the state as owner and (over) regulator, while institutions affect the market-creating functions and the more necessary regulatory functions.

In what follows, we shall be focusing on the first category of institutions—the bureaucracy and judiciary—that affect the creation and sustenance of markets.

HOW ARE INDIAN INSTITUTIONS FARING?

While the popular perception in India is one of institutional decline, the verdict in the academic debate is understandably much more circumspect. The caution derives in part from the fact that India's size and heterogeneity resist easy attempts at generalization. Joan Robinson famously noted that everything and its opposite are almost statistically guaranteed to be true in India. Kapur and Mehta (2005) observe that: 'Although an observer of contemporary India may be tempted to conclude that India's public institutions are severely stressed and weakening, in reality their performance has varied both across institutions and over time.'

It is true that not all signs point to institutional decline. Kapur (2005) suggests that certain referee institutions, especially the Supreme Court, the Election Commission, and the Presidency, have witnessed rejuvenation. The Election Commission, especially since the late 1980s, has fiercely safeguarded its independence, and presided over many difficult elections. In a country where everything else is so politicized, it is remarkable that election results are never contested. The other referee institution, the Supreme Court, has moved beyond the politicized appointments of the late 1970s that gave India a 'committed' (Indianspeak for political bias) rather than an independent judiciary. In a landmark ruling in 1993, the Supreme Court effectively shut out the executive from appointments to the Supreme Court. Through minor tinkering and technological upgradation, the Supreme Court has also reduced the large backlog of undecided cases before it from 120,000 to 20,000 (Mehta, 2005). And, through public interest litigation, it has moved aggressively, behaving more like the executive than the judiciary, in resolving long-standing public policy issues; cleaning Delhi's atmospheric pollution being the best known, but not the only, example. While purists balk at this overreach,[2] the Supreme Court appears to have gained rather than lost popular legitimacy because of the perception that such overreach is a necessary consequence of and response to an inefficient and weak executive.

[2] The Supreme Court recently even decided on the fate of 300 rhesus monkeys held in captivity.

Further, some of the new institutions such as the TRAI, SEBI, and IDRA
have performed very respectably, especially considering the novelty of the
terrain they have had to navigate. The Central Union Public Service
Commission still oversees a selection process that is fair and merit-based.[3]
Greater decentralization and transparency have been introduced through
the Panchayati Raj initiatives and the Right to Information (RTI) Act. And
the introduction of computer-based technologies has improved efficiency
in a number of areas, with railway users being the most visible beneficiaries
of computerized bookings.

Moreover, the optimists might argue that lamentations of institutional
decline are, like the Rashomon effect, largely self-serving. The lamenters
are mostly the elites who see decline only because they no longer have
monopoly control over the institutions. Hitherto disadvantaged groups,
having acquired voice through the political process, are finally asserting
themselves and demanding that public institutions serve their interests
too, threatening the exclusive hold of the elites.

But the caution in pronouncing on institutional change over time also
stems from the lack of serious attempts at quantifying institutional trends in
India. Quantification has its pitfalls, but especially so in relation to institutions
because: (i) distinguishing institutions from say policies is not always easy;
(ii) there is a maddening variety and diversity of Indian institutions; and (iii)
the measurement of their performance is much more difficult. But policy
analysis and prescription require empirical/quantitative evidence and difficult
though the terrain is, there is no choice but to try and build such evidence.
In terms of the definition of institutions and its difference from policies, this
chapter adopts a very pragmatic approach. For example, in relation to trade,
it assumes that tariffs, quantitative restrictions, etc. are trade 'policies' but
how are these administered by customs as 'institutions.'

So what is the time-series evidence relating to market-creating
institutions? We present now three types of evidence: first, relating to
institutional outcomes; the second comprises subjective, perceptions-based
measures of economic governance/institutions; and the third is a more
detailed analysis of one particular institution which tries to isolate the effect
of institutional quality. Each type of evidence has its own limitations which
we discuss as follows. Moreover, only a few institutions are covered which

[3] This is not true of the *state* public service commissions, which have been scandal-prone.

may not be representative of the multiplicity of institutions in India. For this and other reasons, it should be stressed that the evidence presented in the following is meant to be illustrative and not by any means conclusive.

Stylized Facts on Institutional Outcomes

First, we present some basic stylized facts on institutional *outcomes*. These relate to outcomes such as power-related losses, murders, conviction rates, and evasion, and the institutions implicated in these outcomes are the bureaucracy, politics, and the judiciary. Of course, outcomes are determined by a number of factors, including the quality of institutions. So, it is difficult, if not impossible, to draw inferences about institutions and their evolution over time from outcomes, unless we can control these other factors. For example, if disposal rates of judicial cases decline it could be due to inadequate resources (judges, lawyers, etc.) or to corruption or to the fact that murder rates themselves are increasing for extraneous reasons (guns are more readily available, income leads to more crime, and so on) or some combination of the above. Institutional decline, in this case, is a valid inference only in the former two instances. With this important caveat, we proceed to the evidence.

Power Losses

In Kochhar et al. (2006), we argued that generation and distribution losses in power (a euphemism for outright theft and/or non-payment) could be one proxy for the quality of institutions at the state level. They broadly reflect the quality of both state-level politics—losses arise in part from politicians turning a blind eye to power theft by their constituencies or politicians' unwillingness to enforce laws—as well as the state-level bureaucracy (the state electricity boards) which enforces the laws, including collecting user charges.

How does India fare relative to comparator countries around the world? Figure 3.1 shows the evolution in losses as a percentage of power output since 1971 for India and selected (broadly comparable) countries. In 1971, in India, losses were about 9 per cent lower than in Brazil, Mexico, and Indonesia and about the same as in Malaysia and China. By 2003, losses in India had increased threefold to 27 per cent, higher than in any of the other five countries and much higher than in China (6.5 per cent) and Malaysia (4.6 per cent). Of course, these numbers cannot be interpreted as reflecting just institutional quality, at least not in a cross-country context,

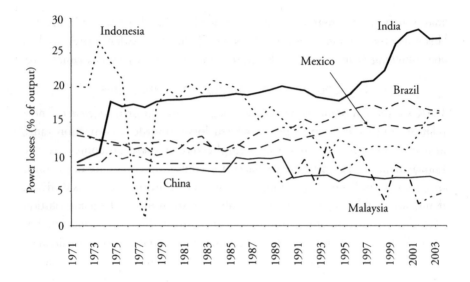

Figure 3.1(a): Power generation and distribution losses, 1971–2003

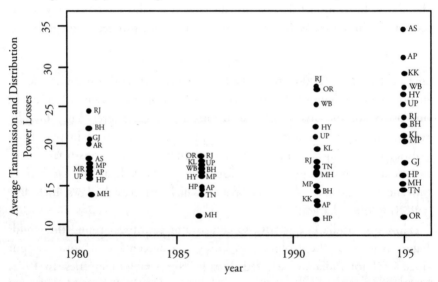

Figure 3.1(b): Transmission and distribution power losses across Indian states

Source: World Bank's World Development Indicators.
Note: Losses are calculated as averages for four successive five-year periods (1981–5, 1986–90, 1991–5, and 1996–2000). Losses are depicted for sixteen large states. Delhi, and Jammu and Kashmir are excluded for presentational reasons and including them does not alter the basic trend depicted. Codes same as Figure 2.7.

because they could depend, for example, on the size of the informal sector, the level of poverty, etc. However, the striking performance over time relative to other comparator countries is still noteworthy.

Mirroring the cross-national development, is the development within the states in India. In Figure 3.2, we plot the average T&D losses in power for four successive five-year periods beginning in 1980. We focus on the eighteen largest states. The pattern of losses in the period 1981–85 appears anomalous. Since then, however, we see a rising trend in losses but also greater diversity in performance—that is, the spread of losses widens, reflected in reduced bunching for the last period. The mean and standard deviation for losses were 17.7 and 4.8 for the period 1985–90, which increased to 25 and 9.6, respectively, during the period 1996–2000.[4] This

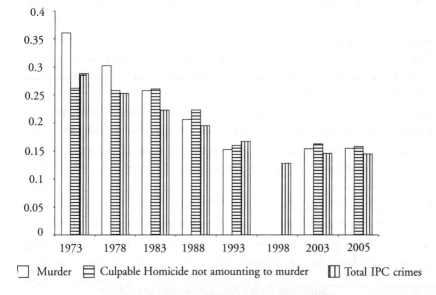

☐ Murder   ⊟ Culpable Homicide not amounting to murder   ⊞ Total IPC crimes

Figure 3.2: Disposal rates of murder-related crimes by courts, 1973–2005
(as a proportion of total outstanding cases)

Source: Based on data from 'Crime in India' a compendium of crime statistics published annually by National Crime Records Bureau (NCRB), Ministry of Home Affairs, India. Disposal rate is measured as the ratio of number of cases in which trials were completed during the year (comprising all cases that were convicted or acquitted/discharged) to the total number of cases for trial (sum of cases reported during the year and cases pending cases from the previous year).

[4] The change in the mean and standard deviation of losses over time are as dramatic even when two apparent outliers—Delhi, and Jammu and Kashmir—are excluded.

is suggestive of decline in the average but also of divergence in institutional outcomes across states, consistent with the diverging economic performance across states (Rodrik and Subramanian, 2005).

Disposal Rates for Murder-Related Cases

'To describe the Indian civil justice system, especially at the level below the Supreme Court, as being in a perpetual state of crisis would be an understatement,' (Mehta, 2005). What is the evidence? And more precisely, does it suggest one of stagnation in judicial institutions or actual decline?

We focus on outcomes related to murder, given the widely accepted convention, which appears also to be true of India, that statistics related to murder are the least unreliable type of crime statistics (Levitt, 1998; Verma, 2005).[5] Murder-related data are from the annual publications of the National Crime Records Bureau. Figure 3.2 illustrates the performance of state-level courts in terms of the disposal of murder-related cases that come before them. Since 1973, there has been a sharp reduction in the disposal of such cases, from 35 per cent in 1973 to about 15 per cent in 2005 (the disposal rate is measured as the number of murder-related cases on which the court gives a verdict divided by the total stock of outstanding murder-related cases). This figure merely confirms what is well known in India, that the state-level judicial system is overwhelmed and that the backlog of cases is mounting, resulting in a situation of justice being effectively denied by being indefinitely delayed. Again, a declining disposal rate does not mean that the court system is becoming more corrupt or even less efficient: a rising flow of cases coming before the courts could mechanically generate a decline in the disposal rate. What is undeniable is that, at the least, the personnel and resources are inadequate relative to the demands being made on the judicial system.

Conviction Rates for Murder-related Cases

We can look at another measure of judicial performance—the conviction rates for murder and related crimes. The exact measure is the number of cases in which the defendant was convicted divided by the total number of murder cases decided. Hence this measure should be less affected by resources because it is scaled by the number of verdicts given. Figure 3.3 shows that there has been a steady decline in conviction rates for murder

---

[5] Misreporting is a common problem for most crimes but less so for murder-related ones.

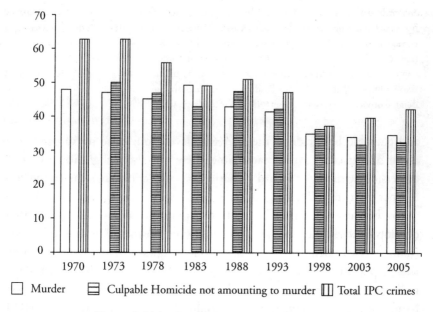

Figure 3.3(a): Conviction rates, 1970–2005

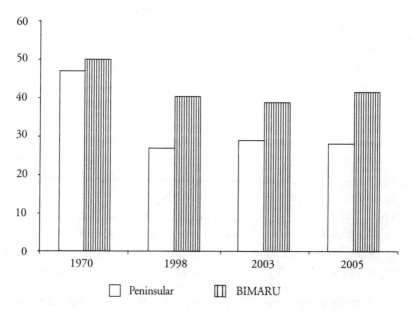

Figure 3.3(b): Conviction rates for murder in peninsular and BIMARU states, 1970–2005

Source: Based on data from 'Crime in India' a compendium of crime statistics published annually by National Crime Records Bureau (NCRB), Ministry of Home Affairs, India. Conviction rate is measured as the percentage of total completed trials during the year which were convicted [i.e., (number of convicted cases/total number of completed trials)*100]. Peninsular states comprise Gujarat, Maharashtra, Karnataka, Kerala, Tamil Nadu, and Andhra Pradesh. BIMARU states comprise Bihar, Madhya Pradesh, Uttar Pradesh, and Rajasthan.
Note: Conviction rates are presented for the 18 large states.

and culpable homicide at the aggregate level from close to 50 per cent to about 32 per cent.[6] At the same time, there was also a slight increase in the dispersion with the standard deviation of conviction rates increasing from 8.9 per cent in 1970 to 13 per cent in 2005.

To be sure, declines in conviction rates can signal a variety of developments, some negative and some even positive. Declines could arise' from the well-documented politicization/corruption of the judiciary so that the perpetrators of crime are able to get away with it because they are politically powerful and can influence judicial outcomes. On the other hand, declines in conviction rates could also signal an improving judicial system, if the control of the judiciary has shifted from the hitherto powerful who have unfairly brought charges against the less powerful.

It is difficult to know which of these stories is correct but looking at the data for groups of states can shed some additional light. Based on the limited data available, we can disaggregate the picture in . Figure 3.3(A) to compute developments in the conviction rate for the states. . Figure 3.3(B) divides the large states into the BIMARU (Bihar, Uttar Pradesh, Rajasthan, and Madhya Pradesh) and the peninsular states (Gujarat, Maharashtra, Karnataka, Kerala, Tamil Nadu, and Andhra Pradesh). Two features are worth noting: surprisingly, in terms of levels, the peninsular states fare marginally but consistently better than the BIMARU states; but, more significantly, the decline in conviction rates is evident for both category of states. The latter suggests that whatever changes are happening over time are common to all states. In Kerala and West Bengal, and even Tamil Nadu, which have not over this period seen any dramatic shift in political power toward disadvantaged groups (as has been the case say in Bihar and Uttar

---

[6] A similar decline in the conviction rate is also evident in cases handled by the Central Bureau of Investigation (CBI), from 17 per cent in 1972 to 9 per cent in 1999. Das (2005) characterizes this decline as arising from 'wilfully incompetent investigation and prosecution by the CBI'.

Pradesh), have witnessed a decline in conviction rates. The evidence is not inconsistent with increasing political influence over the judiciary.

Perception-based Measures of Institutions

Next, we present some subjective, perceptions-based measures of economic governance. These data are mainly compiled by the World Bank (Kaufmann et al., 2006) and go back only to the mid-1990s. These measures suffer from at least one problem. Although they purport to measure how institutions themselves are performing, the problem is that they are subjective—based on perceptions of investors (who tend to be more foreign than domestic)— and vague (they attempt answers to questions such as 'how strong is the rule of law?').[7]

The data compiled by Kaufman, Kraay et al. (2006) includes four measures of economic governance of which two—government effectiveness and and control of corruption—are relevant for us. These indicators are now available for the period 1996–2005. But we want to ascertain how economic governance, in particular, has evolved over a longer time span.

It turns out that similar subjective-measures of economic governance were compiled for the early 1960s by Adelman and Morris (1971). In Johnson et al. (2007), we suggest that a reasonable measure of economic governance, paralleling those being compiled by the World Bank, is one called 'degree of administrative efficiency'. The three criteria that went into the construction of this indicator were in the authors' words: 'degree of permanence and training of administrators (an indirect measure of whether recruitment is based upon qualifications for the job); the extent to which corruption, inefficiency, and incompetence seriously hamper government functioning; and the extent to which instability at higher levels of administration promotes inefficiency.' (p. 77). The classification of individual countries was based upon judgments for the period 1957–62.

We compute the measures for economic governance for India for the 1960s from and for the 1996–2005 period from the Kaufman et al. (2006). To facilitate comparisons over time, we standardize the variables within each time period. Implicitly, this transforms the rating for individual countries to a relative one. The score itself is then a measure of how far away

---

[7] The World Bank has begun computing more objective indicators of governance (World Bank, 2006) but these are available only since 2002.

from the mean (of zero by construction) a country is. A positive (negative) score implies that a country is above (below) the mean. Since the Adelman and Morris (1971) measure contains elements of effectiveness and corruption, we present for the later period, the World Bank's ranking for both these measures.

In 1960, India's rating was close to 1.5 standard deviations above the mean, a very high rating, placing it amongst the very top of the seventy-four countries surveyed by Adelman and Morris (1971). In the last decade, India's score has been close to zero, denoting an average rating.[8] If these measures are at all plausible, the picture they convey is one of decline—substantial decline—since the 1960s.

One feature of the Adelman and Morris (1971) indicators is that they are more plausible as ordinal (based on rankings) rather than cardinal measures. So, we convert all the data into ordinal form by representing each country in terms of their percentile ranking in the distribution. In the 1960s, India ranked around the 95th percentile, while it fell to about the 50th–60th percentile in the last decade.[9]

How reliable are the Adelman and Morris (1971) data? It is always difficult to compare across surveys and especially when the information is subjective and spread across time. But one rough way of checking data quality is to compare their data on political institutions with the widely used Polity IV database that has become something of a standard for quantitative indicators of political institutions and that is also available for the same time period. For example, when we correlate the Adelman and Morris measure of 'the strength of democratic institutions' and the Polity IV measure of constraint on the executive for 1960, the correlation is reassuringly high (0.69).

---

[8] We computed the indicators for the sample in Adelman and Morris (74 countries); and also for a larger sample of 211 countries for which the World Bank has collected data. Over the last decade, Indian performance on government effectiveness has shown a slight improvement while that on corruption has remained flat. It is possible that perception-based measures, especially for a category as vague as 'government effectiveness', are more influenced by the overall performance of the economy, and hence should be discounted more heavily.

[9] It is worth re-emphasizing that these are relative measures: at each point in time a country is assessed against other countries. If there has been a generalized upward drift in the quality of institutions, it is possible that the relative decline in Indian institutions portrayed might not represent an absolute decline.

Isolating the Effect of Institutional Quality:
The Case of Indian Customs

Although suggestive, the evidence presented thus far—which has been more in the nature of stylized facts or subjective perceptions—cannot be a basis for pronouncing on the quality of institutions. Can we isolate the effect of institutional performance per se over time? We present here a third piece of evidence relating to a particular government institution—the customs service. This is based on a more careful empirical exercise which tries to control for other factors affecting outcomes and thus to isolate the impact of institutional quality. The price of rigour, of course, is representativeness, or rather the lack of it. But we will make a case that this example could be typical of the broader set of institutions—including the judiciary and bureaucracy.

The quality of a bureaucracy has an important impact on public service delivery and on regulation and therefore on the environment for investment and growth. At least at the federal level, the civil service in India has been a prestigious institution, with recruitment based on merit, and attracting some of the most competent and talented people. But the popular perception is that the civil service too has become more politicized, and hence compromised and more corruptible. The concise verdict of Krishnan and Somanathan (2005) is that 'the current state of the civil service leaves much to be desired'.

How can we measure the performance of the bureaucracy? One institution that is amenable to 'objective,' quantifiable assessment is customs, which is entrusted with implementing trade and other commercial policies. The extent of evasion that takes place in regard to imports is one such quantifiable indicator of performance. Customs is also a good candidate to examine because it is a highly important and visible part of the bureaucracy. The Central Excise and Customs Department is considered to be one of the elite bureaucratic departments; it is a central rather than a state-level agency, which in general is deemed to be more corruptible and inefficient. Finally, customs has witnessed significant policy reform and technology upgradation through the introduction of computers (see for details). All these factors make customs a public institution that is more—indeed most—likely to have seen an improvement in its performance or at least less likely to have seen a significant worsening of performance.

In Mishra et al. (2007), we collected data on imports into India at the 6–digit level (approximately 5000 products) for a period of fifteen years (from 1988–2002) from all its trading different partners (greater than 100). The WITS database not only provides this import data but also the value of the same imports recorded at the point of origin of these goods, that is it records the exports from these partner countries to India for the same time period and at the same level of disaggregation. We define the difference between the recorded exports at the origin and the recorded imports at the India end as a measure of evasion (because there is typically an incentive to under-record imports to reduce the duty and other tax obligations).

As Figure 3.4 illustrates, the extent of evasion has declined over time by about 20 per cent. We tried to see that to what extent this decline in evasion was due to an improvement in the quality of enforcement by customs administration as opposed simply to the reduction in and simplification of tariffs following the 1991 macroeconomic crisis. The latter would have led to a reduction in the demand for evasion; we need to control this to isolate or identify the supply effect, namely that of the quality of enforcement.

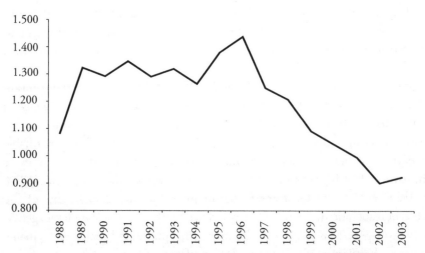

Assumption. Products reported by exporting countries but missing in Indian imports are smuggled completely

Figure 3.4: Import evasion, 1988–2002

Source: Mishtra et al. (2007). Evasion is measured as: log (1 + recorded exports) –log (1 + recorded imports).

One way of assessing the quality of enforcement by customs is to see the change in the evasion elasticity over time. The evasion elasticity is the impact on evasion of a 1 percentage point change in the tariff rate. Over time and within a country, the impact of such a change in tariffs should have a similar impact in terms of the 'demand for' (i.e., incentives for) evasion, so that changes in this evasion elasticity should broadly be attributable to changes in the effectiveness of enforcement.[10]

Empirically, Fisman and Wei (2004) suggest that the evasion elasticity can be interpreted as a measure of institutional quality (the lower the elasticity, the better the enforcement). In Mishra et al. (2007), we find that the evasion elasticity is invariant with respect to tariffs but does vary with measures of enforcement—-for example, the evasion elasticity is significantly higher for more differentiated goods and for goods where uncertainty about price is greater. This suggests that where enforcement is 'more difficult' because of some inherent characteristics, the elasticity is indeed higher. This is therefore consistent with interpreting the elasticity as a proxy for enforcement/institutions (as the paper shows, other measures for enforcement are consistent with this finding).

Having validated the interpretation of the evasion elasticity as a measure of enforcement, our key finding is that this evasion elasticity does not seem to have declined over time; in some selected instances we find evidence of an increase in the evasion elasticity (Figure 3.5). That is, a given increase in tariffs leads to no less evasion in the early 2000s than it did in the late 1980s/early 1990s. Overall, the evidence suggests no improvements in the quality of enforcement by customs administration, at least not enough to affect the marginal impact on evasion.[11] Even where we can identify pockets of better enforcement such as at airports, we fail to find evidence of improvements over time.

Although one cannot generalize from the experience of one institution, the fact that customs—which we argued earlier should have been the

[10] A clarification might be helpful here. Even if the elasticity of evasion with respect to tariffs is constant (i.e., invariant with respect to tariffs), in theory, this evasion elasticity can vary with enforcement (institutions/administration, etc.). What this means is that if one draws a curve in evasion-tariffs space, the shift of the curve (when institutions change) is not necessarily parallel (Allingham and Sandmo, 1972; Slemrod and Kopczuk, 2002).

[11] The basic specification involves regressing our measure of evasion which varies by time, partner country, and product on nominal tariffs, which vary by product and time. The specification is very general because it includes a full set of country-time, and country-product fixed effects,

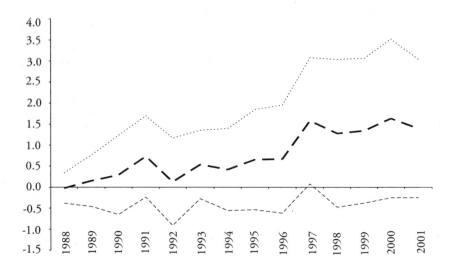

Figure 3.5: Quality of customs administration, 1988–2001
(elasticity of evasion wrt own tariffs)

Source: Mishra et al. (2007). The figure shows the estimated elasticity of evasion with respect to tariffs—a measure of the quality of customs administration—as well as the two standard error bands around it. An increasing elasticity denotes deteriorating customs administration.

candidate most likely to have witnessed improvements—has not exhibited any improvement is itself noteworthy.

This customs example as well as the stylized facts presented earlier on institutional outcomes and the subjective measures of perceptions all seem to be consistent with each other, in suggesting a picture of institutional stagnation. Particularly noteworthy for the similarity in developments over time is the evasion elasticity (Figure 3.5) and the World Bank's corruption measure for India for roughly the same period.

FROM INSTITUTIONS TO GROWTH

In this section, we look at institutions as the driving force and examine their impact on growth in two different contexts: India in the cross-section of countries and regions (states and districts) within India.

with standard errors clustered at the product level. Our core sample comprises more than 300,000 observations. Our key finding is that the coefficient on the tariff, which is significant and positive (as expected because higher tariffs should increase the incentives for evasion), does not change over time. For details see Mishra et al. (2007a).

India in the Cross-section: Explaining the Puzzle of Stagnant Institutions, Rising Growth

The most striking fact about India's growth has been the remarkable turnaround in nearly all measures of growth performance since 1980. Output per capita, output per worker, as well as total factor productivity accelerated sharply after 1980. For example, total factor productivity which grew at about 0.3 per cent per annum during the period 1960–80, grew at close to 2 per cent per annum in the following two decades. The question is why?

In fact, the puzzle can be posed starkly in two ways. First, it can be posed in an intertemporal (within India) context: why despite relatively limited reforms in the 1980s did growth accelerate so sharply during this period? There is an extensive debate on the possible explanations (see Rodrik and Subramanian, 2005). But for our purposes, the interesting point relates to what all sides do agree upon. To the extent that policy reforms were indeed an important contributing factor, all sides agree that the magnitude of reforms especially from the early 1980s till the mid-to-late-1990s, when growth was accelerating, was limited. Ahluwalia (2002), one of the important players in the reform process, himself characterizes the Indian effort as one of 'gradualism.'

The second context for the puzzle is a cross-country one. India has implemented policy reforms since the early 1980s, and especially, the 1990s. But so too have countries in Latin America and sub-Saharan Africa, where reforms have sometimes been broader and deeper than those in India. An illustration of the relative pace of reform is provided by indicators of trade policy. The most commonly used measure is due to Sachs and Warner (1995) as updated by Warcziarg and Welch (2003). This is a binary measure which classifies country as either closed or open. Argentina, Brazil, and Mexico were deemed to have made the transition from closed to open economy in 1991, South Africa in 1991, and Uganda in 1991. In 2000, nearly twenty years after the growth turnaround, India was still classified as a closed economy from the point of view of trade and commercial policies. This picture of India as a closed economy well into the reform process is confirmed more formally using a gravity model of trade (see Rodrik and Subramanian, 2005). To be sure, not all reforms are alike, but India as a policy laggard would be underscored if other measures of reform such as privatization were analysed because, in part, structural reforms tend to be correlated. In fact, Rodriguez and Rodrik (2000) argue that the Sachs and

Warner (1995) measure is itself a broad indicator of macroeconomic stability and structural reforms.[12]

Yet the growth response in these other countries has not been close to that in India. Since 1985, Latin America and sub-Saharan Africa have grown by about 1 per cent per capita per year, while India has grown at about 4–4.5 per cent.[13]

So, if the reforms were not dissimilar, how does one explain the differential supply or growth response? One possible explanation could be that it is the quality of institutions. To understand this point, it is helpful to think of economic development as resulting from the interaction between triggers and fundamentals. Recent research suggests that in the long run, the quality of a country's public institutions is the key fundamental of long-run growth. What was holding India back, prior to the 1980s, was a policy regime that was unfavorable to the private sector. Once that was changed through policy reforms, the economic landscape was transformed. The key point here is that even a small trigger—that is, relatively modest reforms—was sufficient to engender a large growth response because of the considerable under-exploited potential provided by the quality of its institutions. India's institutions, built up through the decades preceding independence, allowed it to get a big bang for the relatively small buck of reforms (at least compared with other countries).

Why did this apparently small trigger elicit such large productivity responses? It is worth noting at the outset that India was very far from its long-run or steady-state level of income given the level of its domestic institutions. If the recent literature's emphasis on the importance of institutions on development is correct, India appears to be far inside the institutions (or production) possibility frontier. Figure 3.6, based on Rodrik et al. (2004), illustrates this under-achievement and its flip side, namely the potential created by India's institutional quality. It depicts, in the spirit of Acemoglu et al. (2000) and Hall and Jones (1998) the long run (in fact very

[12]Of course, a host of other possible factors determine growth outcomes, including initial conditions, human capital, inequality, etc. But in a standard Barro-type cross-country growth regression, India proves to be an outlier even after controlling for some of these determinants (see Table 4 in Rodrik and Subramanian, 2005).

[13] Latin America is, on average, richer than India, so convergence on its own would suggest higher growth rates in India. But the magnitude of the differential cannot all be explained by convergence dynamics alone.

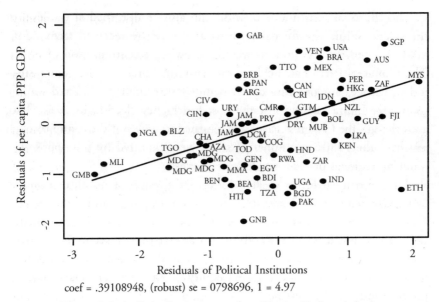

coef = .39108948, (robust) se = 0798696, 1 = 4.97

Figure 3.6: India in the cross-section: The institutional slack

Source: This figure plots the residuals of a regression of a country's per capita PPP GDP (in 1980) on its political institutions (measured as the constraint on the executive), its openness (as measured by the trade-to-GDP) ratio, and its geography (as measured by the distance from the equator). The slope of the line in the figure is exactly the coefficient on institutions in this regression. India is more than two standard errors away from the regression line. For details, see Rodrik and Subramanian (2005).

long run) relationship between income per capita in 1980 against a measure of political institutions in 1980. The slope of the fitted line is exactly the slope of the coefficient of institutions on income, after controlling for other long-run ('deep') determinants, including openness and geography, and after controlling for the potential endogeneity of institutions and openness.[14]

As can be seen, India is well below the regression, line: that is, it is an outlier in this relationship. And it is a negative outlier, suggesting that given its level of institutions, its income should have been much greater in 1980, by a factor of 4 or so. That India was under-achieving relative to its institutions in 1980 is shown more formally in Rodrik and Subramanian (2005) for a variety of institutional measures (economic and political) and estimation procedures. India has thus created considerable growth potential by having done the real hard work of building institutions.

[14] As in Rodrik et al. (2004), institutions and openness have been instrumented.

The effects of institutions in India can also be discerned at the level of the states. While the formal reforms at the centre received tremendous publicity, perhaps less noticed was the growing decentralization of policy. The Congress Party had held power without a break at the center since independence, but the aura of invincibility surrounding it started waning soon after Indira Gandhi lost the post-Emergency election in 1977. Also, even though the Congress Party was returned to power at the centre through much of the 1980s, a number of states were captured by the opposition, often by regional or even single-state parties.

The centrifugal forces created by this dispersion of political power in India also led to decentralization of economic power and hence policy. Greater economic decentralization meant states could differentiate themselves, not least in their ability to attract private sector investment. This was, of course, facilitated by the gradual dismantling of the industrial licensing system that used regional equity as one of the primary criterion guiding industrial investments.

If economic decentralization became important, states' economic performance should have be more closely tied to state-level institutions in the post-1980s period than before. After all, if the pre-1980s era was about the centre deciding, for example, where and how much electricity capacity to install, there is little that the states could have done to affect economic performance within their borders. This is what the evidence suggests. For example, when we relate state-level growth to state-level institutions [which in line with the discussion above we proxy by the T&D losses of state-level electricity boards (as a fraction of generating capacity)], we find that the latter have no role in explaining growth prior to 1980 but a robust role in explaining post-1980s, especially post-1990s growth. Figure 3.7 depicts this relationship. It plots the annual average state level growth against a state's institutions (as proxied by the extent of T&D losses) in the 1990s. In other words, the slope of the line is the coefficient of a regression of state growth on institutions interacted with decadal dummies and after controlling for a number of other variables.[15] The figure illustrates the strong positive

---

[15] Other controls include state and time-fixed effects, the Besley-Burgess indicator of labour market reform interacted with decadal dummies, and initial income plus its interactions with decadal dummies. The relationship between state level growth and institutions is robust to alternative ways of measuring the quality of institutions (Kochhar et al., 2006).

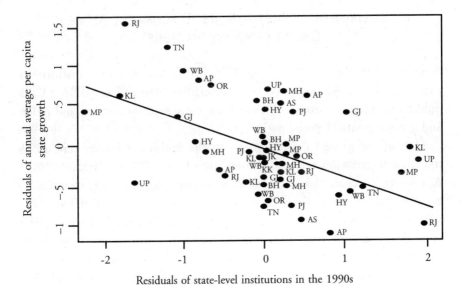

coef = −.33532229, (robust) se = .12843541, 1 = −2.61

Figure 3.7: The importance of institutions: State-level evidence

Source: This figure plots the residuals of a regression of a state's decadal average per capita GDP growth on state-level institutions interacted with decadal dummies, state and time fixed effects, the Besley-Burgess indicator of labour market reform interacted with decadal dummies, and initial income plus its interactions with decadal dummies). The slope of the line is exactly the coefficient on institutions in the 1990s (i.e, the partial impact of institutions in the 1990s on average growth in the same period). The figure illustrates the strong positive relationship between institutions (the opposite of T&D losses). For details, see Kochhar et al. (2006). Codes same as Figure 2.7

relationship between institutions (the opposite of T&D losses) and growth after the 1990s.[16]

In sum, institutions have had an important role in India's growth turnaround, which is discernible in the cross-section of countries and across states within India. The focus on the policy reforms of the 1990s has tended to overshadow this fact.

[16] Banerjee and Iyer (2005) present strong empirical evidence that institutions, not just contemporary ones, but those created nearly two hundred years ago, have had lasting effects on contemporary economic performance in India. They show that variations in land tenure systems can explain the pattern of variation in agricultural investment and productivity, as well as in health and education indicators across districts in post-independence India. For example, the average yield of wheat is 23 per cent higher and infant mortality about 40 per cent lower in those districts that did not have a zamindari (landlord-based) tenure system compared with districts that did.

FROM GROWTH TO INSTITUTIONS: DISCONNECT BETWEEN GROWTH AND INSTITUTIONS?

Around the world as countries grow, political and economic institutions tend to improve. As people become richer, they demand more from their public institutions—better public services, more security and law and order, and greater political participation.

One of the more robust findings in the political science literature is that democratization follows incomes (see Lipset, 1959; Barro, 1996).[17] As countries become richer, they also, on average, become more democratic, granting greater political freedoms to their citizens. In much of East Asia, for example, rising incomes have led to greater political freedoms. The same should also be true of income and economic institutions. Indeed, the paper by Acemoglu et al. (2001) on the impact of institutions on long-run growth is noteworthy precisely because it found a creative solution to the endogeneity problem, namely the widely accepted recognition that as incomes rise institutions improve. Rigobon and Rodrik (2004) find that the impact of income on institutional development is positive. As Korea got richer the costs of doing business for large and small firms declined.

In India, the last twenty-five years have seen a fourfold increase in the income of the average person. The evidence in the section 'How are Indian Institutions Fare?' suggested that institutions have not improved. Prima facie this suggests that economic growth is not necessarily and automatically doing the job of improving institutions. Why is this the case?

Public Institutions: Rising Demand

First of all, it should be noted that the process by which rising incomes leads to better institutions is a two-stage one, involving first a greater demand for better institutions, followed by a process (with complicated economic and political economy influences) whereby this greater demand begets greater and better supply of institutions. The first part of this dynamic has certainly been at play and two examples illustrate this.

---

[17] Acemoglu et al., (2005) argue, however, that this is a pure cross-sectional result and that the time series evidence is less conclusive.

Example 1: Crime and income

In relation to the judiciary, one can ask how growth affects the demands made of the judicial system. If rising incomes leads to a decline in crimes, *ceteris paribus*, institutional performance should be helped as the judiciary is less burdened. So we examine the simple relationship between serious crime (murder) and income. We compiled data on murders committed per capita in the Indian states for the period 1973–2003. We ran regressions of crime per capita on state-level income and included time and state fixed effects. The latter allows us to ask whether over time and within states there is an association between income and crime. The finding is that there seems to be a statistically positive relationship between income and crime, that is, rising income within a state tends to be associated with

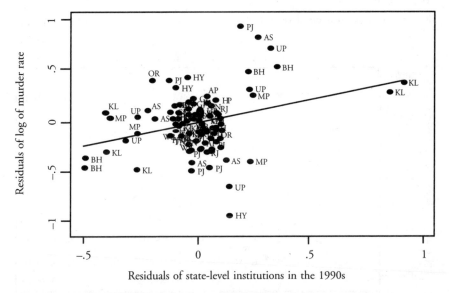

coef = .46993818, (robust) se = .11865759, 1 = 3.96

Figure 3.8: Relationship between income and murder, 1973–2003

Source: This figure plot the residuals of a (unbalanced) panel regression of average murders over seven successive five-year periods beginning in 1973 through 2003 on state per capita net domestic product, controlling for time and state fixed effects. The slope of the line in the chart is the coefficient on income in this regression. The sample includes seventeen large states; Jammu and Kashmir is excluded because it appears to be an outlier but the results remain unchanged even if it is included.

Note: Codes same as Figure 2.7.

more crime. The relationship is depicted in Figure 3.8 for the eighteen largest states.[18]

This simple relationship offers a clue for why judicial performance could be weakening over time: development places greater demands on it, and unless there is a commensurate improvement in resources and quality, outcomes could worsen. The data on declining disposal rates by the courts presented in Figure 3.2 is consistent with increasing burdens being placed on state-level courts. A similar dynamic, albeit with a different twist, is at work in the example that is described below.

Example 2: Education and income

Public institutions in the field of primary education—that is government-run schools—are characterized by rampant teacher absenteeism, ranging from 20 per cent to over 50 per cent in some states. It is not clear whether absenteeism has worsened over time but it would not be surprising if it had.

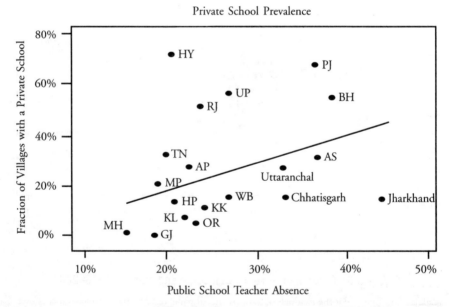

Figure 3.9: Public and private schools

Source: Kremer et al. (2005).
Note: Codes same as Figure 2.7.

[18] The relationship is positive but statistically weaker when we include the smaller states and union territories.

On the basis of a careful and detailed study of schools all over India, Kremer et al. (2005) document a fascinating development, which is captured in Figure 3.9. The figure shows that states, where public educational institutions are worse (that is, greater teacher absenteeism is common), have seen greater entry of private schools. And this has happened in the last ten years, since the early 1990s. They also show that private schools outperform public ones on a wide number of outcomes.[19]

This study highlights one important aspect of the functioning of public institutions. As incomes have risen rapidly, so has the demand for primary education because the perceived returns to education are now seen as much higher. But public institutions have not been able to meet this increased demand reflected in the private sector has stepping in to fill in the gap left by unresponsive public institutions.[20] Viable alternatives to public institutions might be possible in some areas such as education, health, power, and water but they may not, and indeed cannot be, be available in relation to core functions that only a state monopoly can provide through institutions such as the judiciary, bureaucracy, police, etc.

Public Institutions: Lagging Supply?

What these examples illustrate is that rising incomes are placing greater demands on public institutions but, if the evidence presented in third section is at all plausible, namely that institutions and institutional outcomes have not improved, it appears to be the case that supply is lagging behind. Why this is so is an important area of future research. In the following paragraphs we speculate on some possible explanations.

In some ways, the fact that supply lags demand is puzzling because over this period India has witnessed a number of developments that should have facilitated, even forced, institutional improvement.

---

[19] Student–teacher ratios are better in private schools as is the problem of teacher absenteeism. Salaries of teachers are about one-sixth that in public schools and teachers have greater contact with their students. Students in private schools have higher test scores and are taught English a grade earlier than in public schools. And accountability is much better too: The dismissal rate of teachers is 35/600 in private schools compared with 1/3000 in public schools.

[20] Note that efficient private sector provision of essential services such as education does not eliminate an important role for the public sector: from an equity perspective, the fact that poor households have to pay for private education is a social cost. Luckily, this can be remedied by public financing of primary education, while allowing the private sector to continue to play a big role in provision.

First, Indian society, open and argumentative as it always was, has received a further, reinvigorating jolt of transparency: institutions have been exposed to the glare of public scrutiny thanks to the explosion in the quantity and quality of the media. From the Godhra incident to the *Tahelka* probe it seems that not much can elude the prying eyes of the print or the electronic media. Greater transparency should have led to more accountable institutions.

Second, the license-quota-permit raj, a big source of corruption and patronage, with its deeply corrosive effect on public institutions, is being progressively dismantled. While it is true that the locus of rent-seeking may have shifted—from acquiring import and industrial licenses in the dirigiste policy regime of the past to acquiring land, which is now the priceless government-controlled asset in a booming economy—it would be surprising if there were not fewer rents in the aggregate and hence fewer rent-seekers in the system. Figure 3.4 illustrates this point clearly. There has been a significant decline in evasion as tariffs have come down—fewer rents should have reduced rent-seeking.

Third, civil society has become a vibrantly assertive presence in India. Indian civil society has taken on at least two roles: a direct one, in delivering development outcomes, and an indirect one, striving to hold public institutions accountable. Civil society has scored many important successes—from the very visible one of getting Delhi's environment cleaned up through public interest litigation to phenomenal efforts in the field of education. Civil society can now be fairly described as the fifth pillar of the Indian polity.

Fourth, with greater decentralization of political and economic power, the healthy dynamic of competition between states has been unleashed. This allows for demonstration effects: citizens in Bihar can look at their counterparts in Maharashtra and question why they must be in darkness for longer periods without electricity, and why their children must suffer from rampant teacher absenteeism, condemning them to educational backwardness. In turn, this questioning and discontent should have led to a more active, demanding citizenry.

On the other hand, there have also been adverse effects on the supply of institutions. First, although growth has accelerated and poverty has declined substantially, divergences have increased too. Some regions and groups—for example, the Adivasis constituting about 80 million people—have partaken minimally, if at all, of the fruits of economic growth. It is no coincidence that Naxalite activity is strongest in the tribal belt spread across central and eastern India, feeding on the fertile climate of alienation and disenfranchisement. A rising tide need not lift all boats uniformly but if important, identifiable ones are left grounded, that could be a recipe for disaffection, and eventually conflict.

Unequal growth also has subtler effects on institutions. Recall the dynamic of growth leading to a greater demand for better public institutions. But if growth is more concentrated at the upper ends of the income spectrum, there is the distinct possibility of what Albert Hirschman called 'exit': the rich opt out of the public system, turning to the private sector to get essential services (for example, gated communities with private policing, private generators for power, private schools for their children's education, and so on). The normal pressures for improving the provision of public goods get attenuated. Indeed, Kapur (2006) shows that the well-connected and influential class in India may have less of a stake in higher education because an overwhelming proportion tend to send their children abroad for graduate education.[21]

The second major factor contributing to the decline of public institutions is its increasing inability to attract talent. This too has deeper causes, including the growing politicization of the bureaucracy, cynicism about its role, and the fading sense of public service. But clearly one of them is the very rise of the private sector which has simply made the public sector a less attractive place to work in. The allocation of talent has become skewed. With the staggering scale of remuneration that the new economy is showering on skilled people, the public sector does not stand a chance of competing with the private sector in attracting high quality people.[22] And, if institutions ultimately depend on the individuals manning them and the incentives they face, the prognosis is somewhat grim for public institutions.

---

[21] Nandan Nilekani, Chairperson of Infosys the IT giant, argues that roads are likely to get built in India relatively quickly because the burgeoning middle class, having acquired cars—the iconic symbol of wealth and status—needs 'somewhere to go' to show them off.

[22] In the study on customs evasion discussed earlier, we found that the average value of customs transactions handled by the typical customs officer in India is about Rs 29 million per month. The monthly salary, on the other hand, for a customs inspector is Rs 9000 per month.

CONCLUSION

What do these two paradoxes imply for a future reform agenda? Scarcely a day passes without exhortations, from diverse sources, to Indian policymakers to refurbish India's creaking infrastructure, reform its stifling and antiquated labour laws, and lift barriers to foreign direct investment. Underlying these calls is the view that the public sector is the problem and the private sector the solution, and that the policy challenge ahead calls for merely rolling back the frontiers of the state and allowing greater freedom for the private sector. This view is understandable given India's dirigiste past; it is also constructive because it allows for new private sector-based solutions to be explored and found in areas such as basic and higher education that have hitherto been seen as the public sector's exclusive responsibility, but it is also part-wrong or at least incomplete—and the pendulum could swing too far in the other direction, because it fails to recognize the limits to private sector action.

The two paradoxes highlighted here suggest that the core market-creating public institutions bequeathed by India's pre-independence leaders are key to India's long-run growth, but they may not have kept pace with Indian economic realities. The good news is that some of these institutions, especially those relating to regulation, need not be fatally decisive in terms of their growth impact because of private sector alternatives. But India may well be fast using up the slack from the legacy in relation to the core institutions: the Indian growth engine could sputter as much from weaknesses in the soft infrastructure of institutions as the hard one of roads, power plants, and ports.

Neglecting institutional reform is tempting because institutions are notoriously difficult to change. Where does one even start when thinking of reforming the Indian bureaucracy or police or judiciary? But in core areas, relying on growth and policy reforms to automatically lead to institutional improvement is hardly a serious option as some of the evidence presented above suggests. A starting point has to be the recognition that allowing institutional decline could well come back to haunt not just policy-makers but the private sector as well, whose fortunes depend crucially on strong and effective public institutions. Rehabilitating the institutions bequeathed by Mahatma Gandhi, Pandit Nehru, and others, and not just finding creative ways of working around them, should consume the energies of Midnight's grandchildren. A rich and relatively unexplored research and policy agenda lies ahead.

REFERENCES

Acemoglu, D., S. Johnson, and J. A. Robinson (2001), 'The Colonial Origins of Comparative Development: An Empirical Investigation', *American Economic Review*, 91(5), pp. 1369–1401.

Acemoglu, D., S. Johnson, J. A. Robinson, and P. Yared (2005), 'Income and Democracy', *National Bureau of Economic Research Working Paper No. 11205*.

Adelman, I., and C. T. Morris (1971), *Society, Politics, and Economic Development: A Quantitative Approach*, Johns Hopkins Press, Baltimore, Maryland.

Ahluwalia, M.S. (2002), 'Economic Reforms in India Since 1991: Has Gradualism Worked', *Journal of Economic Perspectives*, 16(7), pp. 67–88.

Allingham, M. G., and A. Sandmo (1972), 'Income Tax Evasion: A Theoretical Analysis', *Journal of Public Economics*, 1, pp. 323–38.

Ahmed, S., and S. Ejaz Ghani (2006), *South Asia: Growth and Regional Integration*, World Bank, Washington D.C.

Aiyar, S. (2006), 'Falling Governance, Rising Growth', *Economic Times*, August 2.

Banerjee, A., and L. Iyer (2005), History, institutions and economic performance: the legacy of colonial land tenure systems in India', *American Economic Review*, 95(4).

Barro, R. J. (1996), 'Democracy and Growth', *Journal of Economic Growth*, 1(1), pp. 1–27.

Das, S. K. (2005), 'Institutions of Internal Accountability', in Devesh Kapur and Pratap Mehta (eds), *Public Institutions in India: Performance and Design*, Oxford University Press, New Delhi.

Engerman, S. L., and Kenneth L. Sokoloff (1994), 'Factor Endowments, Institutions, and Differential Paths of Growth Among New World Economies: A View from Economic Historians of the United States', *National Bureau of Economic Research Working Paper No. H0066*.

Hall, R., and C. I. Jones (1999), 'Why Do Some Countries Produce So Much More Output per Worker than Others?' *Quarterly Journal of Economics*, 114(1), pp. 83–116.

Kaufmann, D., A. Kraay, and M. Mastruzzi (2006), 'Governance Matters V: Aggregate and Individual Governance Indicators 1996–2005'. *WBPRDWP#4012.*

Fisman, R., and S.-J. Wei (2004), 'Tax Rates and Tax Evasion: Evidence from 'Missing Imports' in China', *Journal of Political Economy*, 112(2), pp. 471–96.

Kapur, D. (2005), 'Explaining Democratic Durability and Economic Performance: The Role of India's Institutions,' in Devesh Kapur and Pratap Mehta (eds), *Public Instiutions in India: Performance and Design*, Oxford University Press, New Delhi.

Kapur, D. (2006), 'Globalization and the Paradox of Indian Democracy,' mimeo, University of Pennsylvania.

Kapur, D., and P. Mehta (eds) (2005), *Public Instiutions in India: Performance and Design*, Oxford University Press, New Delhi.

Kochhar, K., U. Kumar, R. Rajan, A. Subramanian, and I. Tokatlidis (2006), 'India's Pattern of Development: What Happened, What Follows,' *Journal of Monetary Economics*, 53, pp. 981–1019.

Kremer, M.. K. Muralidharan, N. Chaudhury, F.h. Rogers, and J. Hammer (2005), 'Teacher Absence in India: A Snapshot.' *Journal of the European Economic Association*, 3(2–3), pp. 658–67.

Krishnan, K.P., and T.V. Somanathan (2005), 'Civil Service: An Institutional Perspective,' in Devesh Kapur and Pratap Mehta (eds), *Public Institutions in India: Performance and Design*, Oxford University Press, New Delhi.

Levitt, S. D. (1998), 'The Relationship Between Crime Reporting and Police: Implications for the use of Uniform Crime Reports', *Journal of Quantitative Criminology*, 14(1), pp. 61–81.

Lipset, S.M. (1959), 'Some Social Requisites of Democracy: Economic Development and Political Legitimacy,' *The American Political Science Review*.

Mehta, P. (2005), 'India's Judiciary: 'The Promise of Uncertainty', in Devesh Kapur and Pratap Mehta (eds), *Public Instiutions in India: Performance and Design*, Oxford University Press, New Delhi.

Mishra, P., A. Subramanian, and P. Topalova (2007), 'Tariff Policy, Institutions, and Evasion: The Case of Indian Customs', International Monetary Fund Working paper.

Mishra, P., A. Subramanian, and P. Topalova (2007), 'Crime in India', work-in-progress.

North, D. C. (1990), *Institutions, Institutional Change and Economic Performance*, York, Cambridge University Press Baltimore, Maryland.

Rigobon, R., and D. Rodrik (2004), 'Rule of Law, Democracy, Openness and Income: Estimating the Interrelationships', *Center for Economic Policy Discussion Paper, No. 4653*.

Rodriguez, F., and D. Rodrik (2000), 'Trade Policy and Economic Growth: A Skeptic's Guide to the Cross-National Evidence', in *NBER Macroeconomics Annual, 2000* edited by Ben Bernanke and Kenneth Rogoff, MIT Press, Massachusetts.

Rodrik, D., and A. Subramanian (2004), 'Why India Can Growth at Seven Percent a Year or More? Projections and Reflections', *Economic and Political Weekly*.

——— (2005), 'From Hindu Growth to Productivity Surge: The Mystery of the Indian Growth Transition', *IMF Staff Papers*, 52(2).

Rodrik, D., A. Subramanian, and F. Trebbi (2004), 'Institutions Rule: The Primacy of Institutions over Geography and Integration in Economic Development', *Journal of Economic Growth*, 9 (June), pp. 131–65.

Sachs, J., and A. Warner (1995), 'Economic reform and the process of global integration', *Brooking Papers on Economic Activity*, 1, pp. 1–118.

Slemrod, J., and W. Kopczuk (2002), 'The Optimal Elasticity of Taxable Income', *Journal of Public Economics*, 84, pp. 91–112.

Verma, A. (2005), 'The Police in India: Design, Performance, and Adaptability', in Devesh Kapur and Pratap Mehta (eds), *Public Institutions in India: Performance and Design*, Oxford University Press, New Delhi.

Wacziarg, R., and K. H. Welch (2003), 'Trade Liberalization and Growth: New Evidence', mimeo, Stanford University.

World Bank (2006), *Doing Business 2007: How to Reform*, World Bank, Washington, D.C.

Summary

The Paradoxes of Institutions in India

The tepid-to-torrid transformation in India's economic growth since 1980 is a big story of recent times. But how are India's institutions faring in the light of this transformation?

While the popular perception in India is one of institutional decline, caution is warranted, in part because India's sheer size and heterogeneity defy easy attempts at generalization. As Joan Robinson famously noted everything and its opposite are guaranteed to be true in India.

To be sure, not all signs point to institutional decline. Certain referee institutions, especially the Supreme Court, the Election Commission, and the Presidency have witnessed rejuvenation. Further, some of the new institutions such as TRAI, SEBI, and IDRA have performed very respectably, especially considering the novelty of the terrain they have had to navigate. The RBI's record in maintaining price stability has been exemplary.

But concerns endure about key institutions—politics, judiciary, bureaucracy, and police—that are vital for a market-based economy to flourish. Law and order is a serious concern, as one in every four districts is home to armed insurgent activity. In state courts, there is a growing backlog of unresolved cases. Weak delivery of essential public services, especially in health, education, and water, is endemic. An illustrative statistic is provided by the tripling of losses in electricity transmission and distribution to 27 per cent between 1971 and the early 2000s, reflecting weak governance at the state level.

Overall, the accountability of core public institutions, especially the political process, tends to be weak and episodic. Democracy does allow a blunt form of accountability—removing incumbents from electoral office—to be exercised at election time. But accountability as threaded into the fabric of daily life remains elusive.

We see rapid economic growth alongside institutional stagnation. This juxtaposition leads to two paradoxes. First, why has growth been accelerating despite institutional stagnation? The second, and deeper, paradox is the mirror image of the first: why, despite twenty-five years of rapid growth, have institutions not improved perceptibly? Consider each in turn.

The conventional view now is that growth owes to the policy reforms begun in the early 1980s which reined in the over-regulating, out-of-control state, thereby unleashing the energy of the private sector. But this cannot be a sufficient explanation, and an international comparison illustrates why. Like India, many countries in Latin America and sub-Saharan Africa have also implemented policy reforms, sometimes broader and deeper than those in India. Yet the growth response in these countries has been feeble compared to India's. What explains this contrast? One answer is that India's institutions, built up through the decades preceding independence, created the conditions for the rapid growth, so that even the relatively modest policy reforms favouring the private sector was an adequate trigger. Our legacy was so good as to provide India with considerable institutional slack. But are we fast using up this slack?

This question naturally leads to the second paradox. As countries grow, political and economic institutions tend to improve. As people become richer, they demand more from their public institutions—better public services, more security and law and order, and greater political participation. But in India, average incomes have risen fourfold and yet institutions may not have improved. Why?

Indeed, this puzzle deepens because over this period India has witnessed a number of developments that should have improved institutions: greater transparency with the explosion in the quality and quantity of the media; the progressive dismantling of the license-quota-permit raj which fostered corruption and patronage; the rise of civil society as a vibrantly assertive presence, striving to hold public institutions and officials accountable; and the unleashing of the dynamic of competition between states, allowing citizens in lagging states to question why they cannot expect the same standards of public institutions and public service delivery as in the more progressive states.

There are many possible explanations to this puzzle. Although growth has accelerated and poverty has declined substantially, divergences have also increased. Some regions and groups have partaken only minimally, if at all, of the fruits of economic growth. It is no coincidence that Naxalite activity is strongest in the tribal belt spread across central and eastern India, feeding on the fertile climate of alienation and disenfranchisement.

Unequal growth also has subtler effects on institutions. If growth is more concentrated at the upper ends of the income spectrum, there is the distinct possibility of 'exit': the rich and influential opt out of the public system, turning to the private sector for essential services, instead of lending their voices to calls for improvement. Examples of such opting out include gated communities with private policing and households with private power generators.

Another contributing factor is the increasing inability of the public sector to attract talent. This too has deeper causes, but clearly one of them is the very rise of the private sector. The unprecedented level of remuneration that the new economy is showering on skilled people is skewing the allocation of talent away from public institutions.

What do these two paradoxes imply for a future reform agenda? Indian policymakers are being nagged to refurbish India's creaking infrastructure, reform its stifling labour laws, and lift barriers to foreign investment. Underlying these calls is the view that the public sector is the problem and the private sector the solution, and that the policy challenge ahead calls for merely rolling back the frontiers of the state and allowing greater freedom for the private sector. This view is understandable given India's dirigiste past; it is also constructive because it allows for new private-sector-based solutions to be explored and found in areas such as basic and higher education that have hitherto been the public sector's exclusive responsibility, but it is also incomplete because it fails to recognize the limits to private sector action. Yes, India needs less government but it also needs much better government in key areas.

Neglecting institutional reform is tempting because institutions are notoriously difficult to change. How does one even think of reforming the Indian bureaucracy or police or judiciary? A starting point has to be the recognition that allowing institutional decline could well come back to haunt even the private sector, whose fortunes depend crucially on effective public institutions. Rehabilitating the institutions bequeathed by Mahatma Gandhi, Pandit Nehru, and others, and not just finding creative ways of working around them, should consume the energies of Midnight's grandchildren.

CHAPTER 4

WHY INDIA CAN GROW AT 7 PER CENT A YEAR OR MORE?
PROJECTIONS AND REFLECTIONS

Among all forms of mistake, prophecy is the most gratuitous.
—George Eliot

India's economic performance during the first three decades since independence was christened the 'Hindu' rate of growth, by the late Professor Raj Krishna of the Delhi School of Economics. The term connoted a disappointing but not disastrous outcome, and played to the cliché of the acquiescence that the religion supposedly inspires, because of a greater emphasis on the hereafter. That cliché has lapsed into disuse thanks to the remarkable transformation in India during the last two decades. Since 1980, its economic growth rate has more than doubled, rising from 1.7 per cent (in per capita terms) in 1950–80 to 3.8 per cent in 1980–2000.

With 'feelgood' all the rage now, economic pundits are in unseemly competition to out-predict each other on India's future economic growth rate. This rush of optimism has many proximate causes, all of which are located in actual or perceived recent success: the rebound in the Indian economy in 2003–4, with expectations of 8 per cent growth; the surge in international reserves and the stock market; and the continuing boom in the IT-sector. The litany of corporate successes compiled and publicized recently by Minister Arun Shourie (2003) has given texture to these successes, confirming that 'feelgood' is not just in the abstract numbers but has flesh and bones.

However, why should recent success translate into permanently higher rates of growth of output in the future? Indeed, one of the cardinal errors of forecasting is to extrapolate the recent past. Moreover, if that is so, what is the economic rationale for optimism about India's future economic prospects? One recent and widely cited 'analysis' pinned these bright prospects on the decline in interest rates (Lall, 2003). Another by Goldman Sachs (2003) invoked favourable demographics in the future as the likely cause of a pick-up in the future growth rate. Each of these analyses is problematic or deficient.

A decline in interest rates can provide some temporary impetus to growth by boosting investment and consumption demand: it can hardly be a basis for sustaining higher trend growth rates of productivity or output per capita. Moreover, it is more-than-ironic that perhaps one of the most vulnerable economic parameters should be isolated as the basis for future growth. While there is a lot that is positive on the economic horizon, the fiscal picture is possibly the most dicey. Declining real interest rates against a background of high and rising deficits is somewhat of a mystery in India's recent economic landscape. Particularly if the fiscal deficit is not addressed, rising rather than declining interest rates are more likely in the future.

The Goldman Sachs analysis identifies favourable demographics in the future as a basis for strong growth. Demographics are clearly an important future trend but their full ramifications are not worked through and the methodology employed is also internally inconsistent. For these reasons, the actual forecast of about 5–5.5 per cent annual growth underestimates, possibly quite considerably, India's true potential.

In this piece, we set out an analytical growth perspective to forecast India's growth. We draw heavily upon our recent paper (Rodrik and Subramanian, 2004) to come up with a central growth forecast, which is about 7 per cent per year for output or 5.6 per cent for per capita output for the next twenty years. We spell out the basis for this forecast, discuss the factors that might make this an underestimate, and also discuss the downside risks. Along the way, we present some remarks on what might be interesting about India's economic future, is unlikely to indulge our whim for prognostication. However, the manner that we arrive at them may nevertheless be of some, residual, interest.

INDIA'S ECONOMIC PERFORMANCE SINCE 1980

Three remarkable features stand out about India's economic performance over the last two decades. First, India experienced very high growth of output per capita at 3.8 per cent per year, surpassed only by China and the East Asian countries (Table 4.1). Second, Indian growth was the most stable, surpassing even China and the East Asian countries. As Table 4.1 shows,

Table 4.1 India in the Cross-section: Mean and Volatility of Growth Rate of Output per Worker, 1960–2000[a]

	1960–70	1970–80	1980–90	1990–2000	1960–80	1980–2000	1960–2000
Industrial Countries							
Mean	4.12	2.12	1.54	1.47	3.12	1.51	2.34
Standard deviation	2.26	2.61	1.98	2.06	2.71	2.08	2.63
Coefficient of variation	0.55	1.23	1.29	1.41	0.87	1.38	1.13
East Asia (incl. China)							
Mean	4.19	4.11	4.15	3.98	4.15	4.07	4.11
Standard deviation	3.99	2.80	3.24	3.91	3.69	3.74	3.98
Coefficient of variation	0.95	0.68	0.78	0.98	0.89	0.92	0.97
China							
Mean	1.66	2.82	6.86	8.85	2.24	7.85	5.05
Standard deviation	12.45	3.40	3.59	2.37	8.90	3.13	7.17
Coefficient of variation	7.50	1.20	0.52	0.27	3.97	0.40	1.42
Latin America							
Mean	2.38	1.69	(1.65)	0.83	2.03	(0.48)	0.81
Standard deviation	3.47	4.00	4.40	3.03	4.07	4.17	4.43
Coefficient of variation	1.46	2.36	(2.66)	3.66	2.00	(8.70)	5.47
India							
Mean	1.91	0.77	3.91	3.22	1.34	3.57	2.45
Standard deviation	3.24	4.16	1.87	2.05	3.68	1.94	3.11
Coefficient of variation	1.69	5.40	0.48	0.64	2.74	0.54	1.27
Africa							
Mean	1.87	0.69	(0.47)	(0.03)	1.28	(0.26)	0.53
Standard deviation	5.41	5.25	4.48	4.48	5.54	4.89	5.55
Coefficient of variation	2.90	7.56	(9.53)	(170.29)	4.33	(18.85)	10.47
Middle East[b]							
Mean	4.61	3.47	1.81	1.19	4.04	1.51	2.81
Standard deviation	5.83	6.64	3.42	2.77	6.55	3.21	5.44
Coefficient of variation	1.26	1.91	1.89	2.33	1.62	2.12	1.94

Source: Bosworth and Collins (2003) and author's calculations.
Note: [a] All regional aggregates are unweighted averages.
[b] Excludes Jordan.

the standard deviation of output per worker was smallest for India. Third, and perhaps the most noteworthy and yet least remarked upon, the contribution of growth of total factor productivity to overall labour

Table 4.2 Contributions to Growth: India in the Cross-section, 1960–99

			Contribution of: (in percentage points)			(in % of total)	
	Output	Output per worker	Physical capital	Education	Factor Productivity	Factor Productivity	Physical Capital
Industrial Countries							
1960–80	4.42	3.05	1.22	1.61	1.30	43	40
1980–99	2.68	1.60	0.78	0.98	0.64	40	49
1960–99	3.57	2.34	1.01	1.30	0.98	42	43
East Asia (incl. China)							
1960–80	5.64	2.98	1.45	1.93	0.96	32	49
1980–99	8.03	6.02	2.44	2.85	3.25	54	41
1960–99	6.80	4.45	1.93	2.38	2.07	46	43
China							
1960–80	4.04	1.83	0.76	0.43	0.64	35	41
1980–99	9.75	7.85	2.63	0.36	4.71	60	33
1960–99	6.78	4.72	1.66	0.39	2.60	55	35
Latin America							
1960–80	6.10	2.90	1.08	1.42	1.45	50	37
1980–99	2.20	–0.54	0.09	0.48	–1.02	189	–17
1960–99	4.18	1.21	0.60	0.96	0.24	20	49
India							
1960–80	3.41	1.28	0.72	0.43	0.12	9	56
1980–99	5.73	3.60	1.18	0.33	2.05	57	33
1960–99	4.53	2.40	0.95	0.38	1.06	44	39
Africa							
1960–80	4.36	1.78	1.06	1.21	0.66	37	59
1980–99	2.02	–0.70	–0.12	0.25	–0.93	134	18
1960–99	3.21	0.57	0.48	0.74	–0.12	–21	85
Middle East							
1960–80	5.71	3.14	2.74	3.25	0.28	9	87
1980–99	3.68	0.85	0.20	0.81	–0.08	–9	23
1960–99	4.71	2.02	1.50	2.0	6 0.	11 5	74

Source: Bosworth and Collins (2003)

productivity growth was the highest in India—about 60 per cent—a performance that was only surpassed by China (Table 4.2). Indian per capita income growth has therefore been extensive—motored by productivity—and hence sustainable in the future, rather than based on deferred gratification, which runs into the limits imposed by diminishing returns to capital.

INDIA BETWEEN 2005–25: A GROWTH ACCOUNTING EXERCISE

What do the next two decades hold for India? To project growth over the next twenty years we adopt a simple growth accounting perspective. Growth depends on the accumulation of factors and the growth in their productivity. The familiar Solow growth accounting equation is

$$y = \alpha k + (1-\alpha)\, l + a$$

where y, k, l, and a represent, respectively, growth in output, capital, labour, and total factor productivity.

We assume a to be equal to 0.35 as in Bosworth and Collins (2003). We next need to project k, l, and a. We assume that total factor productivity will grow at the same pace as in the last two decades that is by about 2.5 per cent per year. We argue below that this might be an underestimation.

What is the rate at which physical capital will accumulate? The answer to this depends primarily on the economic opportunities available and the private returns to investment. We shall argue in the rest of this chapter that the opportunities and returns are likely to remain high, and possibly increase further, in the near future. Moreover, there is every reason to believe that there will be adequate domestic saving to finance capital accumulation without running into an external constraint.

To calculate the 'financeable' growth in physical capital accumulation, we assume that the change in private and hence aggregate savings will be determined over the next two decades by the evolution of the dependency ratio. According to population forecasts, India's dependency ratio will decline from 0.62 in 2000 to 0.48 in 2025. This 14 percentage point decline in the dependency ratio will translate into a roughly equivalent rise in private and aggregate savings, from about 25 per cent of GDP to 39 per cent.[1]

---

[1] This near one-to-one relationship is the result of the analysis of saving behaviour in India by Muhleisen (1997). Note that this ignores any feedback from rising incomes back to savings.

Assuming further that India's borrowing from or lending to the rest of the world remains broadly unchanged during this period, this rising savings would allow an equivalent increase in domestic investment. Simple arithmetic suggests that this translates into a rate of growth of the capital stock of about 8.3 per cent per year in the outer years, up from about 6 per cent currently.[2] This growth in the capital stock together with the growth in factor productivity will yield output growth of 5.4 per cent.

What about growth in human capital and the labour force? Over the next twenty years, the working age population is projected to grow at 1.9 per cent per year. If educational attainment and participation rates remain unchanged, labour growth will contribute another 1.3 per cent, yielding an aggregate growth rate of 6.7 per cent per year, or a per capita growth rate of 5.3 per cent.[3] This is a lower bound estimate and, even so, would be significantly greater than the per capita growth rate of 3.6 per cent achieved in the 1980s and 1990s. Over a forty–year period, a 5.3 per cent growth rate would increase the income of the average person nearly eightfold.

UPSIDE POTENTIAL
Within the TFP Frontier

Many factors suggest that there is upside potential to this forecast. First, TFP growth of 2.5 per cent per year has been achieved with relatively modest reforms, particularly in the 1980s, and there is still unexploited potential. Empirical evidence for this comes from simple regressions of TFP on the deep determinants of development (as in Rodrik et al., 2004). They suggest that India's level of TFP is between 1/3 and 40 per cent of what it should be, creating the scope for productivity improvements based just on catching-up. And as reforms proceed apace, the level and pace of these improvements will be enhanced.

Prospects for TFP-enhancing Reforms

But why should reforms proceed apace? Arguably, the political economy of reforms has changed significantly since the late 1990s. Reforms were crisis-

---

[2] It is important to note that this rapid capital accumulation will not lead to too sharp a reduction in the marginal product of capital because of the simultaneous growth in total factor productivity.

[3] Note that favourable demographics arises from India's labour force growth exceeding population growth by about 0.5 per cent per year.

driven in the early 1990s and for that reason stalled in the mid-1990s as the memory of the crisis receded. Over the last few years, however, there has been a distinct pick-up in the pace of reforms—in telecommunications, electricity, transport, and privatization (see Kelkar, 2004). There is a greater sense than in the past that reforms are delivering tangible results, with the telecommunications revolution being perhaps the best example of benefits flowing to a large cross-section of the population. Reforms are thus going from being crisis-driven to success-driven which makes it more likely that they will be sustained and not be subject to major reversals.

Institutions

Another cause for upside optimism relates to the quality of institutions, which has been India's underrated strength. This is going to be important in several ways. If the recent literature on the role of institutions in determining long-run development is correct, then simple econometric analysis suggests that India remains an underperformer, with a level of income well below what it ought to be. India is far from reaping the benefits of its institutional quality. As shown in Rodrik and Subramanian (2004), the India 'dummy' in regressions of the Acemoglu et al. (2001) and Rodrik et al. (2004) variety suggest that India's per capita income should be about four-to-five times what it currently is. In other words, India, having done the real hard work of building good economic and political institutions— a stable democratic polity, reasonable rule of law and protection of property rights—failed until the 1980s to take advantage of it. Even small changes in policies could help India grow rapidly. Thus, India's growth in the near future (for the next decade at least) will not need fundamental and difficult challenge of overcoming institutional backwardness, but can rely on the easier task of taking advantage of existing institutions. Contrast this, for example, with China which has grown extremely rapidly in the last quarter century, but which faces the inordinate challenge of large-scale institutional transformation.

Another aspect of institutional quality is the resilience it creates to handling shocks. Countries with good institutions do not in general experience large declines in growth (Rodrik, 1999; Acemoglu et al., 2002). With strong institutions, a lot will have to happen to move India off its higher growth trajectory.

Skilled Human Capital

High levels of human capital are a key prerequisite for a developing country to exploit the benefits of technological progress (see Coe et al., 1997). India's stellar productivity growth in the last two decades, and not just in the IT-sector, has benefited from its stock of highly educated human capital. Going forward, this process is likely to be reinforced for at least two reasons. First, the growing location of R&D facilities in India—in pharmaceuticals, software, and other IT-services—by foreign companies will further enhance the scope for dynamic benefits. Second, over the last three–four decades India did not fully reap the benefits of its stock of human capital because a substantial share had moved overseas. This dynamic is changing qualitatively. Cyclical factors such as 9/11 and the economic downturn in the United States have reduced overseas demand for India's human capital.

But there are also structural factors reinforcing this effect—as incomes rise and opportunities grow within India, there is less of a push factor at work. Moreover, technological change means that India can deliver services overseas without its labour having to migrate. The more high skilled labour remains within India, the greater the scope for spillover benefits to the Indian economy. Thus, outsourcing produces a double whammy of benefits—India reaps the static efficiency benefits from the international division of labour without foregoing the dynamic benefits that arise from labour emigration.

In terms of the growth accounting framework sketched above, the growth in the skilled labour force in the future available for domestic activity will be greater than in the past because of less emigration and possibly also because of the return of previously emigrated Indians.

Less-skilled Human Capital

Another factor relates to the contribution of less-skilled labour to growth. The future evolution in participation rates and basic educational attainment remain the two key unknowns. In our base-case estimate, we had assumed that participation rates would remain constant over the next twenty years. Participation rates in India have been stubbornly low despite rising levels of education, which has been something of a mystery. However, if this changes in the future, the impetus to growth could be substantial. For example, a 10 percentage point increase in the participation rate over the next twenty years would add another 0.3–0.4 percentage points to growth rates.

What is the likely trajectory of educational attainment? Amartya Sen has drawn attention to the disappointing post-independence performance of the Indian state in delivering education, reflected in very slow improvements in literacy rates, especially amongst women. While the supply of educational services by the state was inadequate, Sen raised the puzzle as to why there was not greater demand for education and hence greater pressure on the state to meet this demand. One answer to this puzzle is that the private returns to literacy and basic education must have been low. There is now evidence that the increasing opportunities that are spurring economic growth also contribute to raising these returns, leading to a greater demand for educational services—public and private—and hence in educational outcomes (Munshi and Rosenzweig, 2003). In such an event, the potential growth rate could reach as high as 8 per cent.

Downside Risks

Consider the possible objections or downside risks to this forecast.

IT's Impact: Accounting versus Spillovers

Some of the recent growth (since the 1990s) in India has been driven by the explosion of IT-related services. One strand of sceptical thought holds that IT cannot be a long-run source of growth because it currently accounts for such a small share of GDP and employment. One response to this scepticism could refer to demand linkages: if one sector grows, it creates demand for inputs of that sector and at the same time increases incomes, generating demand for the entire economy. Nevertheless, this is not compelling because it runs into the cold logic of accounting: a very small part of the economy will have to grow at impossibly large rates to lift the whole economy.

The more subtle and more persuasive response to the sceptics' concerns relates to the impact that the IT-explosion could have on the economy's long-run supply capacity. It is possible that the IT-explosion, by visibly raising the rewards for being educated, will durably boost the demand for educational services. Anecdotal evidence for this comes from the mushrooming of English-language schools in backward states such as Bihar and the agricultural hinterland of Punjab. Munshi and Rosenzweig (2003) provide systematic evidence from Mumbai on how the increased return to education is leading to expanded school enrolment by women and overhauling traditional caste structures. To be sure, increased demand will relate in the first instance to the acquisition of specific skills (such as fluency in English and computer proficiency). Over time, however, this demand could percolate down the hierarchy of skill, improving basic educational outcomes. According to Sen, this pressure from below was missing in the past, contributing to the rather limited progress in educational outcomes.

Strict devotees of the accounting logic—that small sectors cannot lift the overall economy—also fail to recognize that registered manufacturing played a key role in overall economic performance in the 1980s and 1990s despite accounting for a small share of total output of less than 10 per cent (Rodrik and Subramanian, 2004b). In the case of manufacturing, there may well have been a supply externality at work—the acquisition of managerial and organizational skills in manufacturing could have been beneficially transferred to services. With certain service sectors—finance and telecommunications—similar spillover effects could be generated, leveraging the contribution of these sectors beyond what might be expected given their size.

Divergence

One disturbing trend in the last two decades of rapid growth has been the growing disparity in economic performance between two groups of states (see Table 2 in Rodrik and Subramanian, 2004). Instead of convergence among the states, we see divergence big-time, with peninsular India growing more rapidly than the hinterland BIMARU states. Moreover, in the future, this trend could widen as existing advantages are reinforced by new technologies. A related disparity that the future threatens is between skilled (typically urban) and semi- and low-skilled labour (typically rural) within and across states.

It should be noted that the disparity between states is not only a cause for concern but also the consequence of a very powerful positive dynamic in India: namely, the competition among states to improve institutions and policies—a kind of 'race to the top'—as a means of attracting increased amounts of foreign and domestic capital. For these reasons, it is possible that the divergence is self-limiting—states left behind will be under pressure to follow the demonstration effect of the more successful states or else face the consequences.[4] In an internal market such as India's with free movement of capital and labour, these consequences could be severe. Admittedly, India has not witnessed, yet, the movement of labour commensurate with the growing divergence (Cashin and Sahay, 1996), but capital flows are proving to be more sensitive to state-level policies, and over time inter-state labour flows could also accelerate.

Institutions

As remarked earlier, India's prospects are bright partly because of the quality of its domestic institutions. In terms of economic institutions, India ranks in the fourth decile in a global sample, and in the second decile amongst developing countries. In terms of political institutions, India's ranking is even higher (51st in a sample of 173 countries and 14th in a sample of 84 developing countries). Looking ahead, though, what are the prospects for the maintenance and development of these institutions?

Institutions are a fuzzy concept. Institutions can be defined in terms of the functions they perform—developing markets (rule of law and protection of property rights); regulating markets (correcting market failure); stabilizing markets (central banks, etc.); and legitimizing markets (democracy, redistributive mechanism, social safety nets, etc.). Institutions can also be defined hierarchically: there are meta-institutions such as democracy; the legislature, judiciary; press; and the bureaucracy; and then there are meso-institutions such as the Reserve Bank of India, Telecommunications Regulatory Authority of India, vigilance and election commissions, etc., which have performed reasonably well in recent years.

Are the meta-institutions in healthier shape today than a few decades ago? Even allowing for the distorted prism of nostalgia, few would disagree that the quality of politicians, bureaucrats, and judges, and hence the public roles they served and the institutions they inhabited, were considerably stronger in the first two to three decades after independence. The decline set in thereafter, a process that was aggravated by the rent-seeking that the Kafkaesque system of controls gave rise to. While difficult to quantify, the anecdotal evidence points towards a decline in the quality of all the meta-institutions—the rising levels of pending cases in the state courts, the increase

[4] The attempt by even the most weakly governed states to do road shows abroad to convince investors of the investment-friendly climate attests to this pressure.

in the number of 'political' scandals, and the politicization of the judiciary and the bureaucracy.[5]

There are, however, three countervailing trends that could arrest, perhaps even reverse, the decline in the quality of the meta-institutions in the future. First and foremost, there has been a sharp rise in transparency: public institutions have been exposed to the glare of public scrutiny thanks to the explosion in the quantity and quality of the media. From Godhra to Tehelka, it seems that not much can elude the prying eyes of the press or television. While the accountability of public officials and institutions may not have increased commensurate with the increase in transparency, the disconnect between the two can only narrow in the long run. Second, a vibrantly assertive civil society, becoming one of the new and key meta-institutions, has been one of the positive developments in the last few decades. Indian civil society has taken on at least two roles: a direct one, in delivering development outcomes and indirect one by striving to hold public institutions accountable. Third, policy liberalization will progressively erode the license-quota-permit raj as a source of corruption and patronage that has had such a corrosive effect on public institutions.

Agriculture

The conventional wisdom is that India is still beholden to the monsoon for its overall economic performance because agriculture accounts for a large share of GDP. Of course, a series of droughts could yet drag down the Indian growth trajectory. However, the inexorable logic of development, and the experience of the last two decades, shows that the hold of agriculture has declined sharply. Between 1980 and 2000, agriculture's share in GDP has declined by 16 percentage points to about 22 per cent. Another twenty-five years of growth along the lines of the 1990s will shrink the share of agriculture to about 12 per cent, further reducing its grip on the economy.

Fiscal Situation

Large and widening deficits and the attendant explosion in public indebtedness pose a threat to future stability and growth. India's government debt-to-GDP ratio, at about 90 per cent, exceeds that of many of the other

---

[5] However, the performance of the election commission and the success of important public interest litigation initiatives suggest that all is not gloomy even in relation to meta-institutions.

emerging market countries, including Brazil and Argentina. Yet, the sense of risk or imminent crisis has not been as acute for India in part because a much larger fraction of debt is held by residents than in these countries. Even so, it is puzzling that rising indebtedness has been accompanied in recent years by foreign capital inflows and *declining* real interest rates. Of course, markets, given their notoriously procyclical proclivities, be understating the risks, with this being the boom phase of the bust that might follow. However, it is worth noting that part of this apparent market sanguineness could stem from a confidence in Indian creditworthiness, which is in turn based on an unblemished record of no-default and low inflation (which is, after all, expropriation by other means). As Reinhart et al. (2003) show, markets set different debt thresholds for different countries, with lower levels set for countries with past records of high inflation or default. The relatively large slack that markets appear to have cut for India may therefore be grounded in the institutional checks in India against instability and expropriation.

India and China *en passant*

Much has been made of the contrasts and similarities between the recent economic performance of India and China. Some of the motivation for this is plain silly, rooted in a martial conception of economics, and portraying India and China as in some zero-sum game rivalry. Economic growth in China and India and increasing trade by and between them will, of course, be mutually beneficial and positively reinforcing. But there is one interesting contrast that is relevant (and one that has not been made so far) for their future economic trajectories.

Table 4.3 presents a simple regression of income on its deep determinants (institutions, geography, and openness) with China and India dummies added. The really noteworthy difference is that in 1999 India was an underperformer and China an overperformer given the underlying quality of their institutions, with the disparity especially pronounced in relation to political institutions. What this means is that India's future growth for a long period of time will be relatively 'easy' because it will involve a regression or a reversion to the mean.[6] China, on the other hand, has the considerably

[6] India will be merely reverting to the mean, that is realizing already-created potential, until its current level of income quadruples, which at a per capita growth rate of 5.3 per cent per year will take about 25 years.

Table 4.3: How Far are India and China from their Income Possibility Frontier, 1999

	Rule of law	Political voice
India dummy	−1.33	−1.28]
	−4.92	−5.94
China dummy	0.02	1.05
	0.09	3.21
Number of observations	114	114

Note: T-statistics below coefficient estimates.

harder task of having to grow in the future by building its economic and political institutions and having to cope with the shocks that that process will entail. Its property regime needs to be improved and its legal system made more transparent. China's economic performance has been running way ahead of its underlying institutional realities, and is therefore arguably more fragile than India's on that account.

CONCLUSION

Economic development results from the interaction of growth triggers with the right fundamentals that allow the triggers to be exploited. In the conventional view of the Indian development process, there was a long and dark period—the period of controls and import substitution—followed by the burst of sunlight and reforms since 1991. The boom in the IT-sector first awakened observers to the fact that the dark age was not all dark, that important cumulative elements (the fundamentals) were being built up that yielded rewards with a lag, and that these fundamentals were as important as the triggers that sparked the IT boom. In this case, the fundamentals were the pools of skilled human capital built through the technology, management, and research institutes—a sort of import substitution effort in skilled human capital development—that were integral to the Nehruvian vision.

Nevertheless, the Nehruvian economic legacy went beyond the technical institutions: it consisted of the meta-institutions of democracy, rule of law, free press, and technocratic bureaucracy that recent research shows are crucial to economic development. To be sure, these meta-institutions have been buffeted and weakened by the vicissitudes of vested interests, time, and politics. It is also true that the potential created by these institutions went unexploited through decades of misguided throttling of private economic activity. Since the 1980s, the shackles on the private sector have been slowly removed, and the appropriate triggers are now in place. The house that Nehru and others painstakingly built before and immediately after independence, wobbles and all, is now well poised to seize the newly created opportunities.

By the same token, it is important for India to avoid the mistakes that Latin America made in the 1990s by hastily embarking on an overly ambitious agenda of economic liberalization and privatization that runs ahead of the supporting institutions or the productive ability of the economy. Economic growth is best sustained by keeping the private sector excited about investing in the local economy. This requires a pragmatic set of policies towards the private sector that combine carrots with sticks, incentives for dynamic efficiency with market disciplines. The knee-jerk reaction of many economists to move as quickly and as broadly as possible in areas such as privatization (especially in infrastructure sectors), labour market reform, and capital-account liberalization has to be tempered with serious empirical analysis and an appropriate concern for social and distributional impacts. The habitual pragmatism and gradualism of Indian policymaking, dictated by the need to manage pluralism and diversity—the organizing principle of the 'idea of India'—is here more an asset than a liability.

REFERENCES

Acemoglu, D., S. Johnson, and J. A. Robinson (2001), 'The Colonial Origins of Comparative Development: An Empirical Investigation', *American Economic Review*, 91(5), pp. 1369–401.

Acemoglu, D., S. Johnson, J. Robinson, and Y. Thaicaroen (2002), Institutional Causes, Macroeconomic Symptoms: Volatility, Crises and Growth, *Journal of Monetary Economics*, Carnegie-Rochester Conference Series.

Bosworth, B., and S. Collins (2003), 'The Empirics of Growth: An Update', mimeo, Brookings Institution.

Cashin, P., and R. Sahay (1996), 'Internal Migration, Center-State Grants and Economic Growth in the States of India', *IMF Staff Papers*, 43, pp. 123–71.

Coe, D., E. Helpman, and A. Hoffmaister (1997), 'North-South R&D Spillovers', *Economic Journal*, 107, pp. 134–49.

Goldman Sachs (2003), 'Dreaming with BRICs: The Path to 2050', *Global Economics Paper No. 99*.

Kelkar, V. (2004), 'India: On the Growth Turnpike,' K.R. Narayanan Memorial Lecture, University of Adelaide, Australia.

Lall, R. (2003), 'India Can Outperform China by '08', *Business Standard*, August 9.

Muhleisen, M. (1997), 'Improving India's Savings Performance', *IMF Working Paper No. 97/4*, International Monetary Fund, Washington.

Munshi, K., and M. Rosenzweig (2003), 'Traditional Institutions Meet the Modern World: Caste, Gender and Schooling Choice in a Globalizing Economy', *BREAD Working Paper No. 038*.

Reinhart, C., K. Rogoff, and M. Savastano (2003), 'Debt Intolerance', *National Bureau of Economic Research Working Paper No. 9908*.

Rodrik, D. (1999), 'Where Did All the Growth Go? External Shocks, Social Conflict, and Growth Collapses', *Journal Of Economic Growth*, 4, pp. 385–412.

Rodrik, D., and A. Subramanian (2004b), 'From Hindu Growth to Productivity Surge: The Mystery of the Indian Growth Transition', *National Bureau of Economic Research Paper, No. 10376*.

Rodrik, D., A. Subramanian, and F. Trebbi (2004), 'Institutions Rule: The Primacy of Institutions Over Integration and Geography in Development', *Journal of Economic Growth*.

Shourie, A. (2003), 'Before the Whining Drowns it Out, Listen to the New India', August 15, http://www.indianexpress.com/full_ story.php?content_id=29666.

SUMMARY

The Next Two Decades of the Indian Economy

What do the next two decades hold for India? 'Feelgood' seems to be the current answer. This has many proximate causes, all located in recent success: the rebound in the Indian economy in 2003/04, with expectations of 8 per cent growth; the surge in international reserves and the stock market; and the continuing boom in the IT-sector. The litany of corporate successes compiled and publicized by Minister Arun Shourie has given texture to these successes, confirming that 'feelgood' is not just in the abstract numbers but has flesh and bones.

However, why should recent success translate into permanently higher rates of growth of output in the future? Indeed, one of the cardinal errors of forecasting is to extrapolate the recent past. Are there structural reasons to believe that India is indeed on a permanently higher growth path?

In a paper in the *EPW*[1], we argue that there are good underlying reasons for expecting India's output to grow at close to 7 per cent a year, which implies a per capita output growth of about 5.5 per cent a year. At this rate, the income of the average Indian would increase 8–fold over a forty year period compared with the fourfold increase that current growth rates would deliver.

This optimistic forecast is based on three key features of the Indian economy: productivity, demographics, and institutions. The downside risks stem mainly from the disparities that are being created by the current pattern of growth. And the joker in the pack—that will determine both the upside potential and the downside risks—is progress in primary education. Consider each.

In general, growth motored by accumulating capital runs into limits imposed by diminishing returns. On the other hand, growth motored by productivity is sustainable in the future. A key aspect of India's recent performance has been the high contribution of productivity—about 60 per cent—to overall growth, a performance that has only been surpassed by China. Recent productivity performance can be expected to continue in the future, and even accelerate, because of the improved prospects for reforms. There is a greater sense than in the past that reforms are delivering tangible results, with the telecommunications revolution being perhaps the best example of benefits flowing to a large cross-section of the population. Reforms are thus going from being crisis-driven to success-driven which makes it more likely that they will be sustained and not be subject to major reversals. Productivity growth will also benefit from the interaction between India's talent pool of high-skilled labour and the attractiveness of India as a location for R&D creation.

---

[1] Subramanian, A. and D. Rodrik, 'Why India Can Grow at 7 per cent a Year or More Projections and Reflection', *Economic and Political Weekly*, Vol. 39, No. 16, pp. 1591–96, April 17–23.

Demographics represent the second source of optimism. Over the next twenty years, India's dependency rate will decline sharply as its labour force grows faster than population. Declining dependency can be expected to raise domestic savings rates by upto 12–15 percentage points. Provided the opportunities for the private sector continue to expand, increased savings can finance more rapid capital accumulation, contributing to an acceleration in output.

Another cause for upside optimism relates to the quality of institutions, which has been India's under-rated strength. Experience around the world increasingly points to the importance of institutions that affect the rule of law and protection of property rights and opportunities for participation as a key determinant of long-run development.

Our analysis suggests that India is far from reaping the benefits of its institutional quality. India's per capita income should be about four to five times what it currently is. In other words, India, having done the really hard work of building good economic and political institutions failed until the 1980s, to take advantage of it. Thus, India's growth in the near future will not face the fundamental and difficult challenge of overcoming institutional backwardness, but can rely on the easier task of taking advantage of existing institutions. Contrast this, for example, with China which has grown extremely rapidly in the last quarter century, but which faces the inordinate challenge of large-scale institutional transformation.

But will India's institutions hold up in the future? Three encouraging trends can be discerned. First and foremost, there has been a sharp rise in transparency: public institutions have been exposed to the glare of public scrutiny thanks to the explosion in the quantity and quality of the media. From Godhra to Tehelka, it seems that not much can elude the prying eyes of the press or television. While the accountability of public officials and institutions may not have increased commensurate with the increase in transparency, the disconnect between the two can only narrow in the long run.

Second, a vibrantly assertive civil society, becoming one of the new and key meta-institutions, has been one of the positive developments in the last few decades. Indian civil society has taken on at least two roles: a direct one, in delivering development outcomes and indirect one by striving to hold public institutions accountable. Third, policy liberalization will progressively erode the license-quota-permit raj as a source of corruption and patronage that has had such a corrosive effect on public institutions.

What then are the downside risks to this optimistic outlook? One disturbing trend in the last two decades of rapid growth has been the growing disparity in economic performance between states. States that were rich in 1980 have grown faster than states that were poor, accentuating existing inequalities. Peninsular India has been growing more rapidly than the hinterland BIMARU states.

While the disparity between states is a cause for concern it is also the consequence of a very powerful positive dynamic in India: namely, the competition among states to improve institutions and policies—a kind of 'race to the top'—as a means of attracting increased amounts of foreign and domestic capital. For these reasons, it is possible that the divergence is self-limiting—states left behind will be under pressure to follow the demonstration effect of the more successful states or else face the consequences. In an internal market such as India's with free movement of capital and labour, these consequences could be severe. Admittedly, India has not witnessed, yet, the movement of labour commensurate with the growing divergence but capital flows are proving to be more sensitive to state-level policies, and over time inter-state labour flows could also accelerate.

Perhaps a more worrying disparity is between skill levels, with new technologies creating large wedges between a small proportion of highly skilled (typically urban) people a vast majority of less-skilled (typically rural). Certain metropolises are already witnessing the phenomenon of islands of dollar-salaried populations embarrassingly embedded in a sea of ordinariness or even poverty. Managing this disparity will be one of the major challenges for India in the years ahead. Success in this effort will depend to a large extent on what we referred to earlier as the joker in the pack—the progress that India will make in improving basic education.

The Nobel winner, Amartya Sen, has drawn attention to the disappointing post-independence performance of the Indian state in delivering education, reflected in very slow improvements in literacy rates, especially amongst women. While the supply of educational services by the state was inadequate, Sen raised the puzzle as to why there was not greater *demand* for education and hence greater pressure on the state to meet this demand. One answer to this puzzle is that the private returns to literacy and basic education must have been low.

This state of affairs may be changing now. There is evidence that the increasing opportunities that are spurring economic growth—related to the IT-explosion—contribute to raising these returns, leading to a greater demand for educational services—public and private—and hence in educational outcomes. Anecdotal evidence for this comes from the mushrooming of English-language schools in backward states such as Bihar and the agricultural hinterland of Punjab. Evidence is now available from Mumbai on how the increased returns to education is leading to expanded school enrolment by women and overhauling traditional caste structures.

To be sure, increased demand will relate in the first instance to the acquisition of specific skills (such as fluency in English and computer proficiency). Over time, however, this demand could percolate down the hierarchy of skill, improving basic educational outcomes. But this is more hope than firm prediction, and on realizing this hope will hinge how fast and broad-based will be India's future economic growth.

So what lessons do we learn for the future from studying India's recent economic history? It seems more clear now that economic development results from the interaction of growth triggers with the right fundamentals that allow the triggers to be exploited. In the conventional view of the Indian development process, there was a long and dark period—the period of controls and import substitution—followed by the burst of sunlight and reforms since 1991. The boom in the IT-sector first awakened observers to the fact that the dark age was not all dark, that important cumulative elements (the fundamentals) were being built up that yielded rewards with a lag, and that these fundamentals were as important as the triggers that sparked the IT boom. In this case, the fundamentals were the pools of skilled human capital built through the technology, management, and research institutes—a sort of import substitution effort in skilled human capital development— that were integral to the Nehruvian vision.

Nevertheless, the Nehruvian economic legacy went beyond the technical institutions: it consisted of the meta-institutions of democracy, rule of law, free press, and technocratic bureaucracy that recent research shows are crucial to economic development. To be sure, these meta-institutions have been buffeted and weakened over time by the vicissitudes of vested interests, time, and politics. It is also true that the potential created by these institutions went unexploited through decades of misguided throttling of private economic activity. Since the 1980s, the shackles on the private sector have been slowly removed, and the appropriate triggers are now in place. The house that Nehru and others painstakingly built before and immediately after independence, wobbles and all, is now well poised to seize the newly created opportunities.

Section II

INDIA'S GLOBALIZATION

CHAPTER 5

URUGUAY ROUND TEXT IN PERSPECTIVE

In the past months, the Text presented by Arthur Dunkel, director-general of the GATT secretariat in Geneva, has attracted considerable attention in India. Strong criticisms of the provisions of this Text (hereafter referred to as the Text) have come from several quarters, including from some members of the ruling Congress(I). The fact of the furore is a welcome development reflecting keen public involvement in important policy areas. But it is imperative that any ensuing debate be based on the contents of the Text rather than on attributions, many of which are factually erroneous or founded on unjustified apprehension. An objective of this note is to clarify some of these attributions reported in the Indian press which if unchallenged and by virtue of repetition, risk attaining the status of truth. Another objective is to raise issues which ought to inform any sober assessment of any response to the Text. There may be a need to recognize, unpalatable though that is, the limits of the achievements possible, and to contemplate the consequences under alternative scenarios.

The first section of this chapter addresses some general points, and the second section considers the criticisms of the provision contained in certain sections of the Text namely, TRIPS, TRIMS, textiles, agriculture, the balance-of-payments (BOPs) provisions, and the provision on dispute settlement.

GENERAL CONSIDERATIONS

The first point to clarify is that copyright for the Text has been conferred on the wrong party: contrary to the impression conveyed by the label being bandied about (Dunkel Draft Text), a large portion of the Text is the result of nearly seven years of negotiations between the 100 plus countries, including India and 75 other developing countries, participating in the Uruguay Round. Only a relatively few provisions—in areas where outstanding differences could not be reconciled by the countries themselves—have been drafted by chairmen of the different negotiating groups based on their assessment of a possible compromise. Second, give-and-take is the very stuff of any international negotiation; individual countries will have to give up something in return for what they seek; and in general, international treaties of the type contained in the Text (or embodied in the GATT) will necessarily involve some loss of freedom of choice for the countries involved, whether developed or developing. Ultimately, the decision to accept a multilateral treaty should not be based only on considerations of sovereignty, but on an assessment of the costs and benefits of joining and, as important, of not joining the treaty.

As a prelude to making the assessment mentioned above, it would be worth examining the objective circumstances—the constraints and opportunities—facing India in the context of the negotiations ('For every Text a context' to quote Rushdie in another context). In India there is a strong perception of commonality of interests and positions amongst developing countries carried over from the days of north–south confrontations. Critics glide effortlessly between India and developing countries as though they were interchangeable. But no effort is wasted in bringing home the reality that the old south has fallen apart. In recent times the prospect of preferential access to the North American market has lulled or lured Latin America into acquiescence. South-east Asia was always more concerned with trade-peace even if it came with some strings attached; not for it posturing and striding the world's political stage if it meant forsaken exports. And the sweeping winds of liberal economic policy in large parts of the world have blown the apart the ideology of protectionism on which tenuous southern solidarity in the GATT was in part founded. It might be comforting to believe that the fragmentation of the south is a case of desertion under pressure. But that is not, a total nor a fair explanation. The cause of southern solidarity itself has been questioned.

The lack of southern solidarity manifested itself in the Uruguay Round negotiations. Take the three areas—Textiles, TRIPS, and Agriculture—where India's concerns were particularly acute. Ranged against India in its quest for greater access in the area of textiles were the importing—countries the Canada, EC, and United States—together accounting for dominant share of world textile imports. But what about the combined weight of the textile exporting developing countries one might ask? The portrayal of concerted pressure for liberalization from developing country exporters is largely a myth. Only India and Pakistan were credibly insistent on a speedier dismantling of the MFA. When it came to the crunch, other developing country exporters plumped for security of access (code word for guaranteed quotas) rather than a truly non-discriminatory open system of textile trade.

In agriculture too, the coalition (the Crain's Group), pressing for the liberalization of trade and reductions in subsidies which are causing discomfiture in India, is constituted by developed and several developing countries.

In TRIPS, a north–south issue if there ever was one, a large number of developing countries, had even prior to tabling of the Text and pursuant to bilateral negotiations, conceded to the demands being made. In the multilateral context, India faced a daunting unified north without any real support from its natural constituency—other developing countries. Despite these odds, however, the results embodied in TRIPS represent a significant 'achievement' when viewed in the light of the significantly greater obligations that have been thrust upon several developing countries under bilateral agreements, including most recently upon China.

It is one of those predictable ironies that disgruntlement in India at under-achievement in the Uruguay Round is matched by resentment elsewhere at India's perceived over-achievement. The fact that India has done well disproportionately 'well' is acknowledged albeit grudgingly in informed circles and a reading of the Western press makes that clear. Also how can a country which accounts for less than 0.5 per cent of the world trade command so much influence in trade negotiations is the bewildered lament of many an observer.

Aggrieved critics in India, however continue to clamour for a renegotiation of the Text in India's favour, apparently unmindful of the possibility that India, in the negotiating context described earlier, may perhaps have exhausted its substantive negotiating options. In any case, for countries such as India whose influence and clout is—by virtue of its relatively small weight in the international economy—limited, reopening the Text, if others do not do so, may not be a credible option. It is also clear that any call by India to re-open the Text will be greeted with little sympathy from several developing countries which have come out openly in favour of it adoption.

Another option suggested by the critics is that India should only accept selected agreements in the Text. But the Text, warts and all, is on offer as one single package: the pick and choose option is simply unavailable. But the choice facing India is starker than acceptance or rejection of the Text per se. The larger decision is whether to participate in or opt out of what is going to be (provided the United States and European community can resolve their differences to allow a conclusion of the Uruguay Round) a unified international trading system superseding the current GATT system. The costs and benefits of rejecting the Text will have to be evaluated on this premise.

One important component of the costs of opting out would be to forsake the positive elements of the Uruguay Round package. In the area of market access, India would not benefit from the low tariffs that are likely to emerge at the end of the Round. In the area of anti-dumping, subsidies, and countervailing measures, India would not benefit from the new disciplines on the users of these measures and the various concessions granted to developing countries. Even the improved access in textiles and clothing inadequate though it seems, would be denied, and India would have to negotiate terms bilaterally and outside the MFA and GATT process. It strains credulity to imagine better results for India in a bilateral context. In the agreement on services, there is a clear recognition, for the first time, that the temporary movement of labour should be subject of international commitment which would allow India (perhaps not immediately) to reap its comparative advantage in this area. A second important, and less recognized, component of the costs of stating out would be the loss of benefits and privileges that the GATT system offers even as it stands. India's trading partners would be relieved of any obligation that the system currently imposes: even India's basic MFN rights—to be treated as well as any other country in the market of its trading partners—would be voided of value. A third consideration relates to India's new role in the emerging international economic order. As a country committing itself to integration with the world economy and whose reliance on foreign markets is and will be critical to its economic performance, India has now more that ever before, and aggressive stake in the preservation of a multilateral non-discriminatory trading system. It has an active stake in forestalling the threat of regionalism under which India is likely to be discriminated against. That a large number of countries are attempting to enter GATT's door—about thirty with varying degrees of loudness—suggests that the benefits conferred by the multilateral system are not to be scoffed at.

Presumably, critics who argue for staying out have in mind the avoidance of the perceived costs of the Text and here TRIPS looms large in the collective consciousness. But would these costs really be avoided? Special 301 dangles Damocles-like above India. Not only would it fall on India if it opted out but is also likely that our inevitable submission would be on terms more disadvantageous than those on offer in the Text. This is not dire speculation. China considered to have at least as much if not more political and economic clout than India, has accepted terms more adverse that those in the Text under its agreement with the United States on intellectual property. An isolated India, outside a multilateral consensus, cannot count on the support of allies to counter the unfettered use of political muscle by the larger trading partners. Quasi-legitimacy would be conferred on actions against India or any others which stand out even if such actions may be formally in contravention of international trade rules. Bearing these considerations in mind we turn to some specific agreements in the Text.

SPECIFIC AGREEMENTS

Trade-related Investment Measures

Several allegations have been made against the TRIMS agreement contained in the Text. Apparently, it seeks the removal of all TRIMS within a period of five years; it prevents the imposition of any performance clauses on foreign investors in respect of earnings of foreign exchange; foreign equity participation and for transfer of technology it requires foreign companies to be treated on par with or even better than local companies; it prevents the imposition of restrictions on areas of investment and it requires the free import or raw materials, components, and intermediates. In short, free rein for foreign investment.

Each of theses allegations is factually erroneous. The TRIMS agreement does not prevent the imposition of any of the following performance requirements on companies, whether foreign or local; export performance, manufacturing (the requirement that components and inputs be locally manufactured), transfer of technology, minimum local equity, licensing (the restrictions placed on the remittance of foreign exchange). Furthermore, there are no curbs on India stipulating which sectors in the area of good may or may not receive foreign investment. Another important misunderstanding relates to the 'national treatment' obligation; several commentators have read into this requirement to treat foreign companies on par with local companies, of locally produced goods over imported goods. The right to regulate foreign companies, including the imposition of stricter requirement on foreign companies, has in no way been curtailed under the TRIMS agreement.

In the past, several developing countries have favoured locally produced goods in the form of local constant requirements. The Indian 'avatar' of this, the phased manufacturing programme (PMP), is soon to be done away with, this decision having been taken unilaterally and in advance of the TRIMS negotiations. Thus, the national treatment obligation under the TRIMS agreement would prevent a course of action, which in any case India has decided to eschew. The second obligation or discipline under the TRIMS agreement related to the prohibition of the trade balancing requirement and its variant, the foreign exchange balancing requirement. These require, respectively, that companies may import, or have access to foreign exchange for this purpose, only to the extent of or in some way related to the amount of their exports. The TRIMS agreement would not require the phasing out of theses trade-balancing measures if there are grounds such as adverse BoPs circumstances to justify their use. India has in the past availed of this possibility and could do so if the BoPs situation continues to remain adverse.

In short, TRIMS would be and large preserve the *status quo ante* as far as the regulation of foreign investment goes. The only area that it would regulate—preventing the preferential treatment of locally purchased goods—is one where India has chosen to regulate itself.

Trade-related Intellectual Property Rights

Reactions to the TRIPS agreement have been unfavourable, but it is imperative to weed out those which have been based on a misreading of the text from others which may be warranted, chief among which is the galling unfairness of developing countries having to institute a system of intellectual property protection which most developed countries at a comparable stage of development did not have to. Take first the long-term patent regime as it would emerge consequent upon the TRIPS agreement.

It is true that product and process protection would have to be provided in all areas of technology except for plants and animals and microbiological processes. Plant varieties would have to be protected through either a patent system or an alternative *sui generis* system, which is generally understood to be one along the lines of UPOV Convention (International Convention for the Protection of New Varieties and Plants). The duration of patent protection would have to be twenty years. It is incorrect to say that compulsory licenses would be disallowed altogether or permitted only in the case of a national emergency. Compulsory licenses can continue to be granted under the new regime except in the important case where a patent owner fails to work the patent locally (Article 27.1). Compulsory licensing as surrogate price control or as a remedy for any abuse by the patentee would not be disallowed. However, compulsory licensing would be subject to the fulfilment of certain conditions, such as the requirement in Article 31(b) that efforts be made by a firm to obtain a voluntary license from the patentee on reasonable terms and conditions, which would certainly render its use a little more difficult.

In the long run an effective way for India to ensure that the compulsory licensing provisions in the TRIPS agreement will not be over-restrictive is to put in place an effective system of *competition law* under which standards for abuses of patent rights including excessive high prices and other restrictive practices can be defined to the advantage of the technology-importing country. The TRIPS agreement generally leaves outside its scope matters relating to competition policy and importantly has less stringent conditions attached to compulsory licenses granted to remedy anti-competitive practice, so that the flexibility necessary to mitigate the effects of patenting which is taken away by the provisions in the TRIPS agreement could be achieved through the competition law route. Several Latin American countries are contemplating the same approach in order to reduce the costs of the stricter patent regime embodied in the TRIPS agreement. This would be in keeping with the current thinking in India to replace the MRTP Act with an effective competition law.

Turning to the transitional arrangements in the area of crucial importance—pharmaceuticals—it is true that the ten-year transition period for the introduction of product patents in this area should be seen in conjunction with the provision which requires that all inventions for which patent applications are filed after 1993 anywhere in the world (of TRIPS signatories) would have to be protected. However, since these inventions will only start coming onto the market on average after ten to twelve years (this being the period for obtaining marketing approval), the first economic effects of the

TRIPS agreement will be felt in the year 2003–5, which is the time that the obligation to grant patents would kick in. But it is erroneous to argue that after 1 January 1993 no new products can be introduced on the market. In fact during the transition period all inventions for which applications have been filed before 1993 can be reverse engineered and put on the market.

The fact that these provisions would impose significant cost is perhaps unarguable. It would be dishonest to pretend otherwise. But the failure to mould a regime more suited to Indian interests is a reflection of the real politics of international economic relations. For one, a regime of the kind found in the TRIPS agreement has been vigorously sought by nearly all the industrialized countries—the United States, the EEC, Japan, Switzerland, EFTA countries, Canada, and so on. For another, resistance to such a regime has been systematically whittled down through, inter alia, the use of bilateral pressure under instruments such as Special 301. A host of developing countries—Brazil, Argentina, Mexico, Chile, the ANDEAN Pact, several Eastern European Countries, Korea, Singapore, Thailand, Indonesia, and the Philippines—have already put into place (or are in the process of putting in place) a long-term patent regime similar to or in several respects more onerous than that envisaged under the TRIPS agreement. Nearly all these countries have also agreed to transitional agreements which effectively amount to providing protection for pharmaceutical product inventions, for which patent applications were filed after 1983 or 1984. The Text would avoid, for India, the nine to ten years of additional protection that many countries have already agreed to pursuant to bilateral pressures. Significant in this regard is the recent US–China agreement on intellectual property under which (the West's cuddly communists) whose negotiating leverage is considered considerable, has agreed to provide protection for *all* patents granted after 1986, which is equivalent to granting protection to all patent applications filed after 1984 or 1985.

Agriculture

In agriculture, the Text imposes disciplines in the three areas: domestic support (broadly internal domestic measures providing assistance to *production*), export competition, and market access (which relates to measures taken at the border). These disciplines do not take the form of a prohibition on the use of subsidies. The critics incorrectly allege subsidies, including those foe seeds, irrigation, power; fertilizers, pesticides, and credit are prohibited by the Text. Below we examine which subsidies are regulated at all and to what extent.

One kind of domestic subsidy that the text does not impinge on is consumer subsidies. There is, therefore, no reason to believe or fear that the sale of agricultural products at below-market prices through fair-price shops—a consumer subsidy—which is an important aspect of India's public distribution system, would be affected. Furthermore, there is no commitment regarding budgetary payment, such as storage or other infrastructural costs incurred by the Food Corporation of India in its market price support programme.

The Text also lists a number of agricultural policies (the so-called 'green box') which countries need not reduce and which cannot be the subject of countervailing measures in foreign markets. The remaining measures would be subject to different disciplines depending on which of the three categories mentioned above they fall under. But what would these disciplines be in general, and what dispensation would be available for India as part of special and differential or more favourable (S & D) treatment for developing countries?

First, where as all countries have to reduce their domestic support (excluding those which need not be reduced by virtue of qualifying for the green box) if it were in excess of 5 per cent of the total value of production, India's reduction commitments would kick in only for values greater than 10 per cent.

Second, even if domestic support measures did exceed the threshold 10 per cent, they would have to be reduced in either absolute US$ or domestic currency terms (whichever is selected by the country concerned) by 13.3 per cent over ten years, whereas developed countries' commitment would be a reduction of 20 per cent over six years.

Third, support measures, such as investment subsidies generally available to agriculture, and agricultural input subsidies (in cash or kind) made available to low income or resource poor producers on the basis of clear and objective criteria, used by developing countries would not have to be reduced. Developed countries would not have this possibility.

Finally, in relation to the commitments on border measures, whereas developed countries would have to reduce tariffs by 36 per cent over six years (with a minimum reduction of 15 per cent for each tariff line), developing countries tariff reduction would have to amount to 24 per cent over ten years. Furthermore, developing countries could choose the level of tariff from which the reduction would be calculated for products for which unbound tariffs are at the moment the sole means of providing border protection.

Thus, contrary to the impression that has been conveyed, there is an important S & D or favourable element in the Text, in the sense of fewer commitments for developing than for developed countries. Admittedly, this is not as far reaching as the S & D element for the least-developed countries, which do not have to undertake any reduction commitments.

All this is at the level of principle: what would this imply for the existing system of agricultural policy in India? Actually what changes would be required? Would there be any straitjacketing? Calculations show that India's domestic support measure [the Aggregate Measure of Support (AMS)] in products such as rice, wheat, soybean, gram, and meat bovine animals are all well below the threshold level of 10 per cent; they are generally negative for wheat and rice, which are important items of the public distribution programme. In other words, measures directed at these products need not be reduced; there is even leeway to increase the support for these products. This is also the case for products such as groundnut and sugar where preliminary annual estimates show that the relevant support measure to be positive but less that 10 per cent.

And even the minimum access commitments (the guarantee that a certain minimum proportion of domestic consumption should be constituted by imports when non-tariff measures are converted to tariffs), which some fear would flood India's market with imports do not have to be undertaken by India because of the right it currently enjoys to maintain trade-restrictive measures on BoP grounds. Critics appear, mistakenly, to rule out this possibility.

Textiles

The Agreement on Textiles and Clothing provides for, among other aspects, a process for integrating this sector into the GATT in three stages, culminating in full integration by January 2003. It is true that the integration of products of interest to India may take place only during the later phase of the programme. However, the agreement does provide relatively greater market access in products that do remain outside the GATT. For these products, the agreement carries of the growth and flexibility for the MFA, and also provides that these growth rates will be progressively increased by 16 per cent in1993, by a further 25 per cent in 1996, and by a further 27 per cent in 2000. For example, an annual 6 per cent growth rate on MFA restrictions in 1992 will become 7 per cent during 1993–5, 8.7 per cent during 1996–9, and 11 per cent during 2000–2. By specifying the increase in growth rates, the agreement removes the arbitrary manner in which export quota growth rates were fixed under the MFA, where bilateral negotiations often led to a low rate of increase in export quotas. The gains may well be marginal and far short of India's needs or expectations but the negotiating context in textiles described earlier did not appear to render possible a more ambitious outcome.

Balance-of-Payment Provisions

Several critics have argued that one of the basic privileges of developing countries in the GATT system, namely, the right to take restrictive import measures for balance of payment purposes, has been virtually withdrawn which is reflected in the provisions contained in the Text on Articles XVIII:B. But this is not an appropriate characterization. It is true that the Text seeks to impose greater discipline on the use of quantitative restrictions (QRs) which would apply especially to new QRs and to the system of discretionary licensing. Here again, in the light of India's decision to do away with such measures independently of the Uruguay Round process, the Text will not impose and additional burden. It is important to note that even the new disciplines on QRs, in the event that India were to resort again to their use, are neither absolute nor rigid. A country may still have resource to the provided a case can be made for their necessity and appropriateness. The Text also legitimizes explicitly the right to breach, on BoP grounds, any commitment on tariffs or other price-based measures. Thus the thrust of the Text in this area is to favour the use of price-based measures while disciplining the use of QRs, a direction in which the government seems to be moving in any case.

Cross-retaliation

The possibility of cross-retaliation provided in the dispute settlement provisions of the Text under which failure to respect obligations in one sector, say TRIPS, can legitimately invite retaliation in another sector, say goods, has evoked strong sentiment. Some regard it as a legitimization and universalization of Section 301 of US trade law; to another commentator it is highest on the list of changes to the Text that India should seek. But the preoccupation with formal separation, most notably in dispute settlement, has always been puzzling and appears to mix form with substance, means with ends. The possibility of retaliation under the Text would arise only when a country is determined to have failed to comply with its substantive obligations. Thus, countries have to fear retaliation only if they intend not to or are unable to meet these obligations. On this line of reasoning, if a country such as India intends to honour its international obligations, a matter on which its record is exemplary, retaliation or cross-retaliation, a remote contingency, should scarcely be of concern, or at least not the overriding concern evidenced recently. This is not to say that instruments such as Section 301 have not done grave harm, but the harm has been legitimization not so much of the means of 301, that is, retaliation, but of its objectives. In the case of TRIPS this has taken the form of the multilateral codification of the high standards of intellectual property protection that Section 301 sought. Once the objectives are legitimized, retaliation is rendered all but unnecessary, its utility being restricted to the rare cases of non-compliance. If any negotiating coinage remains, it is more productively employed in altering the substantive rules to India's advantage rather than frittering it away on an issue which barely deserves the undue attention it has received.

CONCLUSION

This exposition is by no means an exhortation to accept the Text, a course being contemplated by many other countries; that is for the government exercising its sovereign right to decide. It is a description and a putting in perspective of the outcome of a multilateral negotiating process where power and the strength of numbers matter, and of the limits of India's options in that regard. India's attitude towards the Text should be well informed by Truffaut's assertion about marriage: impossible, but anything else is worse.

CHAPTER 6

JAGDISH BHAGWATI AND INDIA'S TRADE STRATEGY TODAY
OR THE CASE FOR A US–INDIA FREE TRADE AGREEMENT

Jagdish Bhagwati—theoretician, scourge of protectionists, purveyor of dulcet prose,[1] and intellectual colossus—gives us yet another contribution to the debate on trade liberalization: *Going it Alone: The Case for Relaxed Reciprocity in Freeing Trade* (2002). More accurately, the contribution is by trade experts from around the globe, describing liberalization experiences in different countries and sectors, some of them fascinating accounts of the challenges faced and overcome.

But the imprimatur of Bhagwati, even in an edited volume such as this one, is unmistakable. His introduction draws together all the arguments, analysing, clarifying, and taxonomizing with characteristic lucidity. Many of the contributors are students or collaborators. The insightful ideology–interests–institutions trichotomy for thinking about trade policy that he first provided in his earlier volume *Protectionism* (1988) is deployed with great success by many contributors. And the broad message that they convey has been his for a long time: unilateral or rather non-reciprocal trade liberalization, the 'Going It Alone' of the title, can work.

For the purposes of this chapter, two propositions associated with Bhagwati are relevant.[2] First, trade liberalization is overwhelmingly beneficial

---

[1] A good example of Bhagwati's ability to explain ideas is his brother-in-law analogy which highlights the distinction between rent-seeking behaviour and corruption. When you lobby for rents and use up resources, it is a directly unproductive (DUP) activity. But if there is a brother-in-law lurking in the background to whom the rents are inevitably headed, nobody will bother to lobby. In this case, there is corruption but no DUP activity. Unless, of course, some far-sighted crook devotes resources to court the sister in order to become the brother-in-law to get the rents.

[2] See Pravin Krishna's review of Bhagwati's book *Free Trade Today* in the *EPW* for an excellent summary of his other contributions.

for countries. And, second, non-discriminatory trade liberalization—done on one's own or in the context of multilateral negotiations—is overwhelmingly superior to regional trade agreements whereby countries reduce their barriers in favor of some but not all partner countries.[3] Do it alone, do it in Geneva, Professor Bhagwati will exhort us, but the Seuss-like admonitions will quickly follow: not in Brussels, not in Washington, not in Tokyo, and not even in Wellington.

Should India today adhere to Bhagwati's injunction against regional trade agreements? This chapter will argue that it is time for India to consider departing from its long cherished principle of non-discrimination. However, even as India seeks to negotiate regional agreements, it must evaluate these departures and design their implementation always mindful of the benchmark of non-discriminatory trade liberalization. One ignores Bhagwati at one's own peril.

INDIA'S TRADE: THE CHANGING LANDSCAPE

A number of developments render opportune a strategic review of India's trade strategy.

- the dramatically altered foreign policy and security landscape in the aftermath of 9/11;
- the widely shared perception that the growth engine in India is sputtering as the pace of reforms has slackened;
- the uncertain prospects for a successful conclusion of the Doha Round in the wake of the near-standstill in the agriculture negotiations, which many believe hold the key to the success of the Doha Round;
- the frenetic pace with which regional agreements are being negotiated by the United States. in particular which have the serious risk of undermining India's export prospects;
- the entry of China into the WTO, further underlining the competitive threat to India; and, finally,
- India's gambit toward ASEAN, with the curious choice of regional partner, suggestive of a reflex response aimed at neutralizing China's

[3] The terms 'regional trade agreement' and 'free trade agreement' are used interchangeably in this essay but Bhagwati and Srinivasan are correct in highlighting the trace of Orwellian doublespeak in the latter: they lead to freer trade for some but less free trade for others.

inroads into Asia rather than a considered departure from India's time-honoured embrace of multilateralism.

MULTILATERAL, UNILATERAL, OR REGIONAL?

Against this backdrop, the choice for India is whether reliance on unilateral liberalization and/or multilateral liberalization in the context of the Doha Round is sufficient to achieve its objectives of furthering trade liberalization. Economic theory overwhelming supports non-discriminatory trade liberalization based on the most-favoured-nation (MFN) principle. In fact, the insights of Smith and Ricardo embodied in the principle of comparative advantage, which Nobel laureate Samuelson dubbed the only proposition in economics that is both true and non-trivial, applies to non-discriminatory trade liberalization. The question is whether there are limitations to these approaches, which require complementary actions on the regional front. Bhagwati would insist that the choices must be mutually exclusive with regional agreements being the ones excluded. Is this right for India today?

Multilateralism

There are two problems with using the multilateral approach to impart impetus to India's trade reform. First, the prospects for the current multilateral round of trade negotiations appear uncertain, if not bleak. The more important point is that the WTO is unlikely to be a forum where significant progress can be made to further India's market access interests in labour-intensive manufacturing (textiles and clothing) and in skills-based services. These are the areas in which India has a comparative advantage and in which, at this juncture, India needs access to help revive the flagging growth momentum. Even if the Doha Round 'succeeds', it is quite probable that India's export interests will remain largely unaddressed.

The second problem with an exclusive reliance on multilateralism, is that the space of pure multilateral trade is fast shrinking. The United States, EU, and even Japan are striking regional deals galore. The EU has negotiated deep integration agreements with countries in Eastern Europe and North Africa. Mexico has FTAs with the United States and the EU. The United States is negotiating the Free Trade Area of the Americas (FTAA), which will include Brazil and Argentina. The United States and Japan are similarly striking deals with Singapore and other Asian countries. As a result of these,

India's major developing country competitors are gaining a competitive advantage over India in the major industrial country markets. And China, by joining the World Trade Organization (WTO), has caught up with India in terms of its treatment by trading partners. To use a cricketing metaphor, when the world around us has chosen to have the freedom of playing on the front-foot or the back-foot, should India continue to grope forward on principle, oblivious to the flight and pitch of the ball?

Unilateralism

Another approach would be to liberalize unilaterally. Bhagwati's book contains interesting experiments in liberalization from Chile, Taiwan, Australia, New Zealand, and Singapore. India, too, has liberalized impressively in recent years, and the explanatory power of Bhagwati's trichotomy is evident. As the vanes of ideology veered against interventionism with the collapse of communism, the rise of China as an economic power, and India's own crisis in the early 1990, the votaries of state activism in India went into retreat. Interests were at work too, as was clearly seen when the United States and other trading partners forced India, using the WTO dispute settlement mechanism, to abandon its quantitative restrictions on consumer goods imports.

Looking ahead, while the desirability of unilateral liberalization is not in doubt, the question is whether further trade reforms can proceed unilaterally. At this juncture, the problem of unilateral trade liberalization is essentially a political economy one. How can pro-liberalization forces/ interests be harnessed to overcome the opposition from vested interests resistant to reform?

Indeed, if one reads the experiences in this chapter, there seem to be few convincing examples of purely unilateral liberalization. In the case of Taiwan, Arvind Panagariya argues that US pressure and Taiwan's susceptibility to it as a result of political weakness, provided the major impetus for liberalization. For other developing countries in Latin America, the liberalization was unilateral but there was reciprocity in terms of financial assistance under World Bank and IMF adjustment programs. Crisis also seems to have been a powerful stimulus to reform: as Bhagwati quips, 'Nothing succeeds like (previous) failure.'

With unilateral liberalization, the game is one-sided, loaded against reform. International negotiations help overcome this political economy problem by harnessing the power of export interests, with a stake in these negotiations, who can help counter the resistance from import-competing interests. Douglas Irwin's chapter documents how the institutional change in the United States, whereby tariffs were transformed from a purely domestic issue into an international bargaining issue, fundamentally altered the imbalance that favoured protectionists over liberalizers. But this multilateral bargaining route appears less promising for the moment.

Even the most die-hard of optimists such as Bhagwati would concede that prospects for multilateralism are not bright. In response they would say that we should simply go ahead and liberalize unilaterally without 'binding' these reforms multilaterally in the WTO. This appears to have the apparent merit of securing liberalization without frittering away bargaining chips for any future WTO negotiations.

However, this approach is not entirely persuasive for two reasons: first, the question of how liberalization will be achieved and how the opposition to reform will be overcome in India remains unanswered. Advocating unilateral liberalization is the Nike approach to policy advice—Just Do It—catchy but somewhat unhelpful to Indian policymakers, who are grappling with the how of reforms.

The second problem with the 'liberalize but do not bind' view is that it exaggerates the value of this multilateral bargaining chip. Trading partners seek lower barriers (the liberalization aspect) and the security that these barriers will not be raised again (the binding aspect). A country's bargaining chip comprises the sum of these two. By liberalizing, a country loses most of these chips in any case. And the more durable the unilateral liberalization, the less partners value the 'binding', or the multilateral commitment, because they can be more confident that reforms will not be reversed.

Regionalism

The possibility that the Doha Round may well flounder does not of course mean that India should not continue to engage seriously in the WTO negotiations. Nor does the difficulty of securing unilateral liberalization mean that policymakers should ease up on their efforts at moving ahead with domestic reform. But the analysis does imply that India should be considering the regional option as a serious complementary effort to securing further liberalization at home and abroad. Thus, depart from Bhagwati's advice we must.

India has recently signalled its willingness to depart from an exclusive reliance on the multilateral approach by announcing its desire to negotiate a FTA with ASEAN countries. Thus, India has already fired the regional salvo. Perhaps the curious choice of ASEAN as India's preferred regional trade partner is justified under the current circumstances. But it raises the question whether there has been a considered and strategic assessment of the desirability of pursuing regional integration agreements and, if so, with whom.

A much stronger case can be made for India seeking to negotiate an FTA with the United States because it would address a number of problems that arise from the developments described above.

WHY AN INDIA–US FREE TRADE AGREEMENT?

That the world's two largest democracies with so much in common—pluralist politics, a free vibrant press, rule of law, secular in spirit, and home to spectacular diversity—should yet be so far apart remains one of the anomalies of the post-war world order. Can an US–India Free Trade Area (USINTA) provide the starting point for restoring this relationship to its deserved and long-overdue normalcy? This question merits debate now because of some fundamental changes on both sides: a stronger sense of common strategic and foreign policy interests in the aftermath of 9/11 and a break by India with its dirigiste past.

Consider first the benefits for India. India has become a victim—as an outsider—of FTA negotiated by the larger trading partners. Under NAFTA, for example, Mexico has benefited from preferential access to the US market, at the expense of countries such as India. Although India is currently quota-constrained in the textiles and clothing sector, once quotas are dismantled, Indian exporters will be disadvantaged by margins varying from 15 to 40 per cent.

When the negotiation of the FTAA between the United States and Latin America is completed, this disadvantage of India's in the US market would be extended relative to countries such as Brazil and Argentina. And because other big traders such as the EU quickly follow suit in negotiating agreements with regional partners of the United States, India's disadvantage would be extended to more markets. A future agreement with the United States would reverse most of these costs. And as a preferential exporter to the United States, a USINTA would also confer an advantage on India vis-à-vis countries such as China. Maintaining this advantage could become an existential necessity for Indian industries that compete with Chinese exports. It would also buy India some time to implement the much-needed domestic reforms to enable India to become competitive in global markets.

But why not reverse this trade diversion against India by eliminating the preference at source, that is, by seeking to eliminate the MFN tariff in the United States in areas of key export interest to India? In the textiles and clothing sector, the United States remains doggedly protectionist. To expect the industry to stomach further multilateral tariff reduction after the quotas are eliminated, especially with China integrated into the WTO, is wishful thinking.[4] However, a more limited opening to Indian exports could be contemplated as part of a broader deal that provides other benefits to the United States. In other words, it might be easier for India to gain market access to the United States in the clothing sector bilaterally than multilaterally, since in the latter case the United States would be obliged to extend benefits also to China.

The second opportunity that could be created is increased temporary mobility for high-skilled Indian technical personnel. Currently, Indian software programmers gain limited access to the United States under the H-1B visa programme. But there is reason for such temporary movement of personnel to be more fully exploited by lawyers, doctors, nurses, and accountants.

Again the key point here is that from India's perspective, it will be easier to secure improved mobility for high-skilled labour bilaterally in the context of an FTA with the United States than it will be through the WTO. This is a very important point that merits elaboration. From the US perspective, imports of labour, although beneficial, will give rise to political and social costs. To minimize these, importing countries would prefer to target the source of the labour, for example, to ensure that they get high-skilled, English-speaking labour. India offers itself as a natural source. In the WTO, however, targeting sources would be difficult, because the importing country would be under pressure from the MFN principle to extend to other countries the benefits accorded to India. Similarly, for the labour-exporting country, (as, indeed, for the importing country) there might be a desire to ensure that the labour movement is not always permanent for fear of the

---

[4] Indeed, it is not even clear that there will be a timely elimination of the MFA quotas.

usual brain-drain. A bilateral cooperative framework is the most efficient way of addressing this concern.

Further, in a bilateral context, such as a FTA, it would be easier for India and the United States to work toward the removal of regulatory barriers that impede trade in skills-based services, which are often very country-, sector-, and situation-specific. An agreement on high-skilled labour with the United States could then serve as the model for similar initiatives with other European countries, whose need for Indian labour is perhaps even greater than that of the United States.

Third, an interesting pro-reform dynamic could be unleashed by a USINTA. The EU and others are likely to seek to negotiate similar agreements with India, spurred by the competitive disadvantage that their suppliers will face as a result of USINTA (the recently concluded agreement between the EU and Mexico illustrates this dynamic). As a result, the discrimination against India in these markets would be eliminated, while India's own trade liberalization would be broadened. Finally, a future agreement would serve to strengthen India's hand in its broader strategic engagement with the United States by creating a stake for American business in India.

What about the likely costs to India? As against the gains of increased trade and investment flows, preferential liberalization by India will impose costs in terms of lost tariff revenue because imports will be sourced from less efficient suppliers in the United States rather than than their competitors elsewhere in the world. These costs will need to be assessed, but can be contained if the kind of liberalization dynamic mentioned above is set in motion. In other words, while it is true that India's high tariffs create the risk of trade diversion, the likelihood that other major trading partners will seek similar access to India will make India's liberalization less discriminatory.

Then there is the misplaced fear that Indian industry will suddenly be exposed to competition from the United States. To be sure, credible deadlines for implementing liberalization will be set in an FTA with the United States. But the liberalization will be gradually phased in, typically over a period of ten years, allowing domestic firms time to adjust to the prospective changes.

Second, in a post-NAFTA, post-Seattle world, where the old, innocent ceremonies of trade liberalization have been drowned, a USINTA will entail agreements on non-trade issues such as labour and environmental standards. Indeed, the Congressional legislation granting authority to the President

(Trade Promotion Authority) to negotiate international trade agreements mandates the inclusion of labour and environment standards. And there will inevitably be linkages with other strategic issues such as India's nuclear capability. On these non-trade issues, while there are real differences of views, the scope for finding a middle ground should not be ruled out, especially with a Republican administration and a Republican-controlled Congress for whom government regulation through labour and environmental standards is as anathema as it is in India.

What's in a future agreement for the United States? The commercial benefits of gaining access to the Indian market could be substantial. It would only take a few more years of the high rates of growth that India has posted in the 1990s for American business to see an early entrée into the Indian market as a good bet for the future. Even for the present, a USINTA could confer enormous benefits on American business because of India's high trade barriers—they would be favoured insiders in highly protected markets.

An FTA would also present other non-economic benefits to the United States. The 'soft power' that underpins current US preeminence sits uneasily with forging convenient alliances with non-democratic states while spurning democratic ones. A future agreement could begin to rectify this anomaly. Post 9/11, there is general recognition that while the United States will find many tactical allies, India remains one of its long-term strategic partners, especially in the fight against terrorism.

Would a future agreement be feasible? In India, of course, there will be opposition to it. But three sets of actors can be relied upon to help overcome this opposition. First, exporters of labour-intensive manufactures, who will face the adverse consequences of India, being left out of the proliferating network of regional agreements. Second, exporters of high-skilled services, who will seek the expanded opportunities, to enlarge their market access opportunities in the United States. Third, the Indian foreign policy and defence establishments, which are increasingly coming to recognize the importance of closer cooperation with the United States.

And in the United States, too, the weight of the strong private sector interest, the Indian diaspora, and enlightened foreign policy considerations could underpin support for an initiative toward India. The Indian diaspora yearns for a mechanism to institutionalize closer cooperation between the two countries. An FTA between the two countries could satisfy this yearning.

CONCLUSION

Bhagwati commands our admiration, of course, for his intellectual contributions, but especially for his steadfast propagation of the cause of free trade even and particularly when it was unfashionable to do so. Easy indeed it was for a free trader to be alive and spreading the gospel in the heady years of enchantment with globalization. But in the dark days of Indian infatuation with intervention and controls in the 1970s, he was there, systematically and presciently highlighting intervention's ills in the famous NBER volumes of 1978. And in these days of the backlash against globalization, he is again in the vanguard, valiantly fending off attacks from a motley crowd, including Joe Stiglitz, Vandana Shiva, the pharmaceutical industry, and Oxfam, among many others.

Moreover, as he makes clear in the introduction to this book, there are good ways and bad ways of market opening. In the late 1980s and early 1990s, his ire and pen were directed at the deployment of unilateral methods by the United States in particular to extract market opening in developing countries and even Japan.

More recently, regional agreements have been his bete-noire also for representing a less-than-desirable way of market opening. It is therefore unlikely that Bhagwati will actively bless the case made in this essay for India pursuing regional agreements. Shedding a lifetime's addiction is not easy. But he did leave open the possibility that regional agreements could be building blocs leading to the ultimate goal of global free trade. This chapter has attempted to build such a case for India today. Could we have his benign, even indulgent, acquiescence?

CHAPTER 7

PUTTING SOME NUMBERS ON THE TRIPS PHARMACEUTICAL DEBATE

My idea of a better world is one in which medical discoveries would be free from patent and there will be no profiteering from life and death.

—Indira Gandhi

The debate on the social costs and benefits to selected countries in the southern half of the world and to producers in the northern half consequent upon these countries according higher levels of patent protection has assumed sharper focus in the context of the TRIPS negotiations of the Uruguay Round (Trade-related Aspects of Intellectual Property Rights, including Trade in Counterfeit Goods). It has unsurprisingly centred largely, although by no means exclusively, on pharmaceuticals. Unsurprising for at least three reasons.

First, it is in this sector that patent regimes differ most starkly. On the one hand, several industrialized countries provide strong protection in this area with increasing moves towards preserving protection by extending patent terms[1] and, on the other, several developing countries provide very little or virtually no protection at all (World Intellectual Property Organization, 1988). In other sectors such as engineering, automobiles, capital goods, etc., the differences are less extreme.

Second, research shows that proprietary rights in the form of patent protection are far more important in the case of pharmaceuticals than other sectors in ensuring that the returns from R&D are appropriated by the inventor. In other words, whereas in other sectors 'natural' factors such as

[1] See Nogués (1990) for a fuller analysis of the factors that have eroded protection.

lead time, trade secrecy, increasing returns to scale, marketing, etc. can help in preventing imitation by competitors, in the case of pharmaceuticals legal protection is relatively crucial in ensuring that competitors do not dilute the competitive edge of the firm that have undertaken the R&D by cheaply or costlessly imitating the invention.[2]

Third, the sector is inherently susceptible to the rousing of impassioned sentiment, in particular in the context of public health and life in developing countries.

There appears to be a wide degree of consensus that increased pharmaceutical protection entails a loss in welfare (to be defined below) for individual developing countries or even a set of developing countries taken together as long as they are reasonably 'small'.[3] This chapter addresses the quantitative dimension of this welfare loss for a few developing countries and its obverse side—the possible gains to pharmaceutical producers in the north. The analysis is based on models of market structure that vary in their complexity and applicability to the real world.

To date, there have been few estimates of the impact of increasing the level of patent protection in the pharmaceutical sector on variables such as national welfare, prices, quantities, sales, etc.[4] These estimates are important not only in themselves, but also for policymakers when they are contemplating commitments in this area in the context of an overall 'deal' in the Uruguay Round. This chapter will also clarify other issues relating to these losses, including the timing of the impact, their sensitivity to assumptions about market structure, and the size of the country/countries contemplating increased protection.

THE UNDERLYING MODEL

In order to estimate the impact of introducing or substantially raising the level of protection for pharmaceutical products, it is essential to posit a

[2] Nelson et al. (1987) present persuasive empirical evidence in this regard.

[3] See for example Chin and Grossman (1988), Deardorff (1990), Subramanian (1990a, 1991). The question of whether higher patent protection augments world welfare is a distinct question and is addressed in some of these references.

[4] An exception is a study quoted in Siebeck (1991) which estimates the consumer surplus benefits to Chile of not having had patent protection over the years as being in the range of US$7 to 15 million. More recently, Maskus and Konan (1991) have drawn on the analysis in this chapter to calculate some welfare numbers.

Table 7.1: Two Possible Market Structures

	Without patent protection	*With patent protection*
Market structure 1	Perfectly competitive market	Monopoly
Market structure 2	Nash-Cournot duopoly	Monopoly

model of market structure in the absence of patent protection and consequent upon such protection (hereafter referred to as situations without protection and with protection, respectively). Several possibilities present themselves. In this section, comparisons are made for two types of market structure. Comparisons between situations with and without patent protection are summarized in Table 7.1.[5]

In the first case, it is assumed that in the absence of patent protection the market is characterized by perfect competition, with many sellers making zero or close-to-zero rents (extra-normal profits). With patent protection it is assumed that a monopoly results. This is one polar case and in a sense defines an upper bound for the estimates.

In the second case, it is assumed that in the absence of patent protection there are two duopolists—one foreign and one domestic—facing identical costs and engaging in Nash–Cournot competition. That is, each firm decides its profit-maximizing level of output, taking as given its competitor's output. With patent protection it is once again assumed that the duopolistic market structure gives way to a monopoly.

In both cases it is assumed that the monopoly that results is a foreign monopoly, a reasonable assumption when modelling a developing country, considering that in 1980 foreigners accounted for about 79 per cent of all patents granted by a group of important developing countries.[6] The model

---

[5] Chin and Grossman (1988) consider several options. Maskus and Konan (1991) also examine two options based on a dominant firm and a competitive fringe operating in the without-patent situation with the fringe being eliminated after patent protection. Thus these options and those in this section share the feature of postulating a monopoly in the post-patent situation. With regard to the pre-patent situation, it is not altogether clear why their models better approximate reality given that, at least in India, several firms—foreign and domestic—of not dissimilar size currently operate in the market. Insofar as the models considered here are only rough representations of the real market structure, that degree of approximation carries over equally to the additional options considered by Maskus and Konan (1991). Refinements of both these approaches are taken up in fourth section.

[6] Calculated from Table 1 in Eaton and Engers (1989).

comprises a linear demand function and assumes constant marginal costs of production (for details see Appendix 7.1).

Table 7.2 summarizes the impact of choosing higher levels of patent protection on prices, welfare and profits accruing to foreign producers. Welfare is defined as the sum of benefits to the consumer (the consumer surplus) and the rents or profits accruing to the producer. Under perfect competition rents tend to zero. Under a duopoly and a monopoly positive profits accrue to producers, but only those profits accruing to domestic producers are relevant for national welfare (Tirole, 1988). This means that under the postulated with-protection scenario, national welfare comprises merely the gains in consumer surplus, as profits accrue to a foreign monopolist. The estimations have been made for different values of the price elasticity of demand for pharmaceuticals ranging from –0.75 to –2.0[7] in the case of the first market structure and from –1.6 to –3.5 in the second.

THE 'SMALL'-COUNTRY CASE

In this section the theoretical models of the previous section are applied to the data provided in Nogués (1990), which are reproduced in Appendix 7.2, to arrive at monetary estimates of the welfare losses to selected 'small' developing countries where the marginal costs of production are assumed to be the same both with and without patent protection. Before the customary caveats are invoked, a word on why Brazil and Mexico do not appear in these tables. The premise is that the absence of patent protection per se is not a serious problem in these countries as the patentable drug market is predominantly supplied by foreign companies who, although entitled to imitate each others' patents, are unlikely to do so in view of their competitive relationships in other markets. The low share of copied drugs (5 per cent and 15 per cent in Brazil and Mexico, respectively) bears out this contention.[8] Argentina and India, on the other hand, have a very high proportion of imitative indigenous producers,

---

[7] These correspond to elasticities at the initial optimum in the without-patent situation.

[8] The question might then spring to mind as to why the US made the need for change in the Brazilian patent regime a priority. There are several, not necessarily mutually exclusive, possibilities: first, it may have been considered important to signal to the rest of the developing world, particularly in Latin America, the seriousness of their intentions in this area. More plausibly, however, the absence of patent protection was used as a vehicle to secure other regulatory changes in the pharmaceutical industry (price controls, for example) which were thought to be depressing significantly the profitability of operations in Brazil.

Table 7.2: 'Small'-country case

Perfectly competitive market becomes a monopoly

Price elasticity of market demand	-0.75		-1.0		-2.0	
	Argentina	India	Argentina	India	Argentina	India
Annual welfare loss[a]	387	1279	289	955	145	477
	(75%)		(75%)		(75%)	
Annual increase in profits of foreign firm[a]	257	848	192	636	96	318
Price increase	67%	67%	50%	50%	25%	25%
Present value of welfare loss:						
(a) Pipeline protection	2681	8861	2002	6616	1005	3305
(b) Non-pipeline protection	1015	3356	758	2506	381	1252

Duopolistic market becomes a monopoly

Price elasticity of market demand[b]	-1.63		-2.00		-3.5	
Annual welfare loss	223	633	176	598	110	34 1
	(72%)		(72%)		(72%)	
Annual increase in profits of foreign firm[a]	148	490	120	398	69	227
Price increase	33%	33%	25%	25%	17%	17%
Present value of welfare loss:						
(a) Pipeline protection	1545	4385	1219	4143	762	2362
(b) Non-pipeline protection	585	1661	462	1569	289	895

Notes: [a] All numbers other than those for price increases are in constant US$ millions at 1988 prices. The bracketed figures represent the corresponding percentage change. The annual figures represent economic effects that will be felt only 10 or 20 years after patent protection is granted (see Section 5).
[b] This translates into a perceived price elasticity for each duopolist of 3.264 and 7.00, respectively, for the three cases.

resulting in strong competitive pressure on the whole patentable drug market. Changes in patent protection in themselves are therefore likely to have important effects on the structure of the market along the lines suggested and estimated in the previous section.[9]

[9] This argument distinguishing Brazil and Mexico from India and Argentina in terms of the hypothesis that the impact of increased patent protection hinges on the relative unimportance

Sales of patentable drugs, rather than total sales of drugs, are used as the base figures, an implicit assumption being that these would be the relevant base figures in the hypothetical future when actual losses start to be felt. It should also be remembered that the numbers represent annual losses for the year in which the full impact is felt (i.e., losses that would be felt either ten or twenty years, depending on the phasing in of obligations, after the conclusion of any international agreement). This is discussed in greater detail in the fifth section.

Table 7.2 reflects the 'small'-country case, where it has been assumed that the marginal costs of production would be the same with or without patent protection.[10] In other words, the prospects of higher patent protection in a developing country and of greater profits consequent upon such a move are assumed not to have any significant effect on R&D activity that would translate back into lower costs of production. The results for Argentina and India are shown in Table 7.2. Argentina's welfare loss ranges from about US$150 million to almost US$410 million and India's from about US$475 million to almost US$1.3 billion, depending on the price elasticity of market demand. These results are, of course, very sensitive to the assumptions of the market structure, as a comparison of the top and bottom halves of Table 7.2 reveals.

Similarly, the table shows the additional profits that would accrue to foreign pharmaceutical producers. They also vary, but two features about them are noteworthy. First, foreign producers always gain less than the

---

of the competitive pressure posed by imports of drugs from unpatented sources. For example, it could be argued that Brazil would benefit from low patent protection despite the absence of indigenous imitative facilities if it could import similar drugs made in, say, Argentina or India. The data, however, show that this has not happened to a significant extent, either because of production constraints in these other countries or because of prohibitive transportation costs, market access barriers, etc. If, however, this distinction is not valid and cheap imports from unpatented sources were a real possibility, losses to Brazil would be approximately two-thirds India's. Correspondingly, Mexico's losses would be about one-third of Indian losses. In fact this fear of competition from imports, consequent upon the implementation of the trade liberalization strategy, possibly also underlay the demands for higher patent protection in Brazil.

[10] On the one hand, it could be argued that the marginal cost of production in the without-patent situation should be higher because indigenous firms would view some imitative costs. On the other hand, to the extent that some R&D costs are reflected in the marginal costs of production these will not be incurred by imitators. Thus, on balance the assumption of some marginal costs should not be unreasonable.

countries lose, so that patent protection diminishes world welfare and merely serves to redistribute world income (there are no effects on consumers in the north and hence the additional profits of northern producers can be equated to the welfare impact on the north as a whole). Second, the greater the gains to producers the greater the welfare losses to individual countries.

Both these features are analytically true (see Appendix 7.1). The insistence of the demands by pharmaceutical producers is directly and strongly correlated with the likely loss to individual countries.

PATENT PROTECTION WITH COMPULSORY LICENSING

It could be alleged of the models used in second section that they are overly extreme and simplistic in their representation of the structure of the pharmaceutical market in several respects. First, the depiction of the post-patent situation as a monopoly might not square with the observation that some patented therapeutic drugs might and often do compete with each other. Postulating competition between patented drugs is empirically more plausible than postulating a monopoly. Second, the change from the without- to with- patent situations might also be thought to be extreme. In effect, it assumes that a patent drives out all non-patentees from the market. A more plausible scenario, as has been argued by Mansfield et al. (1981), is that a patent forces non-patentees to invent 'around' the patent and thus raises the costs of imitation or the costs of staying in the market, rather than resulting in their complete exit. Finally, although the TRIPs agreement will result in the granting of patent protection to pharmaceutical inventions, the extent of proprietary rights conferred will not be absolute or total. Under the draft TRIPs agreement, countries will retain the right to grant compulsory licences to non-patentees in a variety of circumstances subject to the payment of a royalty to the patentee. As has been argued elsewhere (see Subramanian, 1991), the freedom to grant compulsory licences is analytically equivalent to reducing the strength of the exclusive rights conferred by a patent. This manner of viewing compulsory licensing can be incorporated into the scenario of Mansfield et al. A compulsory licensee can continue to operate even in the post-patent situation subject to facing a higher marginal cost of production on account of having to remunerate the patentee for the compulsory licence.[11]

[11] Of course, the royalty payable to the patentee, which is often fixed by the host country, would have to be less than that payable under a freely negotiated voluntary licence.

Table 7.3: Bertrand Model

	Without-patent protection	With-patent protection
Market structure 3	Nash-Bertrand differentiated products duopoly with identical marginal costs of production	Nash-Bertrand differentiated products duopoly with higher marginal costs of production for domestic firm that is operating under a compulsory licence

These refinements are incorporated into a model of market structure comprising two firms selling differentiated products and engaged in Bertrand price competition. This model allows the fact of competition between patented drugs to be captured. The two firms operate in the market in both the without- and the with-patent situations. The effect of patent protection is reflected in one firm (the non-patentee) having a higher marginal cost of production (either because of facing higher imitative costs or of having to pay the patentee a royalty under a compulsory licence). The non-patentee can thus also be regarded as the compulsory licensee. This model can be represented in the following manner. (Details of this model are presented in Appendix 7.2).

An important assumption made in the estimations is that the introduction of patent protection results in a 30 per cent increase in the marginal costs of production for the imitator/compulsory licensee. This figure is drawn from the study of Mansfield et al. (1981) who find that on average this would be the additional cost imposed by patent protection in the pharmaceutical sector. Even more so than in the case of the other models, the results are sensitive to the specification of parameters. When attention is confined to the set of parameter values that result in the own-price and cross-price elasticities of demand being reasonably close to each other, the results are reasonably robust.[12] As expected the welfare numbers are significantly reduced compared to the earlier section. The price increases[13] range from about 2 per cent to about 9 per cent with an average increase of

---

[12] Details of the values of parameters used are available from the author on request. Some analytical comparative static changes are also described in Appendix 7.2.

[13] Weighted average of the two products, with weights reflecting the output at the initial equilibrium.

about 4 per cent. Annual welfare losses to Argentina and India were on average US$67 million and US$220 million, respectively. Increased annual profits to pharmaceutical producers in these markets would be US$23 million and US$76 million, respectively. In this model, too, the gains to producers are outweighed by the welfare losses to individual countries, implying global welfare losses. (This result holds analytically for the model, see Appendix 7.2).[14] The profit numbers not only evoke the question 'why all the fuss?', but also cast some doubt about the dynamic benefits that could be achieved through higher patent protection. Even an increased profit of US$76 million (the figure for India) pales into insignificance when compared with the figure of US$125 million estimated as the cost of developing a single patented drug (Nogués, 1990).

TIMING OF IMPACT: PRESENT VALUE WELFARE NUMBERS

If, notwithstanding the welfare losses, developing countries were to undertake obligations to increase pharmaceutical patent protection, it is necessary to consider when the changes estimated in the second section would be felt. The timing question is important in the case of pharmaceuticals because, as is shown below, there could be substantial lags between the undertaking of greater obligations or the grant of patent protection for pharmaceuticals and the generation of the economic effects noted in the earlier sections, these lags stemming from the time required to obtain marketing approval for patented drugs. These lags can impinge significantly on present value welfare calculations.

There are two ways in which these obligations could be phased in. First, as was demanded by producers in the north, by requiring all drugs already patented in a foreign country (country A), but which have not yet been marketed in a country undertaking the new obligations (country B), to be protected by country B. This is retroactive protection or pipeline protection as it is sometimes called. Alternatively, the protection of drugs created after the date on which obligations are undertaken could be required, which would be the preferred position of the south in the event that patent protection

---

[14] Unlike in the earlier models, however, losses and gains are not correlated with all changes in the values of the parameters, which introduces the possibility of greater variation in the numbers. However, the possibility of Pareto-efficient bargains between north and south cannot be created in this model, unlike that in seventh section.

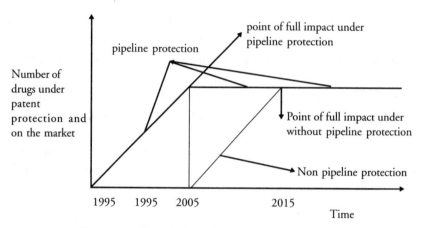

Figure 7.1: Magnitude and timing of patent protection

has to be provided at all. Let us assume a uniform rate of introduction of drugs, a patent term of twenty years and an average time period of ten years (calculated from the date a patent application is filed) for drugs to acquire marketing approval. The temporal impact of these alternatives is depicted in Figure 7.1 as the pipeline and no-pipeline proposals.

Under the first scenario (pipeline protection) the impact of patent protection is felt immediately because imitators cannot market drugs granted patents ten years ago and which have just attained marketing approval. They could, however, continue to sell drugs granted patents in the nine years prior to that. To put it slightly differently, patents that are in the second half (or last ten years) of their life span need not be protected, while patents in the first half (i.e., of vintage 0–10 years) would have to be protected. Thus in the first year of the assumption of obligations, one-tenth of the sales[15] of all imitative firms would be taken away by the foreign monopolist. The full impact on such firms would be felt ten years after the assumption of obligations, full impact denoting indigenous producers' total loss of market of patented drugs. In that limit, if such firms' businesses were based exclusively on imitation, they would effectively be pushed out of the market. (In Figure 12.1, full impact is depicted as the point after which the curve flattens out, the flattening occurs because patented drugs entering the market are matched by drugs whose patent term has expired.) Applying this line of reasoning, one can conclude that under the second

[15] Assuming uniform prices for all drugs.

scenario (not involving pipeline protection) the first economic impact on indigenous imitative producers would be felt ten years after the undertaking of obligations, this being the time required for drugs to obtain marketing approval. The full impact, that is, total loss of the patented drugs market, would be felt a further ten years later. Thus the annual welfare losses estimated in the third section represent an economic impact that will be felt either ten or twenty years after the coming into force of a TRIPs agreement. On today's reckoning, this would be the years 2005 and 2015, respectively.

The annual losses presented in Table 7.2 have been cumulated to arrive at present value losses which are presented in row 4 of the table. The economic losses in the years before full impact have been assumed to be as shown in Figure 7.1, that is, increasing proportionally on account of the assumption of a uniform rate of introduction of patented drugs into the market. The first point to note is that the present value of welfare losses are substantial and vary depending on the underlying assumptions. For Argentina the losses vary from US$300 million to over a billion dollars and for India from about US$900 million to US$3.4 billion. The other interesting conclusion is that the difference between the pipeline and non-pipeline proposal is enormous: in each case the present value loss with pipeline protection is 2.6 times that without pipeline protection. Under the former, the range of losses thus varies from US$760 million to US$2.7 billion for Argentina and between US$2.4 billion to US$8.9 billion for India. The obligation to grant protection for patents in the pipeline could thus be quite onerous.

PRICE BEHAVIOUR

The estimation of welfare, profit, and price changes induced by patent protection is necessarily fraught with difficulties, contingent as it is on a number of assumptions about demand and supply parameters and about market structure, both with and without patent protection. In this section a crude cross-check on the plausibility of the calculations is attempted by comparing the price changes generated by the models with prices of patented drugs in different countries. The numbers in Table 7.2 show that patent protection can induce price increases varying from about 20 per cent to 70 per cent, with a mean figure being about 45 per cent. It is to be remembered that these represent price increases in patentable products and not in the

general prices of drugs. The price increases generated by the model seem
absurdly modest in the face of evidence showing dramatic variations in the
prices of patented drugs across countries.

Table 7.4 compares prices of a few drugs in India with those of the United
States and Malaysia, all of which were under patent protection at the time of
the comparison. The first point to note is that prices in the United States are

Table 7.4: International Prices Compared to Indian Prices of Important Patented Drugs

Drug and dosage	India[a] (Rs)	US[b] (Rs)	US/India (Times)	India[b] (Rs)	Malaysia[b] (Rs)	Malaysia/ India (Times)
Anti-inflammatory						
Flurbiprofen 100 mg Tabs 10s	12.69	**	–	**	**	–
Diclofenac 50 mg Tabs 10s	7.62	105.60	13.86	12.00	49.04	4.09
Piroxicam 10 mg Tabs 10s	2.88	149.20	51.81	**	**	–
Anti-ulcerants						
Cimetidine 400 mg Tabs 10s	17.34	153.03	8.83	**	**	–
Ranitidine 300 mg Tabs 10s	26.16	348.70	13.33	**	**	–
Sucralfate 500 mg Tabs 10s	7.78	**	–	**	**	–
Farnotidine 40 mg Tabs 10s	25.08	348.75	13.91	**	**	–
Cardiovasculars						
Nifedipine 10 mg Tabs 10s	3.88	60.38	15.56	**	**	–
Atenolo150 mg Tabs 10s	5.60	89.38	15.96	7.50	65.03	8.67
Acebutalol200 mg Tabs 10s	18.10	**	–	**	**	–
Pentoxyphyllin 400 mg Tabs 10s	29.57	57.50	1.94	145.00[f]	169.09[f]	1.17
Anti-viral/fungal						
Acyclovir 396 cream 5 gm	98.00 (5 gm)	271.99	2.78	176.80	224.04	1.26
Ketaconazole 200 mg Tabs 10s	41.28	272.94	6.61	72.00[g]	143.95[g]	2.00
Clobetasol 1096 cream 10 gm	10.16	**	–	**	**	–

Notes: [a] Wholesale prices.
[b] Retail prices.
[c] Source for Prices: US, Annual Pharmacists reference (I 989); Malaysia, DIMS (February 1989); India, CIMS (April 1989) and MIMS (May 1989).
[d] Exchange rates: 1 US$ =Rs 16.50; 1 Malaysia $ =Rs 6.10.
[e] ** Represents not available.
[f] Packs of thirty tablets.
[g] Packs of thirty tablets (400 mg).

significantly greater than those in India. It would be erroneous, however, to infer on the basis of such evidence that similar price changes would result in India if it were to increase its level of protection for pharmaceuticals. Clearly, the difference in prices results as much from market conditions, which are not controlled for, as from differences in the patent regime.

What is revealing, however, is the contrast between Malaysia and India. Malaysia does accord reasonably high pharmaceutical protection. Table 7.4 shows that Malaysian prices are significantly higher (ranging from 20 per cent to 760 per cent) than Indian prices. Furthermore, and this is important to note, if the prices charged in Malaysia reflect prices that give a patent holder maximum profits, based on what the market can bear, the prices that would hypothetically be charged in a vastly larger market such as India's (at least 10 times as large as Malaysia's) could be expected to be significantly greater.[16]

THE 'LARGE'-COUNTRY CASE

It could be argued that the 'small-country assumption' is too extreme, at least in the case of certain large developing countries (such as Brazil and India), and with more justification in cases where, as is envisaged under the TRIPs exercise, a group of developing countries is simultaneously expected to increase the level of patent protection. If the group is important enough or big enough to affect decisions made about R&D by firms in industrialized countries, one cannot reasonably make the small-country assumption. In other words, the small-country assumption takes into account the static costs of higher patent protection while ignoring the dynamic benefits.

Before turning to the results stemming from the large-country assumption, an examination of the empirical realities might be instructive. On the face of it, figures showing that the markets of developing countries as a whole constitute about 15 per cent of world sales of pharmaceutical products might suggest that those markets cannot be very important determinants of R&D activities of multinational firms. This share of the world market, however, is increasing and probably offers lucrative rent-making prospects, given that the patentable drug markets are supplied by firms imitating patented technology (see next section).

[16] In more rigorous terms, as the price elasticity of demand is inversely related to the size of a market, the monopoly price for maximizing profits will increase with the size of the market.

At the margin, the relative importance of the markets of developing countries as a source of profits is likely to be enhanced in future. Profits of firms in industrialized countries that undertake intensive research and development are diminishing due to competition from generic drug manufacturers and to regulatory changes that have effectively shortened the patent life.[17] A further and perhaps the most important motive for studying the large-country case is that for certain types of drugs used in the treatment of illnesses specific to developing countries, the markets of developing countries must, by definition, constitute a very high proportion of the total market. Thus R&D in such drugs could be sensitive to the level of protection afforded in these markets.

Table 7.5 below presents the results for the large-country case. The large-country assumption is reflected in marginal costs being 50 per cent lower with patent protection than without. This rather extreme assumption, extreme because such a large response is made a consequence of a few relatively small countries granting patent protection, is intended to give a flavour of the consequences of patent protection. Two points are worth noting.

First, the consequences for welfare in individual developing countries are still negative, except where elasticities of market demand are very high (−2.00 and −3.5, respectively). Second, unlike in the small-country case examined in the third section, profits accruing to foreign producers outweigh the welfare losses. In principle, therefore, world welfare would increase and the possibility of striking Pareto-efficient bargains between south and north is created. The plausibility of this scenario, however, depends critically on the assumption of the large decrease in marginal costs of production consequent upon greater patent protection. An alternative manner of viewing the large-country case would be to ask the question as to what cost reduction created by the boost to R&D would be required to generate national and global welfare gains. These numbers are presented in row 4 of the table. Clearly, larger cost reductions are required to generate welfare increases for individual countries of whom higher patent protection is sought. The reader is left to evaluate the plausibility of the magnitude of cost reductions estimated; given the stylized facts regarding the relatively small size of markets in countries contemplating

---

[17] As Nogués (1990) rightly observes, profits in the industrialized world resulting from the extension of patent terms would be worth considerably less in present value terms than profits that would arise if developing countries were to increase their current levels of protection.

Table 7.5: 'Large'-country Case

	Perfectly competitive market becomes a monopoly					
Price elasticity of market demand	-0.75		-1.0		-2.0	
	Argentina	India	Argentina	India	Argentina	India
Annual welfare loss	270	891	169	557	0	0
	(53%)		(44%)		(0%)	
Annual increase in profits of foreign firm[a]	486	1604	434	1432	386	1273
Price increase	42%	42%	25%	25%	0%	0%
Percentage reduction in cost required to generate						
(a) national welfare gains	–	–	–	–	50%	50%
(b) global welfare[b] gains	20%	20%	15%	15%	8%	8%

	Duopolistic market becomes a monopoly					
Price elasticity of market demand[a]	-1.63		-2.00		-3.5	
Annual welfare loss	116	290	45	149	-131	-273
	(67%)		(62%)		(-27%)	
Annual increase in profits of foreign firm	386	1273	392	1293	439	1459
	(325%)		(406%)		(800%)	
Price increase	25%		13%		-7%	
Percentage reduction in cost required to generate:						
(a) national welfare gains	85%	85%	63%	63%	31%	31%
(b) global welfare gains[b]	12%	12%	9%	9%	4%	4%

Note: [a] This translates into a perceived price elasticity for each duopolist of 3.26,4 and 7.00 respectively for the three cases.
[b] In the global welfare calculus, the effects of cost decreases on consumers in the north have not been taken into account because the large-country case has relevance largely where R&D efforts will be directed towards developing drugs for illnesses specific to the south.

higher protection, the presumption would be that of the small-country scenario. Further empirical analysis would be necessary, however, before any definitive assessment can be made of the magnitude of the spur to R&D that would be provided by a TRIPs agreement.

CONCLUSIONS

This paper has attempted to quantify the social welfare losses to selected developing countries and the gains to pharmaceutical producers if these countries were to adopt higher levels of patent protection for pharmaceuticals. The estimates are based on simple theoretical models of market structure. It emerges that the welfare losses to individual southern countries and profit gains to pharmaceutical producers are sensitive to underlying assumptions about market structure and price elasticities of demand. A few points, however, can be made.

First, under the small-country assumption, welfare losses to individual countries outweigh the gains to pharmaceutical producers. Second, the two are correlated in many situations: the greater the perceived losses to pharmaceutical producers the larger the loss to countries if they were to accord higher protection. One man's outcry is clearly another man's fear. Third, the full economic impact of losses and gains would only be felt either ten or twenty years after the adoption of proposals to grant patent protection. The regulatory process, to which all patented drugs are subject in order to obtain marketing approval, delays and stretches out the economic impact of higher patent protection. Fourth, the demand for retroactive (pipeline) protection, under which the full impact would be felt after ten years, would increase by over two-and-a-half times (relative to the situation where such pipeline production is not granted) the present value of the welfare losses to individual countries. Finally, further work would be necessary before the nature and magnitude of dynamic benefits that would be conferred by a TRIPs agreement could be established. In other words, the small-country assumption might need to be modified, which might render TRIPs less an exercise in international rent transfer away from the south and more of an inducement of research and development and an enhancement of global social welfare.

REFERENCES

Bhagwati, J. (1988), *Protectionism*, MIT Press, Massachusetts.

Bhagwati, J. (1990), 'Multilateralism at risk: The GATT is dead, long live GATT', *World Economy*, 13(2), pp. 149–69.

Chin, J.C., and G.M. Grossman (1988), 'Intellectual property rights and North-South trade', *National Bureau of Economic Research Working Paper Series No. 2769*.

Deardorff, A.V. (1990) 'Should patent protection be extended to all developing countries?', *World Economy*, Symposium Issue on TRIPs and TRIMs, 13(4), pp. 497–508.

Diwan, I., and D. Rodrik (1990), 'Patents, appropriate technology and north-south trade', *Journal of International Economics*, 30, pp. 27–47.

Eaton, J. and M. Engers (1989), 'Section 337 and the global protection of intellectual property', mimeo, University of Virginia.

Levin, R.C., A.K. Klevorick, R.R. Nelson, and S.G. Winter (1987), 'Appropriating the returns from industrial research and development', *Brookings Papers on Economic Activity*, 3, pp. 783–820.

Mansfield, E., M. Schwartz, and S. Wagner (1981), 'Imitation costs and patents: an empirical study', *Economic Journal*, 91, pp. 907–18.

Maskus, K.E., and D.E. Konan (1991), 'Trade-related intellectual property rights: issues and exploratory results', mimeo, Michigan.

Nogués, J. (1990), 'Patents and pharmaceutical drugs: understanding the pressures on developing countries', *Journal of World Trade*, 24(6), pp. 81–104.

Rapp, R.T., and R.P. Rozek (1990), 'Benefits and costs of intellectual property protection in developing countries', *Journal of World Trade*, 24(5), pp. 75–102.

Siebeck, W. (ed.) (1991), *Effects of Strengthened Intellectual Property Protection on Developing Country Economies: A Survey*, World Bank, Washington D.C.

Subramanian, A. (1990a), 'Discrimination in the international economics of intellectual property protection', *Economic and Political Weekly*, XXV(11), pp. 549–54.

——— (1990b), 'TRIPs and the paradigm of the GATT: a tropical, temperate view', *World Economy* Symposium Issue on TRIPs and TRIMs, 13(4), pp. 509–21.

——— (1991), 'The international economics of intellectual property protection: a welfare-theoretic trade policy analysis', World Development, 19(8), pp. 945–56.

Tirole, J. (1988), *Theory of Industrial Organization*, MIT Press, Massachusetts.

World Intellectual Property Organization (WIPO) (1988), *Existence, Scope and Form of Generally Internationally Accepted and Applied Standards/Norms for the Protection of Intellectual Property*, WIPO, WO/Inf/20.

APPENDIX 7.1

Market structure I: Perfect competition becomes a monopoly

Market demand

$$Q = B - P$$

where P represents price. Marginal costs of production are assumed to be constant and equal to L.

Simple profit maximization yields the following under the without-patent situation

$$P = L$$
$$Q = B - L$$

Revenue

$$R = L(B - L)$$

Consumer surplus

$$S = \frac{(B - L)^2}{2}$$

Welfare

$$W = \frac{(B - L)^2}{2}$$

Under a patent, a monopoly is assumed to result yielding

$$P = \frac{B + L}{2}$$

$$Q = \frac{B - L}{2}$$

$$R = \frac{B^2 - L^2}{2}$$

$$S = \frac{(B - L)^2}{8}$$

Foreign profit

$$FP = \frac{(B-L)^2}{4}$$

Welfare

$$W = \frac{(B-L)^2}{8}$$

The values of L and B are obtained by equating the elasticity to the values (–0.75, –1.00, and 2.00) used in the text. Since the data are in terms of revenues, the values of the various parameters are obtained in terms of the revenues in the pre-patent situation which yields the numbers presented in the text.

Market structure 2: Duopoly becomes a monopoly

With the same market demand curve as above, the values of the parameters in the with-patent situation are the same as those noted above. Under the pre-patent (duopoly) situation the parameters take on the following values:

$$P = \frac{B+2L}{3}$$

$$Q = \frac{2(B-L)}{3}$$

$$R = \frac{2(B+2L)(B-L)}{9}$$

$$S = \frac{2(B-L)^2}{9}$$

Total profit

$$TP = \frac{2(B-L)^2}{9}$$

Foreign profit

$$FP = \frac{1(B-L)^2}{9}$$

$$W = \frac{4(B-L)^2}{9}$$

It is evident in this situation that the welfare loss to the country introducing protection

$$\frac{15(B-L)^2}{72}$$

is greater than the profit gain of foreign producers

$$\frac{10(B-L)^2}{72}$$

so that a global welfare loss is implied.

Further any change in the parameters B and L leads to similar changes in the direction of the losses and the gains, supporting the contention that the two are always correlated.

Market structure 3: Bertrand competition and compulsory licensing
Market demand

$$Q_F = a - bP_F + CP_D$$

$$Q_D = a - bP_D + CP_F$$

where Q_F and Q_D are the demands for products sold by the foreign and domestic firm, respectively. The own-price and cross-price responses are assumed to be symmetrical. Both b and c are greater than zero, the latter representing the fact that the two products are substitutes in consumption. The assumption of b greater than c is sufficient to satisfy the stability condition.

In the pre-patent situation, marginal costs of production are assumed to be identical

$$L_F = L_D$$

In the post-patent situation the domestic firm faces higher marginal costs.

In the pre-patent situation, profit maximization yields

$$P_F = 2b(a + L_F b) + C(L_D b + a) / 4b^2 - C^2$$

$$P_D = 2b(a + L_D b) + C(a + L_F b) / 4b^2 - C^2$$

Similarly values or prices can be found in the post-patent situation.

Substituting these into the demand, profit, and consumer surplus functions yields values in terms of the underlying parameters equivalent to those presented for market structures 1 and 2.

In this model, the introduction of patent protection can be analysed as a change in the domestic firm's marginal cost of production. The resulting comparative static changes describe the consequences of such protection. It can be shown that

$$\frac{dFP}{dL_D} > 0 \quad \text{and} \quad \frac{dW}{dL_D} < 0$$

which imply that foreign producers gain and the country loses. Further

$$\frac{dFP}{dL_D} + \frac{dW}{dL_D} < 0$$

which establishes the claim that the country loses more than the foreign producers gain, resulting in a global welfare loss.

APPENDIX 7.2

Estimates of increased income of pharmaceutical companies holding patents (US$ millions)

Variables	Argentina	Brazil	India	Mexico	Total
Pharmaceutical market size	1200.0	2000.0	4200.0	1000.0	8400.0
Patented pharmaceutical market	771.0	1750.4	2546.0	852.5	5919.9
(a) Sales by domestic firms of copied drugs	231.0	93.8	920.0	136.5	1381.3
(b) Sales of drugs by firms who are patent owners	540.0	1656.6	1626.0	716.0	4538.6

Source: Nogués (1990)

CHAPTER 8

CAPITAL ACCOUNT CONVERTIBILITY
A NEGLECTED CONSIDERATION

*Ideas, knowledge, science, hospitality, travel—these are the things
which should of their nature be international. But let goods be
homespun whenever it is reasonably and conveniently possible
and, above all, let finance be primarily national.*

—John M. Keynes

On any liberal view, capital account convertibility (CAC) like free trade must be a consummation devoutly to be wished. At some deep level, the case for both is a moral one—the freedom of individuals to undertake economic transactions, including the right to buy and sell goods regardless of their destination or provenance (free trade), and the right to buy and sell future and contingent claims to these goods to/from people regardless of their nationality (CAC).

The operative word, of course, is consummation. Over the course of history, all societies have placed restrictions on these freedoms for a number of reasons, some good and some less so.[1] Usually, restrictions stem from the assessment that individual freedoms are subordinate to the greater economic good. But societies do progressively eliminate the restrictions as they have become richer: this is true not just of today's Organization for Economic Co-operation and Development (OECD) countries but other emerging market countries as well. The key question then is not whether but when.

This chapter examines one consideration that should influence the timing of any move to CAC. Its restricted focus stems from the view that this

[1] Bhagwati's widely cited 'Capital Myth' is the classic analysis for why restrictions on capital flows are more justified than restrictions on free trade.

consideration is of first-order importance for long-run growth, from the relative inattention to it, and from the well-rehearsed arguments for the other considerations. The Tarapore Committee (1997) provided an excellent summary of the state of the debate on this issue, including exchange rate policy, but devoted less attention to the issue that will be the focus of this chapter.[2]

Not to prolong the suspense, this consideration is the level of the real exchange rate or what might be called the objective of avoiding overvaluation. This is an issue related to the real side of the economy and should be distinguished from those (stability and volatility) that are related to the macroeconomic and financial sectors.

Three points should be stressed at the outset. First, the uncertainties about CAC and the arguments in the chapter relating to them are all about non-FDI-related flows. The positive growth impact of FDI appears to be well established.

Second, the arguments advanced in the chapter need to be appropriately calibrated/modified to take account of the fact that the issue being debated currently, and the action being contemplated by the government, is not a move from being closed to capital flows to becoming completely open. India is already quite open to flows involving non-residents. What is under consideration would involve perhaps a less dramatic change, largely affecting residents.

Finally, and most importantly, the calculus of benefits and risks will reflect a number of factors, including the efficiency and capital- and resource-augmenting benefits of CAC, the strength of the financial system, and the macroeconomic pre-conditions. This chapter should be seen as adding an element into the calculus without claiming decisive status for it.

GROWTH, THE TRADABLE SECTOR AND DIVERSIFICATION

Successful economic growth and development are almost always associated with the growth of the tradable sector. Lee Kuan Yew, delivering the Jawaharlal Nehru Memorial Lecture in 2005, expressed this succinctly and dramatically: 'Since the industrial revolution, no country has become a

[2] Reddy (2004) is a brief but excellent discussion of many of the important issues. Prasad and Rajan (2005) suggest a modality for moving toward CAC without taking a strong view on timing.

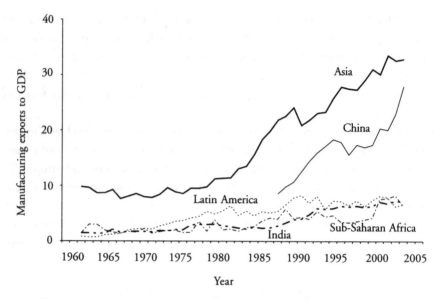

Figure 8.1: Manufacturing exports to GDP, 1960–2005 (in per cent)

Source: World Bank, World Development Indicators

major economy without becoming an industrial power'. Given that
manufacturing is the tradable sector par excellence, the underlying sentiment
is that manufacturing growth is a concomitant, perhaps even a *sine qua non*
of, overall growth. Figure 8.1 illustrates this proposition, plotting the share
of manufacturing exports in GDP against the level of income, for the set of
successful growers in Asia—Singapore, Korea, Thailand, Malaysia, Indonesia,
China, Taiwan, and India; for the sake of comparison averages for Latin
America and Africa are also plotted.

Another related stylized fact is that successful growth is accompanied by
the private sector undertaking new, varied, and sophisticated activities (Imbs
and Wacziarg, 2003; Hausmann and Rodrik, 2003). All economies start
off agricultural, and the successful ones diversify away from agriculture
toward manufacturing, and within manufacturing from simple to more
sophisticated activities. Diversification is thus intrinsic to development.
Figure 8.2 (drawn from Imbs and Wacziarg, 2003) plots a measure of
concentration of activities in manufacturing (which is the inverse of
diversification) on the vertical axis for a group of countries. The typical
pattern is that, over time as countries grow, they tend to diversify (reflected

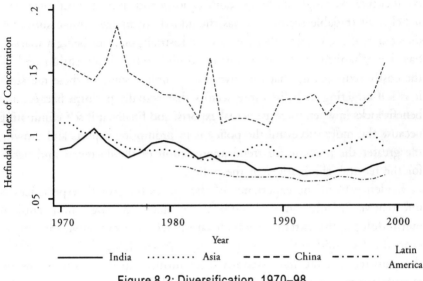

Figure 8.2: Diversification, 1970–98

(the Herfindahl Index measure concentration—the inverse of diversification)

in declining concentration) before they specialize. The figure shows that Asian countries have been far more diversified than countries in Latin America (the line for Asia lies completely below that for Latin America). Read together with Figure 8.1, this suggests that the fast growing Asian countries have not only had a bigger tradable sector but also a richer and more varied set of activities within it.[3]

ENTER EXCHANGE RATES

The ability of and incentives for the private sector to engage in activities in the tradable sector, to move away from traditional agriculture, and to do new and varied things are shaped by numerous factors—history, endowments, culture, institutions, and so on—but also by the policy environment. One key policy that deters investment in tradable sectors and militates against diversification away from traditional, simple activities is an overvalued exchange rate. The exchange rate is key for a number of reasons: in contrast to trade liberalization, which can help exports, a

[3] Although not shown, both Asia and Latin America are substantially more diversified than countries in sub-Saharan Africa.

competitive exchange rate helps both exports and import-substitutes (i.e., it helps all tradable sectors); it has the added advantage, unlike subsidies, directed credit, etc. and other forms of industrial policy, of being a market-based mechanism, and not requiring administrative intervention and all the costly rent-seeking that can give rise to; unlike some of these measures it is self-targeting, it helps those sectors that actually perform because the benefit kicks in when there are actual exports; and finally, it is self-eliminating because the more successful the policy is in promoting exports and growth, the greater the pressure for trend appreciation of the currency, and hence for the natural 'elimination' of the policy.

Evidence from the experience of the successful growth experiences is informative. In Johnson et al. (2006), we calculated, based on a standard methodology, the extent to which countries' real exchange rates were overvalued or undervalued using a simple methodology.[4] We found that the countries that had sustained economic growth and growing manufacturing exports had consistently avoided overvaluation. Figure 8.3 shows that Asian countries have not had overvalued exchange rates, while Latin America and Africa have had bouts of overvaluation.[5] In addition, the successful growers in East Asia had shorter spells (that is, consecutive years) of overvaluation and smaller magnitudes of overvaluation during these spells. For example, the Asian economies had an average spell of overvaluation of four years (compared with seven for Latin America and fourteen for sub-Saharan Africa, respectively); and the average overvaluation during this spell was 7 per cent compared with 16 per cent and 29 per cent for LA and SSA, respectively). Interestingly, India has never suffered a spell of overvaluation, and China has avoided overvaluation since its growth took off in 1978.

More formal evidence on the impact of the real exchange rate is in Prasad, et al. (2007) and Rodrik (2007). Both of these contributions document a statistically and economically strong relationship between growth and real exchange rates: a percentage point increase in overvaluation reduces long-run growth by about 0.1 per cent. Prasad et al. (2007) also show that real exchange rates work by affecting the fortunes of the exportable sector in developing countries.

---

[4] It should be stressed that all methodologies for estimating equilibrium exchange rates are fraught with problems.

[5] It is interesting that during the period 1960–80, when Latin American and Asian growth was close, their competitiveness positions were not that dissimilar (see Figure 8.2).

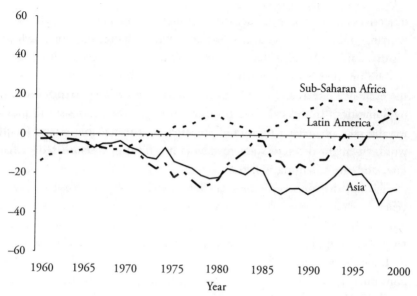

Figure 8.3: Exchange rates: Deviation from long-run
equilibrium, 1960–2000

(+ deviation signifies overvaluation)

Source: Johnson, Ostry, and Subramanian (2006)

Of course, investment in tradables is affected not just be the level but also the volatility of the exchange rate. Risk and uncertainty about returns have a significant dampening effect on investment in tradables. Here too, the evidence is telling. A measure of volatility is the standard deviation of changes in the parallel market exchange rate. For Latin America, the standard deviation is about ten times that for Asian countries.

So the evidence points to a competitive and stable exchange rate, and the consistent avoidance of overvaluation, as a correlate and, perhaps even a key ingredient, of facilitating sustained growth by eliminating the disincentives for investing in the tradable sector.

CAC AND COMPETITIVENESS

What is the role of capital account convertibility in all of this? The simple answer is that the ability to manage an exchange rate is circumscribed by CAC. The famous trilemma (impossible trinity) of international macroeconomics says that a country cannot simultaneously attain the three objectives of open capital account, monetary independence, and a fixed exchange rate. India, which has had a flexible exchange rate for much of its history, can continue to have monetary independence even with CAC.

The problem will arise when there are significant upward pressures on the exchange rate as a result of capital inflows (or foreign currency borrowing by domestics). In this case, the government might want to resist this pressure for the sake of preventing undue pressures on the tradable sector. In other words, it might de facto want to maintain a fixed or a semi-fixed exchange rate, and the trilemma will then bite.[6]

It is not that preserving competitiveness will become impossible. In recent years, India and especially China have sought to keep a lid on the exchange rate and have done so with some success. But there are limits and costs. These have been well illustrated by developments in India over the last few months.

Inflation in India picked up over the last few months while capital inflows continued to surge. These twin developments placed the Reserve Bank of India (RBI) in a quandary. Combating inflation required a tightening of monetary policy, which can be achieved by a combination of rising interest rates and an appreciating currency. On the other hand, maintaining competitiveness required resisting the appreciation pressures stemming from the capital flows.

What did the RBI do? To prevent the nominal appreciation it intervened in the foreign exchange markets (that is, it bought up the dollars). But this increased the supply of liquidity which ran exactly counter to what the doctor ordered for combating inflation. To offset this liquidity expansion, it sterilized the intervention, by issuing interest-bearing securities to the banks, which in return sold the rupees back to the RBI. But when you increase the supply of interest-bearing securities, their price, namely interest rates, tend to go up, or more strictly tend to be higher than otherwise. Domestic agents, especially corporates, found it advantageous to borrow in dollars, which resulted in further inflows. The tail started to wag the dog.

The inducement to borrow in dollars was, of course, facilitated by the RBI's then apparent policy of holding the rupee. Domestic firms were, in effect, given a huge, albeit implicit, subsidy: they could pocket the difference between domestic interest rates and those in dollars without suffering any losses from rupee depreciation, which had been (sort of) ruled out by RBI

---

[6] This suggests that greater exchange rate flexibility need not per se address the problem of capital flow-induced threats to competitiveness.

policy. In other words, those borrowing in dollars and investing in rupee assets were given a one-way bet—a free lunch.

Thus, the limits to sterilization are set by the fact that with an open capital account, sterilization adds to the very pressures that it is meant to address, creating a cycle of flows, sterilization, further flows, etc. It is the inability to manage this that led the RBI to abandon this policy and allow the rupee to float.

The costs of sterilization are really the flip side of the subsidy to domestic borrowers of foreign currency. The financial cost is the difference in interest rates between the paper issued and the returns on the foreign asset, while the underlying or the real cost is the foregone investment and growth opportunity as interest rates are forced to be higher than they otherwise would be in the absence of capital flows.

The point is that with CAC, exchange rate movements are dominated by financial flows and asset markets: in theory, movements generated by asset market behaviour should be consistent with the underlying fundamentals, namely the real side of the economy. But experience has shown that there can be systematic and prolonged divergences between the two (the current level of the US dollar being a good example) and that the process of correction—described by Calvo (2005) as 'sudden stops' —can be abrupt and disruptive, involving overshooting and real costs, to the detriment of a country's ability to manage the exchange rate with an eye to maintaining the vibrancy of the tradable sector.

The assertion here is not that openness to capital inflows is the sole cause of overvalued exchange rates. Both could be the outcome of deeper political economy factors, reflecting the power of elites who have an interest in overvalued exchange rates (and thus cheaper access to imports), and in open capital accounts as protection against future expropriation. It could also be the case that exchange rates are ultimately determined by demographics: for example, overvalued exchange rates can only be avoided if there is a large and growing labour force (which could explain the behaviour of Asian exchange rates). Regardless of the deep determinants, at the very least, it seems that some restrictions on capital are a necessary, proximate, condition for being able to sustain competitive exchange rates and avoid persistent overvaluation. Evidence for this is in Figure 8.4, reproduced from Prasad et al. (2007), which shows that countries that witness more flows, regardless of type, tend to see greater overvaluation of their currencies.

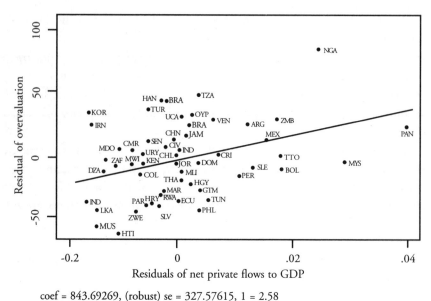

coef = 843.69269, (robust) se = 327.57615, 1 = 2.58

Figure 8.4: Overvaluation and capital flows, 1970–2004

Source: Prasad, Rajan and Subramanian (2006)
Note: The plot is the conditional correlation obtained by running a regression of overvaluation on net private flows (portfolio equity, debt, and FDI), after controlling for demographic variables. It corresponds to the specification in Table 6, column 4 of Prasad, Rajan and Subramanian (2007).

But there is evidence on the detrimental trade and export impact of capital flows from another, unlikely, quarter. Note that the argument about the impact of capital flows on tradable goods via the exchange rate is not confined to private flows. Analytically, the argument also applies to official flows, that is to foreign aid. Rajan and Subramanian (2005) show that aid flows have a negative impact on labour-intensive and export sectors. In particular, they show that in countries that received more aid, labour-intensive and exportable sectors grew much slower, and that this effect was mediated through exchange rate changes. On their estimates, a 1 percentage point increase in aid reduces the growth of manufacturing by about 0.5 per cent. Figure 8.3 illustrates the association between sub-Saharan Africa's poor manufacturing export performance and its consistently overvalued exchange rates. Thus, the experience of Asia, Latin America, and even Africa, are all consistent in suggesting possible effects from openness to capital flows to exchange rates and the growth of the tradable sector.

There is another subtler way in which CAC can affect the exchange rate and tradable goods. When confidence in the currency is high, domestic corporates can take advantage of interest differentials and borrow in cheaper non-rupee liabilities. Their balance sheets will start getting dollarized on the liability side. Once this happens, the ability of the exchange rate to act as an effective tool of increasing domestic demand and helping the fortunes of the tradable sector will be reduced. The reason is the balance sheet effect (Kaminsky and Reinhart, 1999). On the one hand, any decline in the exchange rate will increase demand through normal channels (exports become cheaper and imports become more expensive); on the other, such a change will simultaneously be contractionary because domestic firms (and households will face) significantly higher debt servicing in rupee terms as a result of currency changes. Frankel (2005) has argued that devaluations, which used to be expansionary before the 1990s have now become less so because of the contractionary tug exerted by balance sheet effects.

To summarize, CAC has two distinct effects: first, it reduces a country's ability to influence the exchange rate; and second, because of possible balance sheet effects, it reduces the sensitivity of both aggregate demand and the tradable sector to exchange rate changes.

INDIA

To recapitulate, the chain of reasoning suggested above is that: first, the tradable sector is key for promoting growth; second, that a competitive exchange rate is important in promoting the tradable sector; and finally, that CAC reduces, albeit does not eliminate, the ability to sustain a competitive exchange rate, especially in the face of large capital inflows.

How do these three links apply in the case of India today? Take them in reverse order. In the period ahead, is India likely to be a large net recipient of capital flows? Even discounting for some of the euphoria surrounding 'India Shining', it looks like the growth prospects for India are indeed quite bright. In Rodrik and Subramanian (2005), we had conservatively projected a trend growth rate of 7.5 per cent per year. If anything close to that is realized, India is likely to attract sizable flows of capital for the foreseeable future. One offsetting factor, of course, is the pent up demand for foreign assets from Indian residents, especially households. The open question, of course, is whether this is likely to be a one-off stock adjustment or something that will persist and offset the long-run flows, which will tend to be dictated by differential growth rates, and the higher implied return on Indian relative to global assets.

Will such flows constrain the ability to prevent the exchange rate from becoming overvalued? As argued earlier, India can deploy a number of instruments in the event that surging inflows put upward pressure on the exchange rate. But even sterilization, perhaps the least distortionary form of intervention, is costly, and the fiscal costs, which would be less of an issue if the fiscal position were sound, become a more serious concern in India's case where the fiscal outlook is amongst the few clouds on an otherwise clear macroeconomic horizon. Also, there are limits to sterilization: by forcing interest rates to be higher, it aggravates the inward flow of capital that gives rise to the problem in the first place.

One response to fears about loss in competitiveness through exchange rate appreciation is that other policy tools should be used to offset the loss: fiscal adjustment, trade liberalization, and structural reform more broadly. While undoubtedly true, it begs the question as to why avoiding overvaluation should also not be part of the package of measures geared to attaining competitiveness.

There is the related issue of whether CAC will lead to the type of dollarization that could blunt the exchange rate as an effective instrument to boost demand and the tradable sector. In the buoyant situation that India currently finds itself, it is quite likely that residents will take on foreign-currency denominated liabilities (this seems to underly the recent clamor for CAC by the private sector). Indeed, it would be a surprise and counter to the interest parity condition, if liability dollarization did not happen. The future consequences will depend on risk management practices in the private sector. The more sophisticated these are, the more likely that companies will hedge some or all of their foreign currency exposure. In this case, there might be fewer risks associated with CAC. More research is required to understand the likely behaviour of the domestic corporate sector to CAC.

Perhaps the most important question for India when considering CAC is the importance of developing the traded goods sector. Many have observed that India has underexploited its manufacturing potential (which is to some extent true as reflected in Figure 8.1). In this view, the revival of manufacturing is vital if India is to achieve high growth coupled with providing employment opportunities for its large pool of unskilled labour (Joshi, 2004; Acharya,

2006). If this analysis is correct, it would seem that a competitive exchange rate needs to be part of a package of measures, along with labour reform and development of infrastructure that is geared to reviving the fortunes of manufacturing, especially in the backward states. Kochhar et al. (2006) suggest that the current pattern of skill-based development, which has been at the expense of low-skilled manufacturing, may persist. Their analysis points to threats faced by labour-intensive manufacturing, arising from a kind of Dutch disease as the price of skilled labour is bid up. In such a situation, preserving the ability to influence the exchange rate to protect unskilled manufacturing would appear very important.

Any argument such as that advanced in this piece, namely that, promoting the tradable sector is a key priority for a developing country naturally raises the question as to when this ceases to be a priority or at least an overriding one. Or, to put it bluntly, when does a developing country cease to be a developing country from the perspective of developing the tradable sector? It is very difficult to be definitive or precise about this, but one crude way of thinking about this is the following.

Assume that the process of development follows the Kuznets hypothesis and that the tradable sector is represented by manufacturing. The Kuznets hypothesis suggests that the manufacturing will first rise with development and then fall as incomes rise. Thus, the share of manufacturing in GDP should follow an inverted U shape. One could posit that tradables should cease to be a 'target' of development around the point that its share in the economy starts declining: at this point, a developing country is more like a developed country. What is the income level associated with this turning point? We can actually do a simple calculation to ascertain this. For the latest year for which data are available, we run a regression of the share of manufacturing in GDP against per capita PPP GDP and its square for over 100 countries for which data are available. The Kuznets relationship is indeed confirmed by this regression. The regression also yields a turning point for this relationship of about US$15,000 per capita in PPP terms. Assuming a country was 'normal' and that it followed the typical pattern, this could be the level at which manufacturing ceases to be the focus of development policy.[7]

---

[7] It is worth mentioning that a number of industrial countries—the UK, France, Italy, Greece, and Ireland—moved to full CAC at income levels well above US$15,000 per capita.

A number of good arguments could be advanced for why India is not a typical country: because of its idiosyncratic development strategy, it might have a smaller role for manufacturing in the future than the normal country; and because it is already highly diversified, much more so than the typical country, it needs to provide less policy assistance to promote diversification (see Kochhar et al., 2006). But even so, at a per capita income level of about $2600, the question remains whether Indian policymakers can afford to take their eyes off the tradable sector.[8]

THE CURRENT CONJUNCTURE

The issue of capital account convertibility has acquired new resonance because of the dramatic shift in the policy of the RBI in response to a combination of recent inflows and inflationary pressures: from a managed float, the RBI seems to have moved to a more flexible exchange rate policy.

But the permanence of this policy cannot be taken for granted because there will inevitably be pressures for further appreciation of the rupee and already we see clamor for 'something to be done' about the exchange rate.

In the current context, three remarks can be made about the role of CAC. First, it is difficult to contemplate any major reversal of Indian policy toward CAC. The costs in terms of damaging market confidence in India's reform credentials would be high, even prohibitively high. That said, policymakers should not further undermine flexibility by taking policy actions in the direction of further liberalizing inflows. There may even be a case for tightening external commercial borrowings (ECBs) that were surprisingly relaxed in the last year. If feasible, some tightening of short-term (hot) flows might be warranted. Skill and timing will be essential in implementing any such tightening so as to not disrupt markets. One possibility would be to reduce caps on ECBs whenever they are not fully met and to continue this process as long as the slack allows.

Second, the point is made that given the magnitude and increase in capital flows, it is simply foolhardy to try and manage or reverse this process.

[8] An alternative way of calculating such a turning point is to look at diversification within manufacturing. At what point does diversification cease to be important for a country in the development process? A similar exercise yields a turning point of about US$18,000. This is broadly consistent with the figure obtained above when the question is posed in terms of manufacturing. Again, India, despite being an outlier, is far away from the turning point.

According to this view, India should codify what is de facto an open capital account and just get on with it. But the real issue here is not how much capital is coming in 'naturally,' which obviously should be allowed to come in, but what the future policy actions should be. If ECBs, even as they are now, play a role in limiting inflows, it seems that they should be managed carefully, and not liberalized on the grounds that agents will always find it easy to circumvent controls. As long as policy has some impact, that flexibility should be retained. Similarly, another major area where there is still effective policy control in inflows relates to inflows into the bond market. Again, these should not be liberalized prematurely without taking into account the effect on the exchange rate.

Third, some have argued that one way to manage the exchange rate consequences of capital flows is to liberalize outflows, taking some pressure off the exchange rate. While such action might help, there are two consequences of liberalizing outflows that should be considered. Liberalizing outflows, often, engenders additional confidence in policy and results in further inflows. A second and more subtle point relates to international political economy. The more a country liberalizes outflows, the less easy it becomes to justify the asymmetry between policies to outflows and inflows. Trading partners will inevitably ask why they should be expected to open their economies to Indian capital when India does not similarly reciprocate. In other words, liberalizing outflows could easily lead to pressures from partners on India to further liberalize inflows. India should be mindful of this consideration.

CONCLUSION

Decisions on CAC will no doubt be complex, involving the juggling and reconciliation of multiple objectives and constraints. In the debate on CAC in India, financial and macroeconomic objectives and constraints have been paramount, with much less discussion on the growth and development dimensions of CAC. Of course, the growth dimension cannot be the only, or even the most important, ingredient determining CAC, but it would seem to merit more consideration, given its consequences.

One reason why Indian policymakers have devoted less attention to this issue than it merits, and have not seen exchange rate policy as being a constraint on development, may be because of having managed it so well. Exchange rate policy must be rated as one of the few consistent policy successes in India, reflected in the consistent avoidance of exchange rate overvaluation. And this success may have bred a certain sanguineness about, and hence some inattention to, exchange rate management in what could be a very different era of CAC. It is striking—even shocking—to read the two Tarapore Committee reports and find such little discussion of the exchange rate, and discussions of the potential problems in managing it in a world of greater capital movements. Santayana famously cautioned against repeating the mistakes of the past. Reading the Tarapore Committee reports in light of recent experience alerts us to the wisdom of not repeating the successes of the past.

At the end of the day, CAC might well turn out to be an overblown issue: a tale full of sound and fury, signifying much less than the strong positions of proponents and opponents alike might suggest. This chapter raises the question whether these gains and risks are symmetrically moderate if the competitiveness and growth consequences from an early move to CAC are fully taken into account. Echoing St Augustine, if Indian policy-makers were to say, 'let us have CAC but not yet,' would it be a case of undesirable procrastination or of wisely heeding the precautionary principle? The answer to that question may well be the former but it would be a whole lot more reassuring if it were arrived at after factoring in the exchange rate and growth consequences of CAC.

REFERENCES

Acharya, S. (2006), *Essays on Macroeconomic Policy and Growth in India*, Oxford University Press, New Delhi.

Bhagwati, J. (1998), 'The Capital Myth', *Foreign Affairs*.

Calvo, G. (2005), 'Crisis in Emerging Markets: A Global Perspective', *NBER Working Paper No. 11305*, Cambridge, Massachusetts.

Chinn, M. D., and H. Ito, 'What Matters for Financial Development? Capital Controls, Institutions, and Interactions, *NBER Working Paper No. 11370*, Cambridge, Massachusetts.

Frankel, J. (2005), 'Contractionary Currency Crashes in Developing Countries, Mundell-Fleming Lecture', *Staff Papers, International Monetary Fund*, 52(2).

Hausmann and D. Rodrik (2003), 'Economic Development as Self-Discovery', *NBER Working Paper No. 8952*, Cambridge, Massachusetts.

Imbs, J., and R. Wacziarg (2003), 'Stages of Development', *The American Economic Review*, 93(1).

Johnson, S., J. D. Ostry, and A. Subramanian (2006), 'Prospects for Africa: Benchmarking the Constraints', mimeo, International Monetary Fund.

Joshi, V. (2004), 'Myth of India's Outsourcing Boom', *Financial Times*, November 16.

Kaminsky, G., and C. Reinhart (1999), 'The Twin Crises: The Causes of Banking and Balance-of-Payments Problems,' *American Economic Review,* 89(June), pp. 473–500.

Kochhar, K., U. Kumar, R. Rajan, A. Subramanian, and I. Tokatlidis (2006), 'India's Pattern of Development: What Happened, What Follows?', IMF Working Paper 06/ 22, *Journal of Monetary Economics*.

Prasad, E. and R. Rajan (2005), 'Controlled Capital Account Liberalization: A Proposal', *Policy Discussion Paper*, International Monetary Fund, No. 05/7.

Prasad, E., R. Rajan and A. Subramanian (2007), 'Foreign capital and Economic Growth', *Brookings Papers on Economic Activity*.

Reddy, Y.V., Speech delivered at the 2004 Central Bank Governors' Symposium, Bank of England.

Rodrik, D. (2007), 'Real Exchange rates and Economic Growth', *Razin Lecture*, Georgetown University, Washington D.C.

Rodrik, D., and A. Subramanian (2005), 'Why India Can Grow at 7 Percent a Year or More: Projections and Reflections,' *Economic and Political Weekly*.

LIST OF ARTICLES AND SUMMARIES
INCLUDED IN THE BOOK

'From Hindu Growth to Productivity Surge: The Mystery of the Indian Growth Transition', *International Monetary Fund Staff Papers*, vol. 52, No.2, pp. 193–228, September 2005 (with Dani Rodrik).

'The Economy's last two decades', *The Hindu*, 15 May 2004 (with Dani Rodrik).

'India's Pattern of Development: What happened, What Follows', *Journal of Monetary Economics*, vol. 53, No. 5, pp. 981–1019, July 2006 (with Kalpana Kochhar, Utsav Kumar, Raghuram Rajan, and Ioannis Tokatlidis).

'India needs skills to solve the "Bangalore bug"', *Financial Times*, 17 March 2006 (with Raghuram Rajan).

'From Bharat to India', *India Today*, 26 December 2005 (with Raghuram Rajan).

'Precocious India', *Business Standard*, 14 August 2007.

'The intriguing relationship between institutions and growth in India', *Oxford Review of Economic Policy*, vol 23, summer, p. 196–220, 2007.

'The Paradox of Institutions in India', *Business Standard*, 16 April 2007.

'Why India Can Grow at 7 Percent a Year or More: Projections and Reflection', *Economic and Political Weekly*, vol. 39, No. 16, pp. 1591–96, 17–23 April 2004 (with Dani Rodrik).

'The economy's next two decades', *The Hindu*, 17 May 2004 (with Dani Rodrik).

'The Uruguay Round Text in Perspective', *Economic and Political Weekly*, vol. XXVII No 19, pp. 967–70, 2–8 May 1992 (with Harsha V. Singh). 'Jagdish Bhagwati and Free Trade', *Economic and Political Weekly*, vol. 37, No. 50, pp. 5010–13, 14–20 December 2002 (with Aaditya Mattoo).

'Putting Some Numbers on the TRIPs Pharmaceutical Debate', *International Journal of Technology Management*, vol. 10, Nos. 2/3, 1995.

'Capital account convertibility in India: A neglected consideration', *Economic and Political Weekly*, vol. XLII, No. 25, pp. 2413–18.

INDEX